Sherry,
Take time to tell your own stories. Best of luck in "Life Long Learning."
Brenda

NURSING SHOES
BRENDA CONDUSTA PAVILL, RN, FNP, PhD

Honoring Nurses for National Nurses Week
Annually begins May 6th and
concludes May 12th, Florence Nightingale's Birthday

©2012 Brenda Pavill. Printed and bound in the United States of America. All rights reserved. No material may be copied or reproduced in any form including electronic or mechanical means without the prior written permission of the author, except for short quotations in professional journal articles or for classroom teaching activities. Reviewers may quote brief passages in a review to be printed in a magazine, newspaper, or on the Web.

Although the author has made every effort to ensure the correctness and comprehensiveness of information contained in this book, no responsibility is assumed for errors, inaccuracies, omissions, or any inconsistency herein. Any errors related to people, places, organizations or retelling of stories are unintentional.

ISBN # 978-0-692-01942-9

LCCN: TXu 1-805-655

First printing: February 2013 (ebook version, April 2012)

Photography: Ashley Blaine

Cover Design & Layout: Smart Designs and Graphics

Editing Assistance by Alice Osborn

ATTENTION UNIVERSITIES, COLLEGES, MEDICAL CARE FACILITATIES, PROFESSIONAL ORGANIZATIONS, AND CORPORATIONS: Quantity discounts are available on bulk orders of Nursing Shoes for gift purposes (particularly during annual National Nurses Week), educational events, or as premiums for increasing journal and magazine subscriptions or renewals. Certain book excerpts can also be created to fit specific needs.

For specific information related to Nursing Shoes purchase, distribution or printing, please contact the author at pavillbrenda@gmail.com

Dedications

To my students who inspired me to tell my stories.
To my colleagues who are partners in crime.
To the patients and families I met along the way who helped me evolve into the nurse I am.
To my husband and daughter who listened to my many stories.
To my brother who made me grow and see life through different lenses.
And to those who are inspired to set out on their own nursing journey.

Contents

PROLOGUE 5
CHAPTER 1 Inspiration 9
CHAPTER 2 Snapshot of the years: Recollecting the journey ... 33
CHAPTER 3 The first round: Nursing school escapades 61
CHAPTER 4 Faces 93
CHAPTER 5 Bugs, Nits & Crawlers 187
CHAPTER 6 Situations 203
CHAPTER 7 Transportation 281
CHAPTER 8 Treasures 331
CHAPTER 9 Soaring: Today 355

Prologue

Ah, my dear nursing shoes. They have been with me every step of the way as I have grown from novice to expert. Just as I have changed so has the style and comfort of my shoes. My original shoes were the traditional snug fitting, highly polished white leather nursing shoes that hugged one's foot. They kept my foot secure and in place. They prevented me from slipping and falling with their soft, almost flat, non-conductive copper-colored rubber soles. Their style truly mirrored me as the nurse I was at the time. When I wore this style, I was a student and a new RN, so I was hesitant to think outside of the box, intentionally conforming to the other nurses I observed. I backed up my actions by the book and did nothing out of the ordinary. Their fit mirrored my inner fear of making a mistake, or of being different. All my actions were housed in the novelty of being a new graduate.

After going through many of these traditional shoes, I began to wear shoes of softer white leather that gave around the contour of my feet. My new style was more contemporary. I now preferred loosely fitting, white leather clogs with closed heels (open heels were not permitted for safety reasons in most hospitals) that allowed my foot to move. The softer grip allowed my foot freedom, but the fit wasn't so loose that my step would wobble and cause me to fall. My shoes were me. They were relaxed, accurately reflecting a nurse with new found confidence who felt less inhibited in sharing ideas with supervisors and colleagues. I was advancing, leaving the novice behind and moving towards the more expert-thinking nurse, but I was not quite there yet. I still had another change of shoes.

My next and most preferred shoes would be chic ones. They offered me the ultimate support, contoured to my feet, and allowed me to move with grace. These are the white nursing shoes of today, the ones that have been designed with the latest foot technology to give ultimate comfort and a free-spirited step. For some, and even me, this may be in the form of a white canvas or white leather sneaker fabricated specifically for the active nurse in mind. Today, as I walk in my supremely soft and comfortable shoes (my white leather sneakers) my step is secure. I feel sure-footed and confident in how balanced I feel. As I progress I occasionally stop, clean the scuff marks off, and smile as I continue down my nursing path.

In the unfolding pages I will tell you about my life as a nurse. Sometimes you will wish you were me because the story will touch some emotion that makes you sigh and long to be part of the adventure. Other times, you will be glad you were nowhere near that experience. In the end, though, I hope you can appreciate the ordinary nature of my stories. What makes them ordinary is also what makes them special.

I will mature as my stories evolve. You will see me change from a novice to an expert as my self-esteem and expertise blossoms. The book starts out with me as an adolescent trying to make adult decisions. Consequently, some stories speak of successes and others resonate of challenges. But these triumphs and trials make the overall story realistic. My adventures have made me the person and nurse I am today.

I think, with the multitude of experiences I have had over the last thirty-plus years there will be at least one story or account you will relate to on some basic level. Maybe you are me as an insecure high school student, or me as the inexperienced new graduate. Wherever you see yourself, enjoy the reflection. Maybe laugh and maybe cry. But, savor the experience!

I can see these stories used in the classroom to highlight nursing history; they can lead into a critical thinking exercise where one is asked "what would be your assessment in this situation" or possibly shared as exemplifiers for other nurses. The fact that some of my nursing experiences occurred before today's young adults were born should not take away from the lessons that can be learned. The essence of the anecdotes about humans and their everyday emotions and experiences transgress time. The meaning of nursing and its core values will not change whether one is reflecting on an account recently transpired or something which happened "years ago." So whether one is young, middle-aged or a senior, there is something in this medley of stories for everyone.

Every nurse has his/her stories. Though the stories may differ amongst individual nurses, common themes emerge. Some of these principles could apply to other occupations; but some are unique to nursing. Caring is a perfect example. Caring is not unique to nursing, but for nurses, caring is the soul of nursing. Nursing resonates caring. Undoubtedly, as you read some of my stories you will come to appreciate the caring nature of nurses.

These stories can touch an array of people. They are written for the nurse who has his/her own stories to convey, and the person who enjoys reading stories of a humanistic nature. This book is for individuals who thrive on stories that are chronicles of someone's life and who want to gain a better understanding of the everyday adventures of a friend or relative working in the nursing profession. But ultimately this book is also written for those young men and women who will someday, I hope, be tomorrow's nurses. They will be me in a new generation, in a different era of nursing. They will be the ones who care for us when we are old and gray. And, who I trust will confidently carry on the nursing legacy. Hopefully, they too will someday impart stories of care, love, struggle, and inspiration.

My dream through writing is to inspire some of our youth to take on the challenges of the profession, to plan their career paths, to strive to become professional nurses, and to never utter the words, "I'm just a nurse." We need fresh minds to continue to progress and to embrace change in changing times. We talk of a nursing shortage and of a need to care for one another. We need to extend our arms and embrace one another as we create new nursing stories.

So let's see, now that we know for whom the book is written, where do we begin? I think we should start at the beginning—logical, yes? So…what did inspire me to become a nurse? Is that where the story commences? I think so, inspiration would be a superb start since my goal is to inspire!

Before you come along on my journey take a moment to view the clips posted on the link below that celebrates and honors healthcare providers such as nurses.

http://www.healthcarecelebrations.com

Chapter One

INSPIRATION

☙❧

If we take action: we can move mountains.

(UNKNOWN)

☙❧

The Inspiring Beginning: What bought me into nursing?

Would you believe a Noxzema jar, a jar of invigorating, white, cool cleansing cream set my course toward nursing? You probably wouldn't, but there is some truth in this seemingly absurd answer. Of course there is more to the story, but truthfully…there is a connection. Did I spark your curiosity? I hope so. So let's begin with the Noxzema story. Oh, but before I share that story there is another story, like a preamble I need to tell to set the stage.

The Dike

I was somewhere around eleven or twelve years old. It was summer and on this particular day I was hanging out with my brother and his two buddies. Believe me when I tell you hanging out with my brother and his buddies were not everyday occurrences. Rather, as I was nicely informed, being in their presence was an "honor" because I was a girl, and not only a girl, but one a year younger than "the guys." Heaven forbid if the young lads should be seen hanging out with a girl. But as luck would have it, by the end of the day the "good old boys" were pretty lucky a girl was hanging out with them. One of those touché moments for the female gender!

Naturally, on this day we found ourselves looking for something to do. After some debating and then making a pact not to tell anyone where we were going, we decided to hang out at The Dike. You know, one of those places where as a kid you were forbidden to even think about going. Well, that's the infamous place we called The Dike. We were forever warned it was a place where "all the bums hung out," "no place for kids," and that "you'll only end up in trouble there." Of course we thought, trouble us? Not likely! In our minds, we deduced since we obviously wouldn't be getting into mischief, why not spend time there. You know, scout around, explore, and see what we could find. No doubt we surmised there had to be some unclaimed treasure we would find. And besides, what harm would there be in going if we vowed not to tell anyone? No one would be the wiser! So the covenant was schemed. We would go and nobody in our pack would utter the secret of where we went.

Unlike the interpretation of adults, The Dike for the neighborhood kids was the wooded area over the railroad tracks that offered endless adventure. There were the illustrious "Captain Chairs" (which were really large salves of concrete) that we heard as kids were ruins left over from some military operation during "the war." What war? I'm not sure any more whether we imagined they were left over from World War I or World War II. But regardless of their war connection, the "chairs" were great to climb on, sit on, or use as protective barriers in the midst of imaginary combat. We could spend hours amongst those chairs fighting our pretend battles.

Then there was the creek… the creek that offered an endless supply of cool water on hot summer days. No kid could resist taking his/her shoes and socks off (if you wore them) to walk in the water. But walking was awkward because of the many rocks that jabbed at the soles of your bare feet. Almost everyone hopped around on the rocks exclaiming "ouch" as the rocks poked at their feet. "Ouch… ouch…ouch" was a familiar echo.

After spending time at the creek we would notoriously have to hang around the dike even longer to dry off in the sun, because you know, nobody ever left the creek with only wet feet. Surely they had to wade in deeper.

Well, on this day our adventure unraveled at the creek. Amongst the four of us we were doing our own thing. One of the guys was walking in the water, or should I say hopping in the water, two were skipping rocks and I was squatting on the edge of the water looking for whatever little fish or tadpole I could find. Exactly how the injury happened I did not see, because remember I was looking down. However, it did not take much imagination to envision what ensured.

As I was focused on the fish my concentration was broken by the sounds of the guys yelling and one of them crying. There were shouts of, "How could you be so stupid, didn't you see him?"… "I can't believe you did this"…and, oh yes, the panicked, high-pitched exclamation of, "He's bleeding!" I vividly recall looking up upon hearing the shouts and seeing one of the boys holding the side of his head with blood running through his fingers. I thought, "There's so much blood." "I can't believe this has happened." And then, the fleeting thought of, "We're in trouble now."

Whether there really was a gross amount of blood, I don't know. I just know from a kid's point of view, looking at blood and being in a place you shouldn't be spelled trouble. Another significant detail that broke through my erratic thoughts was the boy who was injured, crying, and holding his head didn't seem to be acting right. I was too young and medically inexperienced at the time to figure out if he was in shock, but from what I can recall of his actions, more than likely he was.

I knew someone needed to take hold of the situation, calm everyone down and get our friend some help. Plus, before we got back we would need to agree on the story of how and where this happened—because heaven help us if our parents found out we were at The Dike. From our perspective, if our secret was revealed we would all be in big-time trouble, and possibly even grounded for the rest of our lives.

Running over to our injured friend I told myself to stay composed and talk to him in a soothing voice so he would calm down.

I felt an urgent need to allay his fears so he would cooperate, which would allow us to venture back through the woods. I didn't doubt that we would make it back, but I didn't know how far our injured friend would progress before he passed out or went berserk! Maybe that is what drove me to push those guys; the fear that if we didn't keep moving, and moving fast, we wouldn't make it back before something worse happened. So with a tee shirt pressed against his head, damp clothes and wet feet we all made our way back through the woods, moving much slower than when we began the day's adventure, but moving nonetheless.

I walked alongside the injured boy trying to speak quietly to him so he would not become any more hysterical than he already was. I particularly remember repeatedly lying and telling him "everything looks fine" each time he asked me if it looked like the bleeding stopped. As I told him the bleeding looked to have stopped, I could clearly see blood seeping through the tee shirt. Of course, I knew I wasn't being truthful and I felt bad about being dishonest, but this was one of those times when you convinced yourself a little white lie is better than the truth. I just didn't think our friend could handle the news that the bleeding persisted. I figured if I told him the truth he'd either start convulsing, perish right there, or take off running and screaming through the woods. So lie I did, all the way back through the woods and up over the railroad tracks to his house. As you might expect, as we walked we all talked, except our injured friend, about what account we would report to explain our whereabouts. By the time we reached the railroad tracks we had our agreed upon story. I no longer recall exactly what story we fabricated but in the end it turned out we never did tell the whole tale. Once his parents saw the blood everything that transpired from that point on happened rather quickly, so there was no time for our edited narrative.

As all four of us approached the injured boy's house the pitch of his sobs intensified, so much so, his mother came to the front door to check on the commotion. Immediately upon hearing the loud sobs emitted by her child our injured friend was whisked away, put in the car, and rushed off to the hospital. No questions were posed to us about where this occurred. Instead, his parents just wanted a quick account of what happened. It was effortless to answer, "He got hit with a rock and it cracked his head open." Simple as that! Never mind we were at The Dike and one of his friends threw the rock which accidentally hit him on the side of the head. They didn't have time to learn the stone was intended to plunge into the creek, but because his friend had such a bad aim, for a boy no less, he was hit in the head instead.

Luckily for us, the car with our now hysterically wailing friend inside sped off before we could reveal too much information. Maybe the fact we didn't have an opportunity to elaborate on our story was a good thing. That way, we didn't have a chance of mixing up our fabricated account, which more than likely would have occurred. Who would spill the beans? I don't know; someone would, they notoriously did.

Our injured friend was gone and we were left just standing there. Everything seemed quiet after all the commotion. Not knowing what else to do, we decided to call it a day and go home. My brother and I had a quiet walk back. I think we were both too physically and mentally exhausted to talk. Besides, we were deep in our own thoughts wondering what would happen to our friend. I didn't think he would die. But yet, I really didn't know what would happen to him.

We never did tell my parents the story about our day, but weeks later, we inadvertently shared that someone had injured our friend by throwing a rock. By then he was already healing and all was calm, so we didn't feel threatened by telling select parts of the story. Fortunately, our parents didn't know the injured boy's parents, only the injured boy. He never really spent much time at our house so my parents didn't know him well enough to feel comfortable calling his parents and inquiring about his injuries. So our secret was safe! When my brother's friend wasn't around for a while, our parents didn't spend a great deal of time wondering about his absence. And, not around for a while is exactly what happened.

We never knew whether our friend ever divulged the real story of where we were when his accident transpired. He swore he never told, but after the incident we didn't see him for quite some time. His absence made us wonder if his parents forbade him to hang around us because they now considered us a "bad influence." But even if his parents did try to separate us, the start of the school year ended any such attempt; at least, for the boys it did. As for The Dike, well, I didn't return and I believe the boys rarely went back. For some reason it lost its appeal. I never again thought of the place in the same way. Even today, when I drive by the railroad tracks where The Dike is just over the hill, I envision that day by the creek and the faces of four frightened kids.

So what does this all have to do with nursing? Well, believe it or not, the boys gave credit where credit was due. They all acknowledged I saved their friend's life. They dubbed me the hero of the day. The retold story always includes the doctor's comment of how fortunate our wounded friend had been because his substantial blood loss could have cost him his life. We all knew because of my pushing, we got home just in time. Me, the unsung hero!

Several years later, after hearing the true version of the story, my mother pointed out even then I had the makings of becoming a nurse. But for me, I was just glad the day was over and I was able to put the experience in the back of my mind. Really though, I guess you could say maybe The Dike experience was a preamble to my future. But frankly, I think the Noxzema jar story is what did the trick. Yes, a Noxzema jar had something to do with my becoming a nurse!

The Noxzema Jar

So how does Noxzema play into my decision to become a nurse? Well, naturally there is a story but first I need to take you back to the time in my life when I was trying to figure out what I wanted to be when I grew up. When I was fifteen or sixteen years old I first thought about becoming an airline stewardess. I wanted to travel and see the world; it was kind of a natural flow of events for a "Navy brat." I figured being an airline stewardess would confer both these wishes. Besides, I surmised, according to television portrayals an airline stewardess life was pretty glamorous and exciting. That's what I wanted: excitement and glamour. Seemed like the perfect solution. So airline stewardess I resolved it would be. And it was... for a couple weeks. But then the dream vanished after a relative informed me that I would not qualify to be an airline stewardess because I was too short. Too short...who would have thought height would be an issue? I figured airsickness maybe, because I certainly had problems with carsickness, but height? Not an issue. Even so, I accepted my relative's information as fact and checked airline stewardess off the list.

And that perceived obstacle of being too short? Well, it could have been true, but somehow I doubt it. Really, I'm 5'3-¼ inches! Now I could see if I was 5 feet! Then I would be little! Well, whatever… that aspiration was short lived. At the time it was unfortunate but I didn't have the spunk or the backbone to challenge the issue. I simply went back to thinking up other options.

Though I thought my next choice was another logical selection, the adults in my life didn't. I simply deduced since I loved to sew and design clothes I would be a fashion designer. That certainly made sense to me, but I was soon informed of all the reasons fashion designing was not an ideal choice. The reasons varied. I heard comments like, "You will have to move to New York City if you want to make it as a designer, you know what New York is like" and "do you know how many fashion designers are starving?" Well, I guess that disqualifies me…how stupid of me to think I just might be one of those who would make it. So, another option bit the dust. I was back to contemplating.

Well, despite my bumpy start, the day would be saved. The next milestone that happened in my life resolved my occupation dilemma. This time everyone agreed it was the ideal answer. The answer had something to do with the Noxzema jar, and oh, yes, a drum majorette and tussled white marching boots. Yes, boots.

So what could these items possibly have in common? Simply, they led me to nursing. You see, it was just around this time of occupation confusion that I was selected to be the drum majorette for our high school band. I was chosen at the end of my sophomore year which meant I had the whole summer to prepare. You know make new uniforms plus create new routines and practice, practice, practice. Yeah, right, what was I thinking, a whole summer to get ready? I should have known even at sixteen things rarely go as predicted.

You see, I was born with these oddly shaped feet. My family lovingly called them my "duck feet." Normally one's feet are wider at the toes than at the heels but unlike most, mine were even wider than normal. This wideness caused my big toes to deviate outward and contributed to the formation of bunions on the inner aspects of both feet. The bunions hurt when I walked and the pain was even worse if I wore certain types of shoes, like boots.

I never thought about how my feet would be affected by wearing marching boots; I only thought about how nice the boots would look. You just don't think about physical concerns at sixteen, you think about fashion. Foot problems and the elderly went together, not young and sixteen. Unfortunately it was an orthopedic doctor who voiced concerns about my marching and wearing boots. What I heard from him was, "No, no, you can't do that." "You can't march for long periods and wear those type of boots." "The boots will aggravate your feet and make them worse." Of course, I truly believed he was overreacting but my parents didn't.

According to the orthopedist I had two options. I could either have surgery over the summer to correct the problem or give up the majorette idea. Naturally, in my youth I only saw what I wanted to see, which was to be a majorette. So I saw one choice, have the surgery. That was my mentality.

I was informed the surgical procedure would involve having bones broken in both my feet and then having them reset. Since bones would be broken, my legs from the knees down would be in plaster casts for several months. Today, I might have gotten away with wearing sneakers instead of having surgery, but sneakers were not a marching option then. Leather white mid-calf marching boots and majorettes were synonymous. You didn't have one without the other. I knew surgery and recovery would consume my whole summer, but I was willing to sacrifice the time if my feet would be fixed, and I would be ready for marching by fall.

The surgeon questioned whether I wanted both feet done at the same time or one at a time. Explanations as to why I shouldn't have both feet done simultaneously followed the question. I wondered why he even bothered to offer me a choice if he thought having them done together wasn't practical. Instead of debating the issue, I inquired whether any of his other patients ever had both feet done at once. Yes, I was told, but "it's not ideal." Well...I didn't need time to ponder my options. I thought the answer was straightforward, maybe not ideal, but certainly logical. That is, do them together and get the ordeal over with. I calculated coming back a second time meant double pain, a longer time to get better, and more delays before I could start marching. "Do them now" and "do them both"— that was my comeback!

Believe it or not, my voice was heard. My surgery was scheduled as a bilateral repair. Can you believe it? I was on my way, and I was getting my way! I secretly think my parents were glad I chose to have both feet done at the same time. I believe they had the foresight to know convincing me to have the second surgery, after experiencing the first would probably be a challenge. Now, with hindsight, I think they were right. Once was more than enough.

The surgery went as anticipated with no problems or complications. I found myself back in my room, flat on my back, with two very sore feet which felt extremely heavy from the weight of the wet plaster casts. But I must say the shot I received of Demerol worked wonders. It relieved the pain, but boy did it make me hallucinate. I had one dream which about sent me through the ceiling. I fantasized I was stepping up over a large step, and in my drugged sleep I took that big step. I actually physically lifted my feet into the air to step up and then slammed my feet back against the mattress as I perceived I was stepping down. Ouch! Talk about seeing stars.

But that dream was not what spurred me into nursing. It was

another event during my hospital stay. Actually it happened the day after this dream when my casts were drier but not dry enough that I was allowed to get out of bed and walk about. I was still officially on bed rest. Nowadays, there are synthetic casts that dry in a matter of minutes, but in my time the commonly used plaster casts took days to completely dry.

I had to go to the bathroom in the early morning before my mother arrived. She was the only one I would allow to help me with such a private deed. I knew because my casts were still damp, and I was supposedly on bed rest, I would be expected to use a bedpan. I could handle going on the bedpan to void (a word I did not know then) but using the pan for "anything else" was out of the question. And this time it was "anything else." How in the world did they expect me to do it on a cold, tiny metal pan? They had to be nuts! Not me, there was no way! I had to make it into the bathroom… there was no chance I was using a bedpan to go!

This is where the Noxzema jar comes into play. Being sixteen, I was embarrassed just thinking about having to use the bedpan. So I conjured up a plan on how I could maneuver my way to the bathroom completely by myself. I was lucky I was in Pediatrics because the unit was small and every room was a private room. So that meant no roommate to tattle on me. I was sure anyone with common sense would have rung for the nurses if they saw what I was about to do. I speculated if I could manage to get out of bed, I could then walk across the tiled floor on my knees. The hard part would be holding my casted legs up off the floor as I maneuvered about.

The bathroom seemed right there, the door was open and I could see the toilet. I figured I could make it, do my business, and be back before anyone caught me. Nobody would be the wiser! Yeah, right!

I would make just one mistake.

Somehow I did manage to get out of the bed. Looking back now I find it amazing to think I believed I could pull off such a stunt. But I was motivated like Houdini. The analgesic effect of the Demerol masked the pain as I used the trapeze bar to maneuver out of the bed and onto my knees. To this day I can't imagine how I managed to get out of the bed and onto the floor, but somehow I did. I believe I slid out the side of the bed on my stomach, hands first.

I made it into the bathroom without a glitch. Right next to the commode was the sink. From my ground position, the sink was high enough to occlude my view of all the items placed along the sink's edge. I decided to grab onto the sink and pull myself up onto the commode. Well, as I reached up to grip the sink's edge I knocked a large Noxzema jar off the sink. You can imagine the sound when the sizable blue glass container hit the tile floor and smashed! The echoing sound was loud enough to bring a nurse running into the room. I always wondered if the nurse was already on her way into my room because she seemed to come so fast.

The breaking jar made a fairly loud noise, but I didn't think the sound was thunderous enough to be heard at the nurses' station down the hall. I never inquired about the nurse's whereabouts when she heard the noise because when she arrived we were both too shocked by one another's presence for me to ask. And later, I did not want to reopen the wounds, as they say, because I was too embarrassed by what I had done.

Caught red-handed, there was no denying this one. Today, after being a nurse myself, I can imagine the concern that must have crossed the nurse's mind as she entered the room and saw my empty bed. Her heart must have sunk to her toes; I know mine would have. There's me, half on the floor and half pulled up on the sink with damp casts, creamy white lotion splattered on the floor and walls, and pieces of blue glass shattered about.

Much to my surprise, the nurse didn't yell at me or say anything to hurt my feelings. It was the way she handled this situation which inspired me to want to be a nurse. Rather than scold me, she asked me what I was attempting to do. After explaining I was trying to go to the bathroom she helped me onto the commode, gave me the privacy I needed and stayed in close proximity to assist me. When I was done she called for aid to help me back to bed, then had housekeeping clean up the broken glass and splattered cream, all without a single lecture. Later that same day a physical therapist brought crutches and taught me crutch walking. Whether receiving the crutches was just a matter of timing or whether obtaining them had something to do with this nurse trying to help me along were questions left unanswered. I like to think she advocated for me and made it possible for me to be able to make it to the bathroom on my own.

My desire to become a nurse did not occur at that very moment of the glass shattering. No, first I focused on how mortified I was at being caught doing something I knew was wrong. Rather, it was months before I realized I wanted to help people with the same compassion and caring that this nurse displayed to me. I was impressed she did not "freak out" when she found me. Instead, she maintained her cool and was kind to me. Her actions spoke volumes. She inspired me to treat others similarly. There's that word INSPIRE! But she did influence me, and at the same time she framed my future. So you see, what we have here is one broken Noxzema jar for one nurse. Not a bad exchange! Plus, in time I got to wear those majorette boots.

Once I got started framing my career path, I went all the way. I figured since I loved children I would not only become a nurse, but a nurse midwife as well. I planned to achieve this goal by enlisting in the military after completing my basic nursing "training." I calculated I would serve twenty years so I could earn a decent pension. You know, for my retirement someday. Wow, what planning for a sixteen-year-old—already thinking about a pension. Way to go!

I guess all the talk about a military career was not surprising since my father had been an enlisted man for thirty years. I had it all figured out. My first step after nursing school would be to join the military as a nurse cadet. Loving to travel, I reasoned becoming a flight nurse made sense. I assumed being a flight nurse would give me an opportunity to take trips and see the world. Aha, the same themes that had me thinking of becoming an airline stewardess! But oh, yes, I was too short. Remember?

I figured after I had been in the military for a while, I would return to school to become a nurse-midwife. I pictured myself retiring from the military, most likely the Navy, as a military nurse midwife. How's that for planning? Would my dreams come true? Well, how can I answer that now, I need you to keep reading. So read on and you shall see how my career ended up evolving.

Three versus Four Years

Somewhere in our junior year of high school each of us was called into the guidance counselor's office to discuss what career path (work or college) we planned to pursue after graduation. If we planned to continue our education, the next question related to which schools we anticipated submitting applications to. Well, I had the retort for the first part. I wanted to be a nurse, so my answer was easy I would take the schooling path. However, what I did not anticipate was being asked whether I planned to go to a college or to a hospital for my education. This probing question took me by surprise because I just assumed if you were going to be a nurse you went to study at a hospital.

In my career counseling session I definitely got the sense my advisor felt my better career path would be to attend a college. She felt I would be better served by earning a bachelor's degree rather than a diploma from a hospital-based program. In order to introduce me to different colleges she then encouraged me to attend college recruitment fairs. It was while at one of these consortiums of schools, and the only fair I attended, I learned of a terrific sounding girl's college in my home state. The distance was a little far but I speculated I could handle living away. And besides, the possibility of living in a dorm seemed exciting. I was animated until I learned what the tuition and room expenses would be. Once I heard the cost I felt deflated because I knew my parents would never be able to send me to a school which cost so much. I already had one sister in college and another brother starting college the same year as me. Also, the cost of hospital based diploma programs were fairly inexpensive and often were funded with state dollars. State funding and low cost meant virtually no expense for my parents.

To this day, I am not sure why I never admitted to my guidance counselor money was the reason I could not go to the four-year college. I suppose pride had something to do with my not sharing the information. Maybe if I had communicated my financial concerns she might have directed me to potential scholarships. Instead, I downplayed my interest in attending a college-based nursing program. I challenged her by asking, "Why should I go to a program which will take me four years to complete when I can go to a program and finish in three years?" As a high school youngster I naively believed a nurse was a nurse, no matter what school he/she attended. In my limited perspective all nurses did the same thing; they cared for people in a hospital.

I suppose if the associate or two-year degree nursing program was proposed to me, I would have jumped at the opportunity to complete a nursing program in two years. I am sure I would have thought "what a bargain, two years rather than three or four." But at the time, the option never surfaced.

It's sad to think I was so narrow-minded, however, I was. Instead of focusing on the amount of time it would take me to finish school, I should have being mulling over how this was my future and not lose sight of the saying that "good things are worth waiting for." Years later when I returned to school part-time to obtain my bachelor's degree in nursing, the program took me eight years to complete. Some shortcut idea! I should have listened to my guidance counselor because, in the long run, I would have saved quite a bit of time! Despite my counselor's frowns and shared wisdom when all was said and done I opted to apply to a three-year diploma program—the quickest route; at least that's what I thought!

Traumatic Entrance Exam

For high school seniors, any college or educational programs requiring a minimum score on a standardized test for admission automatically elicits high levels of anxiety. The diploma program I was interested in applying to, like most of the nursing programs at the time, required I take one of those anxiety provoking standardized tests. Although I did well academically in high school, scoring respectfully on a standardized test had never been one of my strong points. Despite my qualms that I might not do as well on the admission test as I would like, I knew if I wanted to go to nursing school I would have to rise up to the expectation.

This pre-nursing test was only offered once or twice a year. We're talking pre-computerized testing here so everyone was given a date and a specific location where the examination would take place. In my era, I would be taking the exam in pencil and paper format. No ifs, ands, or buts, the testing center did not want to hear about any scheduling conflicts. You didn't debate the schedule; you merely made plans to be present as assigned. Plainly put, if you did not take the examination on the designated date, you would have to wait six months to a year before a similar test would be offered again. The repercussion one paid for missing the date was that you simply messed up your chances of applying to the school's nursing program for the year. Ouch!

As my luck would have it, the examination date was scheduled around the same time I could expect my period. For me that was awful news because I always experienced terrible cramps with my menses. My monthly menstrual discomforts and over-all ill feeling were so bad I often either missed school or ended up being sent home from school. I would try taking whatever over-the-counter pain pills I thought would help; however, despite my best efforts, the medications never seemed to touch the cramps. As a result, each month I came to dread this natural cycle.

I had of course gone to a gynecologist for some relief, but at the time, the prevailing belief was menstrual symptoms were psychosomatic. Can you believe it? I always figured the accepted theory must have been proposed by a group of male physicians since the implication that the symptoms were all in one's head seemed preposterous. Today, the proposed link of prostaglandins and menstrual symptoms sounds so much more rational and scientifically grounded. The prostaglandin theory actually makes sense. Another interesting statement offered to me at the time was that I would "grow out of" the bad cramps. I was told my periods would be much better after I had a baby. Think about the implications of such a projection! Imagine a sixteen-year old thinking that having a baby just might be worth the process to end menstrual period discomforts; something was wrong with that power of suggestion!

I prayed for a miracle so somehow my period would be late, but I had no such luck. The night before the scheduled testing, my "friend" came to visit, along with the dreaded cramps. On the day of the examination I felt awful and just wanted to stay in bed and succumb to the cramps, but of course I couldn't.

And what time do you think most of these testing centers expected us to register? You got it—early! Since we had a two-hour drive to the site we were up at the crack of dawn in preparation for the trip. The particular expressway we needed to take into the city was one of those roads where anything could happen, and did on a daily basis. You never knew what to expect. Any delay from an accident could cause me to forfeit my slot for the test. Thus, to reduce the chance of our being late, we planned for ample travel time. So that meant, we got up at an ungodly hour.

The transportation arrangements had all been made beforehand. It was agreed my father would drive because he was familiar with the city and the expressway. His assuming the driving was fine by me; with taking the test on my mind, I didn't need the extra stress of driving in an unfamiliar city.

On the morning of the big day I had my period and felt lousy. Though I wished I could have cancelled taking the exam, I knew my wish wasn't an option. Everything was set in motion. I had paid the testing fee, the date was here, and I needed the test score to complete the school's application process.

One look at me that morning told my father I was not feeling well. My color was pasty and I was shaky, but I passed my appearance off as having the flu. At sixteen I would rather have died than tell my father I had my period. Maybe he believed the flu explanation, or just pretended he did. I suspect my mother clued him in as to why I really didn't feel well; moms often do those kinds of thing. My father suggested I try to sleep in the car so that maybe by the time we arrived I would feel better. I hoped and prayed he was right!

When we arrived at our destination, I didn't feel any better, in fact, I felt worse. I hadn't slept a wink during the drive. The cramps were intense but I didn't want to take any medications, because from experience, I knew the medication did not relieve the pain but merely made me drowsy.

We arrived on time. We got through the expressway unscathed and found the testing center without incident. Everything seemed to fall into place except my body. Somehow I managed to complete the registration process and took my seat in the testing room. When the actual testing was in progress concentrating on the questions was impossible; instead, I found myself praying the examination would end before I embarrassed myself by fainting or vomiting all over my examination. I felt so... sick.

At some point I should probably have gone to the proctor and reported I could not do the examination because I was ill. But instead, I kept trying to answer the questions. In the end I just ended up randomly picking answers. When I finished the examination I remember handing my paper in and running out the door because I could feel the vomit ready to erupt. No sooner had I got out in the hallway I puked all over the hall floor. I know I must have grossed people out, but what can you do?

My father witnessed my frantic exit from the testing room and was there to help me. Crying, I told him how poorly I knew I must have done on the examination. He tried to help by asking the proctor to write a note on my test stating I was ill when testing. The proctor was very nice and said she would include a note. I didn't think whoever graded the examinations (most likely a machine) would see the proctor's remark, but at least the proctor's efforts gave me hope that things would work out. So what do you think, did things work out or did that test come back to haunt me? Let's see....

Rejected and Accepted

Initially, when looking into potential schools, I had planned on submitting an application to only one program; but something told me not to put all my eggs in one basket. Heeding this inner voice, I selected another possibility. As a high school student I did not have much money to spend on application fees so I needed to limit my selections. My guidance counselor recommended I apply to the first program on my list since other graduates from my high school had gone there and done well. Mainly though, I included the school as a choice because a few of my peers were also applying there. Aside from the peer factor, I was receptive to her suggestion because I knew our high school counselor and the program's recruiters had a positive working relationship, and I had heard positive testimonies about the school. Would you believe I had never seen the school and its affiliated hospital other than in a brochure photo? Since I hadn't been to the school and formed some kind of connection with the facility, I was interested, but not enthralled about going there. However, listening to my counselor about applying there seemed practical.

The other school I decided to apply to was slightly further away in a metropolitan setting. I had seen the facility many times while visiting a nearby naval hospital. With my father being in the Navy my family made frequent trips to the naval hospital for non-emergency healthcare. Though we never stopped at the other hospital, there was a sense of familiarity. My guidance counselor was not keen on this selection since she was unfamiliar with the program and did not know students who had trained there. One thing she found favorable was like my high school, the institution was Catholic-affiliated.

My parents were receptive to my interest in this second program. Besides being familiar with the community where the hospital was located, they were also amenable to the idea because we had relatives who lived in the vicinity. They knew my relatives would watch out for me and offer me support if needed.

There was another benefit to this second program. This facility was located in an ideal place to watch the city's famous New Year's Day Mummer's Parade. Front row seats! Now, only a Philadelphia-born kid (born, of course, in the naval hospital) would think of such an advantage!

So two schools were earmarked to receive what I imagined would be horrible grades from the horrendous standardized testing day. Once the admission's personnel saw my score I was afraid, despite my high school grades, the odds would be against me being accepted into their programs. So, I anxiously watched the mail for the day when the yay or nay letters would arrive.

Though it seemed I was never going to hear from the schools, the day finally came. The first letter I received was from the school my guidance counselor favored. The letter was politely worded, but basically informed me due to limited space I was not selected for fall admission but to consider applying in the future. Was I surprised?

Not really, but my apprehension intensified. All I could think about was what if the second school also passed me over? Where would I apply next? Was I running out of time for fall admission? Such were my panicky thoughts. Today, I know there would have been a school out there for me, but at the time I was blinded to the possibility. For me, it was as if these were the only two schools in existence!

There were only three people who knew the schools I had applied to: my parents and my high school counselor. So they were the only individuals I shared my denial with. I felt dejected but focused on remaining positive about the other school. I prayed things would work out.

The letter from the second school requested an interview with me rather than simply rejecting or accepting me. An opportunity to dialogue was a good thing, I figured. At least, I was not turned away without a chance. I assumed the faculty must have been at least slightly interested, or had questions, if they were taking the time to talk with me.

As I suspected, the school requested the interview because of the disparity between my high school grades and my pre-nursing standardized test score. Overall the meeting went well and provided me an opportunity to meet some of the nursing faculty. To my benefit, the meeting also provided me the opportunity to explain how sick I was the day I took the pre-nursing entrance examination.

Talk about understanding and compassion; those were virtues I found in the school's director. When I was leaving the interview, the director assured me my profile looked favorable for entrance but I would have to wait for an official acceptance letter. I was ecstatic. Besides, I reasoned, who needed that other school; this one was surely for me! I was convinced I was meant to go to this school. We were a natural match; it was my destiny.

Not long after my interview and true to her word, I received a letter from the director congratulating me on being accepted. Now this news was something to celebrate and share with friends. I joined the ranks of my fellow classmates who knew exactly what they were doing after graduation and what schools they would be attending. Yes, senior year came together after all! No more worries. I was on my way!

Chapter Two

SNAPSHOT OF THE YEARS:

RECOLLECTING THE JOURNEY

ಸಃ

*When mapping out
our life, be sure to
use a pencil.*

(BON JOVI)

ಸಃ

Now that I have told you how I was inspired to become a nurse and my struggles with acceptance into nursing school, let me take you down the path of where my journey took me. In this chapter I open with a reflection of my beginning years at a diploma nursing school and bring you to where I am today. In the remaining chapters I will share with you the plethora of unique experiences and fascinating people I have met along the way. Truly, the different experiences and the many people I describe can provide a glimpse of what it means to be a nurse.

This part of my story I equate to a journey down a straight road. The road does not bend and twist at this point; nor do other roads run parallel. Rather, this is a synopsis of my story, my journey. In the chapters to follow I will talk about the side roads and wonderful scenery I experienced along the way. But for now, this is the straight and forward; this is my "from point A to point B" route.

I always liked the idea of equating one's life as a journey. The word journey just seems to fit. For me, because nursing has been a major part of my life and I have been in the profession for so many years, I see my nursing career as my journey. It is my own route. Though some individuals may have similar experiences, no other person will have an identical journey. The path I follow defines me and defines my career. I have taken all kinds of footsteps up my path (fast, slow, hesitant, skipping, awkward…) and will continue to advance cautiously but steadily down the road. As I am writing I have flashes of Dorothy and the Scarecrow from The Wizard of Oz locking elbows and skipping merrily down the yellow brick road. That's me skipping down the road of my career, a road that extends far ahead of me and one I approach with a sense of adventure and with the caution of wisdom. Overall the route has not been an easy one; however, the course has been adventurous.

My education started at a hospital-based nursing program where I would receive a diploma in nursing. For those who might be unfamiliar with what a diploma nursing program entails, let me explain. Someone who graduates with a diploma in nursing sits for the same state licensure examination as does a student who graduates from an associate degree nursing program (typically a two-year program at a community college) or a baccalaureate program (typically a four-year program at a college or university). Essentially, no matter which of these three programs a student attends, if they pass a state licensure examination they are entitled to use the abbreviations RN for registered nurse.

All registered nurses, regardless of their education programs, follow the same scope of practice guidelines set forth by the states in which they take their licensure examination and/or are employed as RNs. When diploma programs first emerged they were popular among hospital administrators because student nurses could staff their facilities. Historically this explains why most of the original diploma programs were affiliated with or existed within hospitals. One could, and many have spent years, philosophically debating performance differences between diploma, associate, and baccalaureate graduates. But let's not go there.

Currently if you were to survey seasoned or more "mature" (not older!) nurses, you would probably find many obtained their basic nursing education at hospital-based schools or diploma programs. Today there are still some diploma programs in existence, but associate and baccalaureate programs are most prevalent. Well, since you could call me a seasoned (but not old!) nurse, you can see how my initial educational accomplishments match with this more mature generation of nurses.

The faculties in the diploma program I attended taught us the foundations of nursing science, and instilled in us the need for lifelong learning. Now as I reflect on my nursing career there is truly evidence I embraced the concept of lifelong learning. Some even tease me about how I always seem to be in school. In a way, the remark is valid. Typically, if I am not formally pursuing a degree, I am reading a journal article or attending a conference/workshop to broaden my knowledge. I do exemplify the concept of lifelong learning!

As you read on you will see many of my stories come from the three and a half years I spent at this diploma school. I often say the program was three and a half years, instead of three years, since we had approximately two weeks off between May to September. So the program in terms of duration was almost equivalent to a four year baccalaureate program, but who's counting!

Did I regret initially obtaining a diploma rather than an associate or bachelor's degree in nursing? No. The only regret is that when I decided to continue my formal nursing education and pursue my bachelor's degree I had no college credits to transfer. Without those credits, what could have taken four years to complete took eight years part-time. Adding the three and a half years it took me to obtain my diploma, means I went to school for nearly twelve years before achieving my Bachelor of Science in Nursing (BSN). Wow!

If only I knew then what I know now, I would have listened to my high school guidance counselor and chosen to complete my bachelor's degree in four short years instead of almost twelve. Compared to when I was fresh out of high school, going back to school was much harder while working full-time, being married and simultaneously engaged in other life responsibilities.

After graduation I decided I wanted to stay in the city and work in one of the urban hospitals. I wanted to work in obstetrics but could not find a position, so I looked to another specialty. At the time I graduated, the standard was not to hire new graduates for specialty areas. Rather, new graduates were encouraged to work in medical-surgical nursing for at least a year to gain a broader perspective. Additionally, at the time there was no nursing shortage so hospitals were quite selective in their choices. New graduates found it a hard sell to convince nursing directors why they should hire them over seasoned nurses.

At one of the city hospitals, I was offered the opportunity to work in a Neurology intensive care unit. The complexity of the brain fascinated me and I liked the opportunity to discover more about neurology. I thought it would be a great opportunity to learn and grow as a nurse while caring for people with various brain disorders and diseases. I wanted to learn and learn from the best at a progressive teaching hospital with a specialty unit that few hospitals offered. So I tuned out comments like "It's not in a safe section of town" and "You're crazy for considering working there."

Despite my initial enthusiasm, I did not take the job. Before I officially accepted the position my parents asked me to consider looking for employment closer to home. There was a large tertiary hospital with a respectable reputation about an hour from my parents. With some reluctance, I agreed to check out the hospital and see if there were job openings. Like most healthcare facilities, the hospital had no openings in obstetrics, but they did have an opening on second shift in a medical-surgical/orthopedic unit. With encouragement from my parents and the person I was dating from my hometown, I agreed to return home. So my great city job never transpired. I suppose at the time, it just wasn't in my cards to be a Neuro Nurse.

There must have been a purpose for me going home. Over the

years I have come to believe the reason was because some new friends had become a part of my life. They were the people who were meant to enrich me; they were my fate. I worked in the large rural hospital for a little over a year. My many experiences at this first job taught me so many things and allowed me to refine the basic skills and concepts I had learned in nursing school. I was beginning to transform from the novice nurse to a more polished professional. This institution even witnessed my transformation from a graduate to a registered nurse.

What made me leave this hospital? It was not because I did not find the job challenging or disliked working with our nursing team, but rather it was because I was getting married and my fiancé, who was in the military, was stationed in another state.

Our move opened a different chapter in my career journey. I was in another state and looking for a new job. I still wanted to work in obstetrics, so I went to the hospital nearest our home to inquire about working in labor and delivery. Even at this hospital, which was fairly large, I was told there were no openings. Before embarking on the interview I had decided if my first choice was not available, I would inquire about working in one of their adult intensive care units (ICUs). It turned out there were positions open in intensive care, but in neonatal rather than adult ICU. The nurse recruiter asked if I would be interested in working in their neonatal intensive care unit (NICU) where there was a greater staffing need. I had been exposed to a neonatal ICU at one of the city hospitals while I was in nursing school, but as students our experience was mainly observational. As students we were too inexperienced for the NICU staff to assign us direct care of the ill and premature newborns. So my experience in neonatal nursing was essentially nil.

With the recruiter's encouragement, a tour of the unit, and a description of the job I found myself saying "yes." That day, I left the interview with a new and exciting opportunity and a position that would lead to a fulfilling career in Maternal Child Nursing.

Maybe because I loved caring for the newborns, I found myself wanting to learn as much as I could about their care and about the diseases and illnesses afflicting them. Unique for the time, most of the nurses working in this particular neonatal unit had their bachelor's degrees. So, as a result of my desire to learn more, to be educationally equivalent to my NICU peers, and because of a proposal that all nurses would soon be required to have a bachelor's degree in nursing as the minimal entry into practice, I decided to return to school.

Remember when I said earlier if I had known then what I know now how much wiser I would have been? Well, this is another example. Formerly in high school if I had realized the value of college credits, I might have sought a diploma program that offered at least some college credits. Back then, I really did not have a clear understanding of academia and did not see myself going on to school beyond a basic degree. Yes, I wore blinders, but who can change the mindset of an adolescent?

Anyway, going back to school for my degree meant earning 128 college credits. Now the real challenges began since I had to work full-time while going to school. Like many newlyweds, I needed to continue working because we did not have the financial stability to survive on one salary, plus pay tuition. Also, I liked what I was doing and believed caring for newborns was my niche in nursing. What this meant was a lot of juggling in my future.

One variable that helped me return to school was working 3 to 11 shifts. Working these hours allowed me to enroll in morning classes.

The other variable was my husband also decided to continue his education at the same college so he was able to maintain a schedule similar to mine. As a matter of fact, we actually took an Anatomy and Physiology class together in which we had the opportunity to be lab partners. Because I enjoyed dissecting specimens and took the initiative to do the actual cutting, I was bestowed the nickname "Chainsaw" by my favorite lab partner, my husband.

Being married with both of us going to college, meeting everyday expenses, and being ineligible for state financial aid meant we needed to look for a school which was affordable, yet maintained the excellence we were looking for. In our area a local community college fit this bill. So for about three years, during which time I worked in the neonatal intensive care unit, we chipped away at our liberal arts courses. Nearly three years later, when my husband was now out of the military and we were at the point in our educational pursuits at which we needed to transfer to a four year college, we opted to return to Pennsylvania, our home state.

We moved back to our hometown, found an apartment, started new jobs and continued our education together at the same four-year college. Nursing jobs were not plentiful in our locality, nor did any of the hospitals in the area have neonatal intensive care units. It was not until a few years later, when reading a textbook about the historical trends of neonatal nursing, that I realized I was one of the early nurses to work in this specialty. However, as notable as my expertise was, the specialty in my hometown offered no jobs. So, since I could find no openings in any realm of obstetrical nursing, I went back to caring for non-childbearing adults.

My first job in medical surgical nursing prepared me to take a position as a home care nurse. Initially, I knew little about home care nursing except they carried blue leather bags and dressed in navy blue. In my early weeks of home care orientation, I learned some basic principles. I was educated to leave my coat in the car, just in case there was no clean spot in the house to place the coat. I also learned to always spread newspaper out before putting one's leather bag down, and to assume the unexpected behind closed doors.

Shining a flashlight from my car to see street signs (many of which did not exist), getting lost, and trying to find house numbers are lingering visions I have of my home care days. Despite the occasional frustrations of finding a house in the dark, I also have many memorable tales and tangible keepsakes from those days.

I was working as a visiting nurse for about a year and a half when an opportunity to work in obstetrics surfaced. Two smaller community hospitals, one of which had an OB department, were sold to a third hospital. The bigger and more financially stable third hospital built a new hospital and closed the two smaller hospitals. Most of the personnel from the two smaller hospitals transferred to the new facility.

Since only one of the former hospitals had an obstetrical department and the unit in the new hospital was larger, additional obstetric nurses were needed. Thank goodness I had previously worked in a neonatal intensive care unit, because having the experience qualified me to obtain a position in the new hospital's maternity unit.

The anticipated staffing plan for the new facility was for all the obstetrical staff to rotate between labor and delivery, postpartum, normal newborn nursery and the sick newborn nursery. Having experience in two of the four areas (regular and intensive care nursery) made me a viable candidate for one of the open positions. My biggest challenge was learning to care for women in labor.

So because of the closing of two hospitals, and the opening of a brand new one, I had the opportunity to become a labor and delivery nurse. With time, mentoring, and peer support I learned the ins and outs of being an obstetrical nurse.

In the span of the five years I worked at this particular hospital in obstetrics, I continued pursuing my bachelor's degree in nursing while working the 3-11 pm shift. By the time I had completed all my liberal arts and core courses, the university where I chose to continue my studies started a new program for RNs going back to school for their BSN. It was referred to as a RN to BSN program.

The concept of working with RN students in assisting them through accelerated programs to attain their BSN was new. At the time when I decided to pursue my degree, universities and colleges were attempting to define exactly how many credits, if any, to allocate nurses for their diploma school education and for non-credit nursing courses. Since the RN-BSN curriculum was novel and evolving, inconsistencies existed between schools. However, at the time I was committed to a specific geographic location so I had to work with what the local colleges offered to returning RNs. Basically, through standardized testing I was able to challenge about thirty credits. Otherwise, no other credits were allocated for either my diploma education or for prior nursing experience.

After eight years of part-time studies and 128 credits later, I graduated with my BSN. After I graduated I continued to work in labor and delivery. About a year after receiving my degree, my husband who also finished his bachelor's degree, was contemplating a career in healthcare. The sister hospital of the entity where I was currently working (the same rural hospital where I took my first nursing job as a graduate nurse) had a healthcare program my husband thought he might be interested in. I went along on the day he went to speak with the school's admission recruiter. That day changed the direction of my nursing career and took me down a path I never anticipated venturing down.

You see, the recruiter did her job. As she spoke with my husband about his interest in their health-related program she inquired about my interest. When I shared I was a nurse she asked if I had my BSN, which as you know from above, I had recently acquired. Upon hearing I had my bachelor's degree she asked whether I would be interested in teaching Pediatrics at their School of Nursing. Her proposal took me off guard. Teaching nursing was something I had never dreamed of undertaking.

But this was a diploma program, and I did have my bachelor's degree. So technically, I was one degree ahead of the students who I would be teaching, which is generally an academic standard. Still, I questioned if I had the ability to teach. I had never thought of teaching!

At the moment, part of me wanted to say no and part of me found the request intriguing. To give myself time to think, I asked if I could get back to her with my answer in a few days. Naturally, my request was fine. My husband, being the supporter he has always been, encouraged me to give teaching a try. He assured me I would be a great teacher and would be a "natural." He certainly had more faith in me being an educator than I had in myself.

So we both telephoned and said we were interested in our respective offers, which for me meant I now had to go through an interview process. Since our contact person had been the recruiter and not a faculty member, or the director of the nursing program, I needed to go through a formal interview. This would be one of my first lessons on how different the interviewing process is for a hospital staff position than that of a teaching/academic position. My ignorance of the academic process at the time was probably a good thing; otherwise, I might not have had enough confidence in my abilities to pursue the teaching offer.

Sometimes I wonder whether they were just desperate to find a qualified pediatric person, or if they really saw some teacher qualities in me. But, for whatever reason, I was offered the position. During the first months of teaching as I modeled myself after other faculties and began to develop lectures, I came to realize what a monumental task I had undertaken. To keep ahead of the students, I needed to do twice the amount of work. To this day, I can't teach content I do not feel I have a strong grasp of. So for this new academic position, I had to do lots of self-preparation to feel at least somewhat functional. Translated, this meant hours on hours of prep time.

Not only did I teach class content, but I was a clinical instructor as well. This meant I also needed to learn the clinical routine of the affiliated hospital. Since this was a large tertiary hospital there were several subdivisions of the pediatric department (e.g., pediatric intensive care unit, set-down pediatric unit, regular pediatric unit, toddler unit….) which our students rotated through. Thank goodness my husband and I were both in school because our common routines made life a little easier. I could see where the life of a teacher can drive a wedge between two people in a relationship. A lot of work comes home with a teacher, and if a balance is not achieved between family and teaching responsibilities, tension can mount. A teacher can easily lose focus of family time with the demands of schoolwork. Luckily, I had a husband who understood.

When my husband and I took on our new positions, we needed to relocate. For me, this was my second time moving to this community. This time though was different, I was married and we planned on staying longer than I did as a new graduate. I ended up teaching in this position for nearly four years.

After teaching for about a year, I was encouraged by the school's nursing administrators to go back to school to obtain a master's degree. Despite the vision and the path the School of Nursing perceived for me, I saw myself taking a different scholarly route. It would be a path to a master's degree; however, I did not see myself pursuing a master's in nursing. Rather, I desired to complement my nursing knowledge by obtaining an advanced degree in a non-nursing related field.

After working in pediatrics with so many sick children, I saw another area of focus where I thought I could make a difference. One of the pediatric units which captured my interest was where children with chronic illnesses were admitted for treatments when their remissions had lapsed. Having a comprehensive pediatric unit meant there were multiple disciplines working with the children. One area I believed could use improvement was the linkage between a child's school needs and their hospital needs. I thought what a great opportunity for someone who could merge the two roles (nursing and education) to meet the child's academic needs as well as their physiologic needs. It seemed quality of care as well as continuity of care would be better for the child if the same person met both needs.

Another concept which interested me was opening a "sick day care." Again, I thought how complementary an education degree and a nursing degree would be. So with these two thoughts in mind, I went down the road to the local university and earned a master's of science degree with a certification in early childhood education.

With the degree came some restlessness to try something new

and to experience more of what was out there. Meeting new people, traveling, and stepping out of our comfort zones was what we did on a regular basis. We had gone to Hawaii on our honeymoon and gone back several times for vacation, each time having a desire to stay longer. So having just finished school and feeling fairly secure in our employment capabilities, we decided to leave the ways of the east coast and try a new life in Hawaii. Paradise, am I right? Well maybe, with some disparities.

I did not secure a job before moving to Hawaii. I figured since I was qualified for either a nursing job or an education job, I would not have trouble finding some type of employment. I really wanted to find something other than teaching in the traditional classroom and caring for children in the customary hospital setting. I hoped to merge my two dream roles (nursing and child education).

I came across an advertisement for a nanny and gave the position some consideration. The agency was thrilled to have a person with my qualifications inquire. However, in the end, I decided to focus on what I knew best (nursing) so we would have a chance to acclimate to the island and learn some of the Hawaiian culture. After moving, I came to the realization too many new things at the same time had the potential to be overwhelming. So I decided for at least a year, to hold my nursing knowledge constant, while I looked around for an ideal combination job.

Wanting to work with women and children, I naturally went to a large women's and children's hospital located on the "big island." I was hoping to find a position at the hospital that encompassed both of my degrees. Unfortunately, what I later came to realize is each discipline had a hard time visualizing a merged role. For accreditation purposes, everyone either wanted to focus solely on the nursing or solely on the education component.

The hospital had no openings for someone who was a nurse/ early childhood education teacher, but instead, had a number of open positions for staff nurses. Further searching would not lead me to find a combined position, unless I branched off as an entrepreneur and started my own business. So instead of venturing into something new, I took a job at the hospital in their neonatal ICU step-down unit. Here the newborns transitioned from intensive care to going home. I loved working with newborns, so although the job was not my first choice, the position was ideal for me.

As life would have it, within a year we had to leave the island and return to the mainland. We transitioned in the southwest for a few months before returning to Pennsylvania. In the southwest I worked in an obstetric unit in a community hospital. All the nurses at the hospital rotated between labor and delivery, postpartum, and nursery. The variety provided me a great opportunity to learn similar, but different, approaches to delivery of care.

By the time we returned to Pennsylvania a little more than a year and a half had lapsed. Once again, we returned to our hometown. My dream on returning was to find a building I could convert to a sick day care. However, after looking I could not find exactly what I needed with the available funds I had. At the time we also needed a house to live in, so purchasing two buildings was a bit over our budget. I did what most people would; I took a job with hopes of eventually saving enough money to someday open "my" sick day care center.

But sometimes, things don't work out like you expect them to, and as I alluded, I have come to believe other forces occur beyond one's control which cause you to end up where you least expect. Well, for me, you might say the force was a divine one, because it came in the form of a nun.

Working in the nursery at the hospital where I had taken a job was a religious sister who was a member of a progressive order, so did not always wear a habit. In obstetrics we wore scrubs for infection control reasons, and she did as well. I mention her attire, because since she did not dress any differently than anyone else, she did not stand out as a nun. If you were talking with her you would believe she was simply one of the nurses. The thing that connected me with her, beyond being working colleagues, was the fact that she taught nursing at a local Catholic college. At some time as a new employee, I must have shared with her I had a master's degree and previously taught nursing.

Well, it turned out a few months after I started this job she came to me and asked if I would be interested in teaching obstetrical nursing at the college where she taught. They had a part-time faculty position open and needed someone with a master's degree. I believe her request was put forward sometime around June. At the time I told her I really was not interested because I was already working full-time, was trying to get settled back into the area, and just wanted to have some free time to enjoy. What I didn't want to do was end up working one and a half jobs.

When August rolled around and they still had not found a qualified instructor, she came back and asked if I would please reconsider applying. She was a good persuader because I found myself saying "okay" and accepting an interview. I was brought on board the first semester to oversee a group of adult learners who were pursuing nursing degrees. Though I had a master's degree, there was somewhat of a stir because my master's was not in nursing, but rather in education. After special approval from our accrediting board, I was allowed to teach with one stipulation. If I continued to teach I would need to obtain a master's degree in nursing as well. That mandate was acceptable to me because I only planned on teaching one semester. What I did not anticipate was being matched with a great mentor.

The director of the nursing program tagged me with a senior faculty member to serve as my mentor since I was a neophyte teaching on the baccalaureate level. That one semester turned into many years and my part-time clinical position ended up evolving into a full-time load in which I taught in both the classroom and clinical setting. Along the way I found myself working on my master's degree in nursing and eventually my doctorate degree. Oops, bringing up the doctorate is getting way ahead of the story, so let's jump back.

For awhile I continued to work full-time in the OB unit at the hospital as a staff nurse while working part-time as a clinical instructor at the college. In addition to these two roles, I maintained my responsibilities to my family and managed a household. So I was busy! As if all of this was not enough, I was being politely reminded to begin taking courses for my nursing master's. For me, the academics of going back to school was not what seemed daunting; rather, the issue was finding time for travel, study and work. My choice was to go to school, or give up teaching at this particular school.

There was one variable in my favor which made going back to school workable. The college where I was teaching also had a master's program in nursing, which meant I could attend evening classes without compromising study time with travel time. So I started back, working full-time as a staff nurse, teaching part-time and going to school. That pattern lasted for about two years before I switched part-time and full-time positions. I began teaching full-time at the college and working part-time at the hospital. After about four years of part time studies I completed my master's in nursing.

I had been home "in the valley," as we natives referred to the vicinity of our hometown, just long enough to feel restless. I had the urge to try something new and venturesome again. I felt the need to take a break from teaching and from the expectation of going on to school for my doctorate. Enlisting in the Air Force seemed inviting. Working with the recruiter I learned of some intriguing opportunities, so I began the process of enlisting. Unfortunately, during the preliminary stages a family issue surfaced which caused me to halt the process. Again, I lived with the saying "it must not have been meant to be." Hard to swallow sometimes, but necessary if one is to accept what hand he/she has been dealt, and move on.

Well, would you believe the next chapter of my life would be influenced by a nun again? Not the same one, but from the same religious order. I must have had some heavenly connection or maybe someone was looking out for me. Who knows? Whatever, or whomever was watching certainly pointed me in the right direction.

There was a hospital located in our valley that was started and operated by the same religious order that founded the college. At the college where I was teaching very few of the nuns still worked in the hospital, however, some remained active members on the hospital's administrative boards. At one time, the sisters predominantly ran and operated the hospital but over the years the number of religious sisters delivering direct patient care decreased dramatically. Some of the sisters were affiliated with both the college and the hospital and on some matters both entities were seen as one system.

An academic colleague, who was also one of the nuns from this same religious order, asked me to consider an OB/Pediatric nurse manager position that had opened within their hospital system. She told me she thought I would be perfect for the position. Again, I was not sure about pursuing the opportunity but at the same time was curious, so I interviewed to learn more about the position. How many other applicants were my competitors I do not know, but after several interviews I was offered and accepted the position.

This was a great opportunity as a manager to make a difference. The obstetric staff was in the midst of transition, changing from an older model maternity department to a newly renovated and updated mother-baby unit. What more could a manager ask for but to oversee a department embarking on a whole new start! Since the new architectural plans had been developed before my hire, I did not have input into the design of the unit. Though, I did have the opportunity to organize and develop the new department. That was exciting! From having worked in several different obstetrical facilities in several different states, I had some innovative ideas I was excited to share and develop.

Change, though, does not come easy. Much of the nursing staff had worked at the hospital and in the specialty for many years and now things were changing fast: a new unit, a new manager, a new vision…. Exciting and threatening at the same time. Consequently, true to human nature, there were a variety of reactions. Some employees were positive and some struggled to embrace change.

My first year was spent focusing on developing the obstetric and pediatric units. Somewhere in the start of my second year new changes came about. The face of healthcare was transforming and terms such as "downsizing," "restructuring," "cost-containment," and "cutting/controlling lengths of stay" were starting to resonate within the healthcare arena. Being a mid-level manager can be challenging during such times of reductions and downsizings. Mid-level managers feel organizational pressures from both ends: administration or upper management on one level and employees or staff on the other level. They're in a no win situation. During times of cost trimming, mid-level managers are some of the first employees to be let go. Over a short period of time we watched our mid-level managers dwindle drastically.

Once some of the mid-level managers were let go the rippling effect occurred. The workload of those dismissed managers was merely redistributed amongst the remaining managers. This was the predicament I found myself in after I was in the managerial position for about a year. My role grew from overseeing operations in two specialty units to overseeing three units, without reduction in workload or change in financial compensation.

Next, when the daily centralized staffing model was discarded for a more decentralized approach, the team members originally managing the hospital's staffing patterns were either reassigned to open positions or terminated. Naturally, the staffing responsibilities were then added to the plates of the mid-level managers. For this institution the change meant on a daily basis mid-level managers would be responsible for tasks such as replacing employee call-ins, telephoning other staff to see if they could replace the individuals who called out sick, controlling overtime and usage of outside agency nurses, redistributing personnel between patient units based on staffing needs and assigning staff on the float team to appropriate units. In addition to these expectations, we were responsible for opening and closing beds for admissions/discharges, placing ER admissions, and evaluating lengths of stay. Managing staffing for the "house" also meant attention was diverted from one's own units, yet mid-level managers remained responsible for the operations of their units as well.

Reallocation of duties did not stop with being responsible for staffing coverage throughout the entire facility. Instead, a new mandate was enacted from upper management announcing mid-level managers would start rotating house coverage on weekends and on some second and third shifts. House coverage meant being present at the hospital for an eight to twelve hour shift to manage any hospital-wide problems ranging from system operations to patient issues. Examples of responsibilities included: triaging, calling in OR teams for emergency cases, replacing staff call-ins that occurred during the shift, evaluating the status of patients for possible discharge if all beds were full and the ER needed to admit, plus a multitude of other responsibilities.

All the joys I found in the position were being squeezed out of me and exhaustion was setting in. For my personal well-being, I knew I needed to make a change. The workload expectations became too much for one person and administrative support fell short.

I was lucky my colleagues from my teaching days did not forget me. As a matter of fact, I saw some of the faculty members from the college regularly as they supervised students in the hospital. Frequently, they shared how much I was missed and asked if I would consider teaching with them again. I would thank them for the compliment and explain that since my return meant I would need to begin doctoral studies, which was not practical at that time in my life, returning as a full-time faculty member was not possible.

With a young child, family responsibilities, and working full-time I realized trying to focus on doctoral studies would be difficult. The nearest school which offered a doctorate in my area of interest was over two hours away. The distance meant on days I attended classes at least five hours would need to be shifted from study time to travel time. Not really practical when time would be precious.

Hence, returning to school at that point in my life did not seem feasible. I had enough foresight to see something would be sacrificed: either myself or my family. Thus, for another year, in the midst of downsizing and restructuring, I continued to push ahead and tried to weather the job out. I hoped the institution would turn the corner financially and things would once again level out, but this did not happen. The hospital never seemed to recover economically, and about ten years later was bought and restructured by a larger healthcare system.

In time, one of the universities in our valley started a doctoral program which matched my personal needs and professional goals. With the inception of the doctoral program, some of the variables such as the traveling time that previously hindered my potential success no longer existed. Also, I realized returning to teaching and leaving the management position would offer me more time during holidays and summer breaks to spend with my family. Plus, the extra time off would provide me with more studying time and the opportunity to just enjoy being a student. Something, as non-traditional students, we often fail to do. Be "a student," that is.

So, when I saw an advertisement for an open faculty position at the college, I applied. Finding individuals with the appropriate qualifications for nurse educator positions can be difficult. The conundrum is many nurses possess the clinical expertise to teach the art of nursing but lack the necessary teaching credentials to be nurse educators. This time though, I had the necessary credentials and the expertise, plus I was willing to begin pursuing my doctorate.

I did get the position, and again resumed the academic side of my career. That was about twenty years ago and since then I have remained in academia. Throughout the years, I have also maintained some type of clinical practice so as to continue some form of direct patient care. For example, the summer before I resumed teaching, two colleagues and I obtained certification as board certified lactation consultants. Together the three of us opened a home-care breastfeeding consulting business. At the time we were the only three registered nurses in our immediate geographic area who were board certified and offered this type of professional lactation service.

On one hand, our credentials of being board certified enhanced our professional image. Yet, on the other hand, the status of being certificated seemed unnecessary to some. For us, being certified was professionally fulfilling. Through the business we conducted workshops on human lactation for the public and for professionals, we helped businesses set up lactation centers, we had our own supply of breastfeeding accessories, we ran a breast pump rental station, and we made home visits from both hospital and private physician referrals. We were busy! All three of us ran the lactation business and were employed full-time as obstetrical staff or taught in an academic setting; all while juggling other responsibilities in our lives.

Along with family responsibilities and the business, I maintained other duties such as going to school and working on my doctorate. I kept up this triad of activity for about five years. Then, a year and a half before I completed my doctoral dissertation, our business partnership dissolved. One business partner's pregnancy, relocating for a spouse's job, my schooling and the need to focus on personal matters made us decide that dissolving the business was our best option. Subsequently, after five years we closed the corporation and each pursued other interests.

I finished my doctorate approximately a year and a half later. The topic I selected for my doctoral dissertation stemmed from the lactation business and my experience working with breastfeeding families. From running the lactation business we learned how to set up and manage a business and how to be entrepreneurs. During this period I also completed my doctoral qualifying exams, developed scholarly papers, published, conducted research, and did my doctoral defense. As we say in doctoral studies, "a lot of hoops to jump through." After much hard work and a successfully completed dissertation, I finally jumped through my last hoop and was awarded a doctorate of philosophy degree (Ph.D.).

Sometimes when individuals complete their doctorate they venture down new career paths, but I did not. I continued teaching at the school of nursing I taught at while pursuing doctoral studies. Earning a doctorate meant I could pursue a promotion in academic rank from assistant to associate professor, plus I could submit my application for tenure. Within a year of receiving my doctorate I was celebrating my promotion in rank, and achievement of tenure status. I had earned two respected honors in academia, both testaments to my commitment and dedication to lifelong learning.

About a year and a half after I received my doctorate I would have another experience that would once again take me back to the classroom as a student. This time the Girl Scouts were the catalyst for change, specifically, a summer Girl Scout camp. I have to say, this new adventure once again started with my weakness of not being able to say no.

The scenario transpired when I took our daughter to sign up for her first summer camp. There were only a few days before camp was scheduled to begin and the staff had one unresolved problem; they had no full-time camp nurse. So the frantic search for someone was on. The camp counselors at registration were desperate to find someone to fill the position, and guess who entered the picture? I really can't remember how "the cat got out of the bag" thing happened. I mean, how the counselors found out I was a nurse, and better yet, a pediatric nurse! Well, there was no saying, "no." Most of the counselors employed by the camp for the summer were college students between eighteen to twenty-one years of age. They had a knack for begging and saying all the right things. They were so skilled at pleading I found myself uttering "Okay, I'll do it!" I didn't just agree to do it; I really did it! I agreed to live at the camp in the health center 24/7 for four weeks. In the end both my daughter and I packed our bags and headed off to camp, a true mother-daughter bonding thing.

Well, there were a lot of adventures which transpired at the camp, but so I don't get sidetracked from how the camp experience led me back to school, I will save some of those adventures for later in the book. While at the camp I found myself in several situations where I wished I could have done more to directly help some of the children who were injured or had health problems. In these situations I needed a broader scope of practice, and regretted I didn't have one.

Several times I found myself calling other healthcare providers about a child with no healthcare insurance to see if they would see the child without charging. I was surprised at how many campers had no health insurance, or had plans with limited coverage. On several occasions, when the child had no healthcare insurance if I had greater autonomy and a broader scope of practice, I could have prescribed specific treatments and medications and managed them myself.

Not only was healthcare insurance a frequent issue, but another concern was the closest medical backup was a distance away, which in all actuality was the emergency room of a community hospital. However, despite having at least some emergency back-up, not all issues were emergencies, and not everyone had healthcare insurance that covered urgent care visits.

Since I never had been a camp nurse before, I lived and learned. Prior to assuming the position I was assured I would see mainly bug bites, cuts, abrasions, poison ivy, and homesickness. In the fifty years the camp had been sponsored nothing major happened in terms of injuries or medical issues. When I tell my camp stories later in the book, you will see I was the first nurse, since the camp's inception, to call 911 several times in four weeks for medical emergencies.

My sense of feeling limited in what I could do in terms of treating some of the campers, convinced me I needed to expand my scope of practice and increase my autonomy. So, the fall academic semester following my summer camp experience I enrolled in a nurse practitioner program.

While I went to school I continued to teach full-time; and as many nurses do while in school, I worked my regular job during the day and attended classes in the evening. I was fortunate to attend a part-time program that predominantly scheduled nursing classes for non-traditional students in the evening. In four years I finished all the clinical and the course work, passed my nurse practitioner certification examination, and began volunteering as a nurse practitioner at a free clinic.

The free clinic was started by a group of concerned parishioners with the intent of delivering free healthcare to the community's uninsured and underserved populations. I volunteered at the clinic a few hours a week while I maintained my full-time job as a nurse educator. With a little juggling in my life things managed to fall into place. But hey, what's a little juggling. At this point in my life, I was used to shifting gears.

Over time my husband and I found the cold winters of Pennsylvania to be harsh on our aging bodies. Now after some life changes, I am still a nurse educator but at a different university in a warmer state, where I still volunteer as a nurse practitioner in a health center. I continue to explore and enjoy the path of my journey. I know there will be bumps ahead, beautiful things to see along the way, and yes, a need to remind myself to stop and smell the flowers.

So, I have taken you down the road from the beginning where I first started, to where I am currently. What I have described thus far basically has been the straight shot. I have not deviated much to talk of the people or events experienced along the way. But now it is time to step back and take you down side streets and through detours. To meet other people and glimpse some of the events I experienced en route. Quite obviously, it is the people and the events which have made this my journey—my personal journey. In the upcoming chapters let's travel some of those twists and turns. Let's meet some of the people and recount events I experienced. Let's saddle up to venture down the side roads.

Chapter Three

THE FIRST ROUND:

NURSING SCHOOL ESCAPADES

Too much of a good thing can get you in trouble.

(UNKNOWN)

Beginning

Reflecting on the memories of my nursing school days, many of those recollections come from my first years of training. I have to wonder if this is because I was so impressionable at the time or because many of the experiences were so new to me that I savored them. Did maturity and the familiarity of experience dull my sense of novelty? I would like to think not, but instead, believe I still feel a sense of fulfillment when I do the unexpected or have one of those "aha" moments, which are so frequent when one is first learning.

Overall, despite some ups and downs and some tears, the positive experiences in my first nursing school far outshined the negative ones. During my years as a student my instructors helped me to grow both as a person and as a nurse. After this first nursing school experience my other educational ventures were of a different caliber, and symbolized something different to me. My later school experiences were never quite like my diploma education days where my nursing foundation and professional values were originally etched. When I think of those days I have to say, "No wonder I have so many early stories to share…the experience was a hallmark time in my life and in my career." These events provided me with a lifetime of memories and enduring friendships.

Captain of the Ship

"Faculties are quitting and the school is closing." Imagine hearing such whisperings a few weeks after starting school. Being freshmen, and already a bit nervous, we quickly realized the situation was serious and could impact our education. As it turned out, some but not all, faculties did quit. Why? Because nurses were not being shown the respect they deserved by the medical director of the hospital affiliated with the school.

The hospital's chief of staff or medical director made belittling remarks about nurses to some of our faculties. He treated nurses subserviently, declared himself "the captain of the ship" and insisted what he said be accepted without questions. What this medical director did not realize was he was dealing with a new generation of autonomous nurses and the "captain of the ship" mentality was a thing of the past. Apparently, this man was out of touch with evolving times. Today, and at that time, such linear thinking only infuriated nurses. Mistakenly, he chose to spar with free-thinking, intellectual professionals who would not tolerate his egotistical thinking.

It was not an easy decision for most of our teachers to resign, but they did what they felt was ethically and professionally right. Though we were concerned about what would happen to us, and who would take their places, we did not begrudge them for their decisions. Rather, we respected them for standing up for all nurses. What was fascinating was the event signified a major stride for nursing, and the change was happening at "our" school!

In the midst of all the commotion, what we worried about most was, "But what about us?" We stressed over our future, questioned whether we would be subjected to the director's disrespectful mentality and pondered if we had made a mistake attending a school with political undertones. Fortunately, our uncertainties were put to rest when remaining faculties assured us the school was not closing. With this guarantee we were able to shift our focus to studying and once again being freshman.

I must say, after the initial unrest the new school director, who took over and forged ahead, did a remarkable job. This person did such a commendable job things did not seem to miss a beat. As we were thrust into the realities of surviving a vigorous nursing curriculum, and staying abreast of our studies, life moved on and we moved ahead. We as a class, however, did come away with the realization if nurses and doctors were to work together the "captain of the ship" mentality would have to sink with the ship.

Big Sisters, Housemothers, The Living Room, Telephones, and New Friends...

Are these words and phrases random thoughts? It may seem so, but actually they are the thoughts which flash through my mind when I think back to my first nursing school days. I can't overlook sharing some of these early experiences because I believe many of them molded me into the nurse I am today. The first nursing school I attended, the diploma program was the grass roots of my nursing career. It was my maiden voyage.

I was merely eighteen when I originally started nursing school. At this young age, and fresh out of high school, I did not have many life distracters to interfere with my being a student. Later when advancing my career I juggled school with other life responsibilities: wife, mother, full-time employee, teacher.... so the experience of being a student was never quite like my first venture.

For some of you, the italicized words and descriptors in the title may seem unrelated or out of context, but for those of you who may have graduated from a diploma nursing program, I know you understand. More than likely you will smile and say, "Oh, yeah, we did that too." But most of all, I bet you could take each of the above words and phrases and weave your own stories. You could share your own nursing school memories and at the same time provide a glimpse of yourself as a nurse.

If I took the time to tell you about each of these thoughts, what would I tell you? First, I would talk about our Big Sisters because they were one of the first individuals we met. I will use the phrase Big Sisters because in my particular class we had no male students. However, in classes which had male students we used the phrases Big Brothers and Big Sisters.

The summer before I started nursing school my Big Sister took the time to write me a letter. She congratulated me on my acceptance and inquired if I had any questions about school or nursing. Receiving the letter was reassuring and affirmed my inclination that I had made the right school choice. I liked the idea of having a Big Sister and appreciated the connection she created so I would know someone on my first day as a beginning nursing student.

You might be wondering just what Big Sisters were. Quite simply, they were the senior level nursing students when we were freshman, hence Big Sisters. Each of us was assigned to a Big Sister unless there was a disproportionate number between classes. In such cases, two freshmen shared a Big Sister, but truthfully, everyone wanted a Big Sister all to themselves.

Our Big Sisters guided us and showed us the ropes. They looked out for us. They did a number of things such as quizzing us on content when we were studying for exams, offering study tips, introducing us at fraternity parties, and letting us know which teachers were helpful and which teachers to avoid. Simply put, they strived to help us have a positive experience. We looked up to them. They seemed to know so much that we were awed by all they had accomplished. To us, being seniors meant our Big Sisters had made it. They would soon be "real" nurses. Exactly where we wanted to be, instead of just beginning!

Our Big Sisters helped us through our first year and showed us by example how to be future Big Sisters. The Big Sister tradition was passed down through generations of nurses, before the role eventually phased out. Today, the concept of mentoring is very similar to the concept of Big Sisters.

Housemothers, you either loved them or hated them. They were your parents' conscience, surrogate parents when your parents could not be there. We had two housemothers: one we loved who was a mother to everyone, and one we considered a pain. Some felt the less favored housemother was simply nosey and thrived on knowing everyone's business. Consequently, she was not appreciated by most of the girls. Instead, some took pleasure playing small tricks on her. And boy, could she get mad! Well deserving, but livid no less. Naturally, her outbursts only added to everyone's delight. As a result, she was the unwitting victim of many antics.

I remember once some of the girls intentionally enticed her away from the small wooden desk that was situated at the entrance of our community living room and routinely used as an office desk by the housemothers. As some students distracted her, others took her desk and hid it. So, of course, when she turned around her work station was gone and nobody seemed to know what happened. Like a drill sergeant, she conducted a search of our dorm which was one floor above the living room. Wouldn't you know, while she was upstairs investigating "the crime," her desk miraculously reappeared in its original spot? It was unbeknownst to all exactly how this happened. Nobody seemed to know a thing. Her furnishings just materialized! Of course, while she went upstairs to investigate, the thieving group secretly slipped back around and returned the desk.

I would imagine anyone who assumed the saintly role of being a housemother would have an assortment of humorous and unbelievable stories to impart around a campfire. I reckon they would tell you, "I have heard it all." Or, they might chuckle and secretly share, "She/he must have thought I was pretty stupid to believe that story!"

Let me tell you a little about our housemothers and what their roles were. First of all, they were the gatekeepers. Nobody and I mean nobody, got to see one of the nursing students living in the dorms without first addressing the housemother. Males were particularly targeted. Absolutely no male visitors were allowed beyond the communal living room. Even fathers were not allowed in the dorm area except on special occasions, such as move-in day. This ruling might seem a little extreme, but you have to remember this was a Catholic nursing school and our dorm floor was just above the convent quarters. What a parent's dream, their daughter living amongst nuns!

It was a policy if you were caught with a male in your room you would be dismissed from the nursing program. No ifs, ands or buts. You were out. At that time coed dorms were virtually nonexistent in hospital-based nursing schools. One reason was that few males were pursuing nursing careers and the coed dorm concept was still somewhat controversial. Today, I imagine issues of discrimination could possibly surface over exclusive female dorms. Yet, back then, this no male practice was reflective of conservative times.

As I previously mentioned, the housemother's reception desk was situated at the entrance to the community living room. No visitors navigated past the desk and through the living room doors without explaining their intent to the housemother. Housemothering was a 24/7 job, except during school breaks which were not very often.

If a male arrived to pick up his date he was instructed to wait in the living room while the housemother called for the requested student on the house telephone. She then informed the student "your gentleman caller is here," so you could come down to the living room to meet him. Male visitors were not permitted beyond the designated living room. If a couple decided to visit in this common area they did so in the presence of the housemother and all the other students who opted to watch television, visit, play a card game, chat, or play the piano. So, you can imagine why few couples stayed long in the living room. Instead, they met and then left on their own adventure.

The living room, though not expensively done, was nicely furnished and had a homey ambiance. There was a Victorian style to the décor. I enjoyed the cozy fireplace and hearing someone play the grand piano, although I did not play. Playing the piano, for me, is an example of one of those things in life you wished you learned but never did. Who knows, maybe learning to play is still in my cards.

Despite the living room's heavy traffic the area always had a tidy appearance. The room was the core of the nursing residence. You might liken it to a beehive. One rarely found the area unoccupied. Somehow everyone always knew what was going on in this central spot, such as who was in the living room, who was coming, who was leaving, who was being picked up, and who was waiting for whom.

I particularly remember the hustle and bustle that occurred one evening when a famous movie star with the initials B.B. was coming to the school to pick up one of our Big Sisters for a date! She truly was the envy of everyone! Rumor had it they had met at one of the "classy" taverns/restaurants in center city Philadelphia. Whether that was true or not, I don't know.

Of course this potential romance was hot news. Everyone desperately wanted to catch a glimpse of the movie star. Having a celebrity come to the school for "one of us" was exciting! A once in a lifetime event to have a movie star in your presence! But guess what? If he was coming for his date that meant he had to stop at the housemother's desk and wait in the living room like everyone else. Yes, the living room! How perfect, because that meant we all would have the opportunity to see him! All we had to do was figure out a reason to be in the living room around pick-up time.

You would have thought the guy had forty dates because that is about how many nursing students felt the need to sit in the living room watching television, socializing, playing cards, or talking with the housemother just so they would be in the vicinity of the desk at pick-up time. Some people even tried concealing themselves behind the living room chairs, hoping to catch a peek at the couple. The poor girl must have been mortified, but what could one expect from a bunch of curious nursing students! Of course, when he arrived, we all agreed B.B. was extremely handsome and our Big Sister... well, she was absolutely gorgeous. She made us proud!

Another memory of my nursing school experience was how about fifty of us shared two telephones for talking with friends, relatives, boyfriends... or whomever. There was a third phone which was only used for in-house calls, like the housemother ringing up to tell someone their date had arrived. Imagine fifty girls sharing two such valuable commodities! Is it a surprise certain people always seemed to break the fifteen-minute time limit on calls? Most likely not, if you ever had the experience of living with a group of people in a dorm-like setting. If you did, then you can appreciate how tempers flared when people exploited the time restrictions. Luckily for the offenders, there were no penalties for abuse other than being berated by one's peers. No one had the authority to restrict someone from using the telephones. Nevertheless, people retaliated by using other more subtle tactics. For example, if there was an incoming call for a repetitive phone abuser, one would simply reply the person was not in or unavailable. A tic for a tack!

The two telephones were situated in the hall so anyone passing a ringing phone answered them. There were no telephones in our rooms and cell phones and computers were not available as everyday modes of communicating. This meant people did not text and/or e-mail. One of the two telephones was situated in a phone booth structure in the hallway, and the other telephone was mounted on the hall wall. At least when talking on the telephone in the booth, one could close the door for a private conversation. When talking on the mounted phone, there was little to no privacy. A person was wise to give out the telephone number for the booth phone if desiring a private conversation. Otherwise, one's conversation was open to anyone passing through the hall. Or was audible to those who thought they had a reason to listen. The only drawback in sharing the one number was that the caller had a harder time getting through on the telephone lines. It was not uncommon for someone to say, "I tried to call you all night, but I couldn't get through."

During the morning hours, the telephones remained quiet because most callers knew we were either in class or on the clinical units. I would say anywhere from after 3 pm to midnight telephone traffic was constant. Around midnight telephone usage died down to almost nothing because people retired in preparation for early morning classes and clinical schedules. Alumni working as staff nurses in the affiliated hospital frequently informed us we had no idea how lucky we were our telephone calls were unrestricted. They described how they had prescribed study hours, quiet time and a lights out hour when all incoming and outgoing calls were prohibited. "You," as they told us, "don't know how good you have it."

The telephones were the center of our universe; they were our outside lifelines. Voices, laughter and sometimes even sobs would echo through the hallways as callers and receivers conversed. The voices gave life to the dorms. There was energy about the whole telephone scene. A phone call was something we all waited for—and unexpected callers brightened our days!

Lastly, the word friends comes to mind when I think of this nursing school. Friends meant survival. They were the ones you laughed and cried with and the ones who had faith you would be a stellar nurse. Friends meant late night talks, dorm parties, arguments, money pooling, and so much more. You were convinced if it wasn't for the support of friends you wouldn't have made it through. How could one do nursing school without friends? Impossible, without such buddies and partners in crime!

Old nursing school friends are the faces you look for at professional nursing conventions, at new jobs, and in crowds. They will forever be a part of you. What is really special is when, after many years of not seeing each other, you have not lost contact and you are just a phone call away.

Can't Believe I Did It: Eluding the Nuns

This is one of those events in my life I cannot believe I was stupid enough to have agreed to. I risked being expelled from nursing school before I really started. Somewhere around my second weekend at school my boyfriend and his friend came to visit. They were both entering their senior years at two different colleges, so were familiar with college life. Both found the stipulation forbidding males to enter our dorm area, and the rule of not being permitted beyond the community living room, absolutely absurd. So naturally, having no access merely piqued their curiosity, and provided them with a challenge.

Our dorms were old, small and plainly furnished giving them the appearance of any typical dorm. I had already described my room to my friends but they were curious and wanted to have a look. After repeatedly saying, "No, you can't sneak up to the dorms, I'll get in trouble if you're caught," I found myself giving in. Not a wise choice, but rather an impulsive decision, and one which could have cost me dearly.

Luckily, it was a weekend and the beginning of a new academic year. With classes just underway there was little homework. Not much schoolwork meant the majority of dorm students headed home on Friday. So, essentially our dorm was empty except for a few students who stayed to work or who lived too far to make weekly trips home, such as myself. My room was situated near an exit at the end of a hall. Almost everyone at my end of the hall had gone home. This made the hallway relatively quiet and devoid of the usual bustling activity.

Having an exit so close to my room was ideal to sneak someone up the staircase, but with one obstacle. Recall, I had mentioned the nursing school I attended was a Catholic institution, and the living quarters for the nuns were just below our floor. Well, that meant we shared the same stairwell. The door off the stairwell leading to the nuns' convent was kept locked to keep students out. The majority of the nuns used their private elevator, but a few of the nuns preferred to use the steps. Not many took the stairs, but in this case, even one would have been too many. Can you imagine the surprise on the faces of both parties if the nuns and guys collided on the steps? Hysteria on the part of the nuns I'm sure, with fatal repercussions for me.

Exactly when one of the nuns might decide to take the stairs was unpredictable. But my friends and I decided we could manage the escapade without being caught. Well, an angel must have been on my shoulder because, surprisingly, we pulled it off! The stairwell remained clear of nuns as my friends ascended and descended the steps. I stayed off the stairwell and met them at the top exit. I used the elevator so I would not be seen with the two "criminals." If they got caught, our plan was to say they were lost and had been separated from me.

Normally, visitors had to check in with the housemother before they could visit with whomever they came to see. But, again, things worked in our favor that day. Our regular housemother had a couple of hours off, so instead of her watching the entrance as usual, two of the hospital security guards were assigned the responsibility. This is where ethnicity certainly has its advantage. You see, this particular nursing school was situated in South Philadelphia or "Little Italy." So here is the scenario: you have two Italian security guards and an Italian boyfriend coming to see his Italian girlfriend. Think there was any problem here? Course not! Right past the guards my boyfriend and his friend went!

Between my boyfriend's smooth talking and his Italian heritage, he and his partner in crime gained access into the nursing school residence. The guards called me on the house phone to meet my friends at the entrance of the school. I was instructed my friends could only visit for a few minutes. Clearly, we knew the guards meant they could visit in the guest living room but we thought we would extend our privilege to the dorm rooms. We figured no one would be the wiser since the guards could not see the living room from their station.

After I checked to ensure the stairwell was free of other students or nuns, I sent the guys up the stairs. Believe me when I say my heart was racing! It was pounding! Amazingly, we all made it. I went up the elevator and the boys up the stairwell without being seen by anyone.

Nobody was around. Our surroundings were unbelievably quiet. I was so nervous I don't think my friends were in the dorm for more than five minutes before I was shushing them out. I allowed one quick survey of my room and I had them out of there. I'm not sure now why I was so worried about how long they were in the room. The point was, they were there and their mere presence would have been an issue. Their physical presence in the dorm meant I had broken the rules. Looking back I think my friends relished the challenge of getting up to the dorm unscathed more than they cared about seeing my room. Nevertheless, no matter what the reason, I took a big risk. Dumb!

Peculiar Me

When I left for nursing school I was "going steady" with my boyfriend. In my home town, when a girl went steady, she wore the male's high school ring. It was a big thing to be wearing a boy's ring! The new ring was slid over the girl's finger so it rested on top of her class ring. Made for a heavy finger!

We didn't care the ring combination was heavy, didn't fit well, or the stone setting and metal surface of the girl's ring was often damaged. No, we were just pleased to signify we were going steady. I had no idea this ring tradition was unique and not symbolic of how others going steady symbolized commitment. As a matter of fact, I found out later when some of my classmates initially caught a glimpse of my ring finger, they thought I was peculiar. They did not know the figurative meaning of the stacked adornments. Just several hundred miles from my home the double ring style had no significance. I was under the naïve impression everyone recognized the double rings as a universal "I am going steady" icon.

So there I was, the first day of my nursing school program, not knowing one of my Big Sisters had spotted the ring combination and brought it to the attention of others. My ring finger was the topic of conversation along with nonchalant glances, which I never even noticed. Thank goodness at the time I was not aware of everyone's interest in my fingers, or I would have been mortified. Being a freshman I just wanted to fade into the woodwork, and not be singled out.

Apparently, they thought I was pretty eccentric wearing the two ring combination. I soon learned that for them, going steady meant wearing your boyfriend's ring on a chain around one's neck, not cumbersomely on a finger. I continued to be "odd" and wore my ring in this fashion until my relationship dissolved. I never did wear a boyfriend's ring on a chain around my neck.

Initiation Downfall

Some refer to the tradition as hazing, but we called the occurrence "initiation." All freshmen went through the process. Initiation at our school was not an event hosted by a sorority. Being a small nursing school we did not have sororities, instead, we had Big Sisters. Big Sisters were the masterminds of the initiation ceremonies.

The affair was something the seniors took pleasure in warning us of. They loved sharing their own experiences, more than likely exaggerating at least a little, to intensify our apprehension. It was not a time we looked forward to, but simply accepted as part of the tradition package. Though we were nervous about what to expect, we never felt threatened. These schemers were people who were learning to save lives and help people. Plus, we realized since we had started school these same sisters, our initiators, were the ones who looked out for us.

Nonetheless, despite our qualms, going through this rite of passage was expected. Special activities were planned. We were also informed when the pre-ceremonial events started, if we did not do what our Big Sisters requested, we would be put on what was referred to as the "S_ _ _ List." So for a number of weeks we obliged their demands. Some stipulations were simple; yet many were humbling. One such example was when they had all "little sisters" dress up in cloth diapers and other childish outfits and paraphernalia, and go into the hospital's cafeteria to "enjoy a meal." Of course, we endured a few snickers from our professional colleagues. More than likely though, I suspect some of the alumni diners were recalling their own such embarrassing days.

At the end of our weeks of favors, we either passed the pre-ceremonial activities or were bestowed a Baby Ruth candy bar. The symbolic candy bar was hung from the dorm room doors of those who had aspired to the category of "S_ _ _ List" members. If you were the recipient of a candy bar, you could expect your final initiation day to be right up there with a walk through hell.

Though meant to be fun, being blindfolded and led down a corridor which had been transformed to the hellish decor of a haunted house was unnerving. As we were guided down the hall, slimy things touched us. And other times, we were asked to feel unknown greasy, gooey things which we were told was someone's brain, intestine, heart.... Thankfully, in all these antics, nobody was physically harmed, just taken aback and a bit anxious because of the unknowns.

Mainly, we were asked to touch mysterious objects. Our

imaginations went a little crazy. In reality all the items were purely fabrications of what we were told the objects were. Probably the worst part of the experience for me was when we were still blindfolded and instructed to crawl on all fours amongst some bizarre feeling stuff. Yuk!

Our nursing school had been graduating nurses for quite some time, so this tradition had been practiced for many generations between Big Sisters and Little Sisters. I suppose originally someone must have thought the process built character or some such attribute. Who knows what the initial intent was. Well, some in our class thought differently. Time and a new caliber of students meant the evolution of new values and perceptions. Shortly after our initiation ceremony had transpired, a memo from our nursing director was released banning any future initiation activities. So, the tradition ended with our class. Unfortunately for us, the decree came after the fact. But at least we had gotten through the events unscathed.

Learning Triage in Real-Time

The hospital affiliated with the nursing school was one of the main burn centers in the geographic area. The school and hospital were located fairly close to some of the city's largest petroleum refineries. On this particular day, like any typical day, when the telephone rang we stopped what we were doing to listen for our name to be yelled.

This time, though, the announcement was different. The shouter hollered. "Everyone is to report to the emergency room, there's been an explosion in the oil refineries and victims are coming. Everyone to the ER…NOW!"

We were told it did not matter what year in the nursing program we were. Everyone's presence was requested because the hospital needed as many hands as they could muster, as soon as they could, because victims were on their way. It was expected our hospital would receive the majority of the casualties because we were the closest burn center to the refineries.

Walking into the emergency room I was awed at how many white lab coats, blue scrubs and white uniforms I saw. People seemed to be busy everywhere setting up equipment, gathering supplies, and giving and taking orders. A sense of controlled chaos and an underlying sense of excitement prevailed. Adrenalin was pumping. I had never taken part in a medical disaster so did not know what to expect. But I did know, as insignificant as my contribution might be, the knowledge I would gain would be irreplaceable.

When the first rescue vehicles arrived and shrieked to a stop outside the ER doors I was introduced to the concept of triage. This was when I learned the basics of the process. I heard administrators directing staff who were assisting victims to take the casualties to a specific area based on the victim's needs. Some of the injured were whisked off to intensive care units or to the burn unit, while some stayed in the ER or were positioned on stretchers in the ER hallways. I was directed to stay in the ER corridor and help patients as well as doctors and nurses. I can't say I did anything heroic. But maybe, I made someone a little more comfortable as he/she waited to be attended to by a "real" doctor or nurse.

Within two hours or so of the first ambulance's arrival, the hospital's administrators realized there would not be as many wounded as initially anticipated, and therefore some of the responders such as the student nurses could leave. In the end, casualty numbers were small and the hospital did well in responding to the needs of the community. As for me, I learned what it meant to triage and be part of a triage team.

Doorknob Terror

The brightness of the hallway light glowing through the glass pane above my dorm room door was minimized, thanks to a former student who placed floral designed contact paper over the glass pane. Since I was now accustomed to resident life, this small bit of shining light no longer disturbed my sleep. At one time I required complete silence and total darkness to sleep. Now, thanks to dormitory life, I could sleep soundly despite bright lights and loud noises. I had learned to adapt.

Tonight, as every night, the hallway light was on. It was probably a good thing the light stayed on because the dorms were old. On quiet nights, the hallway oozed a feeling of eeriness. That is why if you had to go to the community bathroom in the middle of the night, you thought twice about venturing into the hall. It wasn't you had to worry about bodily harm, but rather the atmosphere was strangely different at night.

On this particular night I had worked the 3 to 11 PM shift as a nurse's aide so as to earn some extra money. I had returned to the dorm around 11:30 PM. Tired and with no plans to do anything special, I changed and went straight to bed. The dormitory was essentially empty. Maybe one other person had stayed the weekend, but I suspected they were now out, probably working nights in the hospital.

I was exhausted so sleep came quickly. I am not sure how long I slept, if I had just dozed or if I had been asleep for a couple of hours, but I was startled awake by an odd sound outside my door. I thought, "What was that sound? Was it the door? Was there someone in the hall messing with my doorknob? Did I lock my door, I believe so. Or was it just a sound I heard in a dream?"

I gasped with the comprehension of the noise and lunged up

in bed as my body released a flood of adrenalin. Hence my heart pounded and my eyes dilated. As my eyes riveted to the door, I had an instant of regret because I could not see beyond the door. What I would have given at that moment to have X-ray eyes. I sat there like a statue. I was afraid to move for fear I would be heard. Maybe whoever was there thought I was out, or maybe, they did know I was there and it was me they had come for. How the mind goes wild!

All kinds of images flashed through my mind. I imagined being killed in my bed and no one finding me until Monday when I was a no show for classes. I was doomed. Did I see shadows at the bottom slit of the door? Was that the shadow of someone's shoes? As I stared through the silent darkness, I swore I saw the doorknob turning ever so slowly. "What would I do…what did I have to defend myself….nothing….how stupid… how could I not have kept something by my bed to protect myself! Even a baseball bat would suffice. There's not even a telephone to call for help—it's out in the hall, so far away."

I swore if I survived I'd never be caught defenseless again. I watched and watched, stared and stared and never moved an inch. I didn't hear feet moving or leaving. I didn't hear another sound; but I continued to stare and hold my position, afraid to move and afraid to breathe. As I sat up in bed intently watching with no further sounds heard, and the door knob no longer turning, my body must have relaxed enough to allow the adrenalin surge to recede. As hard as this may be to believe, I did eventually fall back to sleep sitting up against my pillow with my eyes closed, yet still averted towards the door. It was amazing I dozed. I can't recall falling back to sleep. I suppose it must have been the emotional and physical exhaustion which caused my body to succumb to sleep.

I awoke to a bright Sunday morning with the hall light still on and sunlight shining in my room. I was there by myself and no one had invaded my room. "Was there really someone at my door, or was the incident merely my overactive imagination?" It seemed too real to have only been a dream. So I think…yes, initially there was someone outside my door!

A Needle, Ice Cubes and Friends

Ice cubes, a needle, friends and me; these were all the ingredients needed to pierce my ears. Nothing fancy—no piercing booths or piercing guns, instead, we managed with friends and a "sterile" needle. I had wanted my ears pierced for a long time, but ear piercing was something not permitted in my parent's house. My sisters and I knew someday when we were older and no longer lived home we would have our ears pierced. There were too many beautiful earnings we longed to wear!

So, I had put piercing my ears to the back of my mind as something I would plan to do someday. Though I must admit, I never imagined getting my ears pierced would play out as it did. There were no catastrophic outcomes like my ear lobes falling off, infections or anything so detrimental. Instead, the event of how my ears were pierced was just a rather unique experience.

I don't remember exactly how our conversation evolved to the point I revealed I had always wanted pierced ears, but somehow it did. Several of us were hanging out together in one of the larger dorm rooms just chit-chatting about our clinical day, instructors, boyfriends or whatever topic struck us as important at the moment. We probably had some popular tune like a Creedence Clearwater Revival song blaring from the stereo, were lounging around in our pajamas and sipping some favorite cola beverage. It was our typical way of spending down- time when we broke away from the daily demands of nursing school. It was times like these we solved many of our most pressing issues or fabricated some mischievous plot that sounded fun and exciting, but when actually played out, turned out quite differently.

So, can you visualize it? Several nursing students hanging out in their flannel pajamas, sitting cross-legged on the floor or on the beds chatting from one topic to the next, and violá the conversation turns to ear piercing. Of course, one of the girls deemed herself an expert at piercing ears and someone else happened to have a clean needle stashed in her room. A clean needle, not a sterile needle, but no problem, a lit match would resolve the sterility issue. Burn the tip with the match flame; sterile technique at its finest. As for ice cubes, we had freezer trays full of them. I was sucked in; no stopping now, no reason to back out. My friends were excited. They had found something fun to do!

So there we were: me sitting in a chair in the center of the room, my friends in a circle around me, and someone holding an ice cube to my ear until my lobe turned numb. My ear was so frozen the lobe could probably have fallen off and I would not have noticed. Then came the perfectly marked circles made with a ballpoint pen, one in the center of each lobe. Stand back and assess the marking. Yes, they all agreed, they had the right spot…and now make the puncture. "Don't look; it won't hurt; it's done." A little blood…a little throbbing… and "hold still we need to do it again." Oh yes, I almost forgot…the second ear, another testimony of my bravery.

"You don't want the holes to close, right?" "Definitely not, put the earnings in." "Now all you have to do is rotate the earnings once a day and clean the pierced holes with alcohol." My friends were good. They even remembered to include patient teaching information. Our nursing faculties had taught them well!

I survived. As a whole, the piercing wasn't bad, at least while my lobes were numb. But then came the throbbing. Yes, the throbbing after the thawing. But I endured. My ears were finally pierced! No way would I ever let the holes close up. One nursing school piercing was enough. Not that the ordeal was that bad, it was just something I would not want to do again. But you know what? My ears did not get infected, so there must have been something to that match sterilizing technique. Thanks to the escapades of my dorm friends, the holes in my ear lobes today are the same holes made that day with a needle, ice cubes, and friends.

Nasal Spray – Sell Your Soul

This is another of those stories which, when I reflect on, I think I was pretty foolish to have done and even luckier there were no ramifications. First, let's start by saying if you were ever a full-time student you can appreciate how financially strapped students can be. There is never extra money and usually what little money one has is just enough to survive from week to week. For me, when I had little funds, my diet for the week consisted of cans of tuna fish or cranberry sauce. I was going for the protein and vitamin C. Being able to appreciate such financial constraints you can probably comprehend why I would agree to participate in a clinical trial study.

Pharmaceutical companies were well aware of the impoverished pockets of medical and nursing students. So, as future healthcare providers, we were an easy collection of consenting human samples. Smartly, the investigating companies enticed us with money and suggested that our participation might help others in the future. They knew our soft spots.

Just as the pharmaceutical representatives calculated, a group of us figured participating in the study would be a quick and easy way to earn extra cash. As I think back on what we did, we sold our souls for about $10.00. Pretty pathetic, wouldn't you say? Of course we signed our lives away, agreeing not to hold the company responsible for any complications or untoward effects. We might even have signed over our first born child for all we knew. Who reads all the fine print? Besides, what could possibly happen to us? We were healthy and in our prime. Complications happened to older people; not us.

According to consensus, "everyone was doing it." Other students who had already participated assured us it was an easy way to earn money. Hence, like a blind herd of cattle a number of us agreed to participate. We didn't have to go far since the pharmaceutical company wisely set themselves up at the entrance of our nursing school. What a recruiting strategy, they got us coming and going!

What did we have to do? Well, once we signed our life away we took several puffs of some type of medication up our nose. Puff, puff and we were done. "Call the telephone number," we were instructed if we had any adverse reactions. I am sure we were told what the action of the medication was, as well as other information about the drug, but to this day I do not know what medication I took, or whether there were any potential long-term adverse effects. Of course, whenever I have issues related to my nose, I can't help but wonder if maybe spraying this stuff up my nose might be at the root of the problem. Though this is highly unlikely, the mind does conjure up some strange things.

Recalling what I can about the medication, I have to think the spray we used was some type of new nasal decongestant. I can only hope it was something so harmless. Thank goodness my nose did not rot and fall off, or something so tragic. Could you imagine doing this for just a few bucks? Not one of my better decisions, right?

The Dreaded Mistake

This story is about a fear all nurses have, let alone a student nurse. It is the nightmare we all dread. More than likely, based on statistical numbers, such incidents happen to most nurses at least once in their careers. Most nurses would say once is too much, but by virtue of human nature, errors do happen. The key is recognizing mistakes, owning up to them, and taking corrective action. Reporting errors is a matter of ethics and accountability.

Well my "dreaded mistake" happened early in my career; it happened in nursing school. I was so distraught by my error I swore I was going to be "thrown out" of nursing school. But what I didn't realize at the time was my instructors understood I was learning and the error was not entirely my fault. Thank goodness, my teachers were supportive and the patient had no ill effects. Those two variables—the fact they understood and the patient had no adverse effects—were probably why I survived the ordeal.

So what was the dreaded mistake all nurses fear? The mistake is making a medication error. As nurses we learn to go through a series of checks to be sure there are no oversights when dispensing medications; however, being human and therefore not infallible, blunders do happen. Mistakes with medications though, can be lethal.

At the time I was the neophyte student nurse so I bore the brunt of the error. But really, shouldering the blame was not the worst of the ordeal. The most awful aspect was worrying if I might have killed the man. Now I know the body is fairly resilient, and can often withstand more stress than we realize, but at the time I was petrified the man would not survive.

Before I tell you exactly what happened, you need to understand that prior to being permitted to administer medications students must first pass specific application exercises demonstrating proficiency in the process. Student nurses are not just turned loose to practice on patients. Believe me when I say we practice... and practice... and practice... before performing such skills in the actual clinical setting. Contrary to what some may perceive, student nurses do not go to clinical and one day decide to pass medications.

The day I made the error was not my first experience dispensing medications. I had administered enough medications to feel comfortable with the process. One of the things our faculty members did when students were assigned to pass medications on clinical units was to flag the patient's medication "kardex." A flagged "kardex" alerted the staff a student would be passing medications to the particular client. This way the staff nurse administering medications knew a student would be responsible for giving the patient his/her pills or shots. Today computerized medication systems are used, so the process of flagging the medication record is somewhat different, but the concept of notification persists.

I was assigned to a confused elderly man who had chronic cardiac problems which contributed to his diagnoses of fluid retention and decreased cardiac output. He was prescribed one pill for contraction of the heart and the other pill was a diuretic to help excrete excess fluid. Around two in the afternoon he was scheduled to receive a dose of each of the two medications.

I saw the student nurse medication alert tag secured to the patient's medication record ("kardex") when I gave him his a.m. doses. When it was time to dispense the mid-afternoon meds I followed each of the "Rs" of administration (e.g., right patient, right dose) we had been taught to review each time we distributed any medications. After I had given the pills to the patient, without any dispensing problems, I went to sign my initials on the medication record signifying I had completed the care measure. In the small block where I intended to squeeze my initials there were other initials transcribed in the box. Talk about one's heart stopping! I just stared at the sheet thinking, "How could this be?" "There must be a mistake." "Someone must have recorded in the wrong space." At the moment, all I could mentally process was if someone else did indeed just give this man his medications, then I just double-dosed him.

As the initial shock started to clear, I also realized the student tag was no longer paper-clipped to the patient's medication record. Possibly someone removed the tag prematurely thinking students had left the unit for the day, or maybe the tag had fallen off.

When I and my clinical instructor reported the error, the staff deflected the blunder entirely back to me, the student. They felt I should have seen the two medications were signed off before I administered a second dose. Of course, their assumption was the staff member's initials were already in place when I started the administration process.

Checking the record to see the medications were not signed off was one of the steps I had taken when preparing the man's meds. All I could figure was two people must have been doing the same thing only minutes apart and never connected with each other. However, despite any rationalizing of how such an error could occur, the end result remained. The patient received double doses of his two oral cardiac medications.

As I said earlier, being an inexperienced student nurse, I feared the elderly man's body would not be able to handle the amount of medication he received and he would go into cardiac arrest. His physician, who was notified of the dosing error, instructed us to monitor the patient's vital signs and report any significant changes. The part I remember most about this whole incident is the vigilance I spent that entire night. I consumed most of the night checking on the gentleman to make sure his heart did not stop or did not fail. Aside from worrying about the man's health, I feared if something did happen to the patient my nursing school career would be over and I would lose all I had come to love.

I checked on the patient every couple of hours from about 3 pm until 6 am the next morning. No sleep that night. Our dorms were connected to the affiliated hospital, so I did not have to go far to do my checks. Every two hours I set my alarm, put my nursing uniform on, and quietly slipped over to the hospital. I was too embarrassed to repeatedly stop by the nurse's station, particularly during the night shift when all was quiet, to inquire on the patient's status. Instead, every two hours I went to the patient's room to check on him. I would go quietly into the room and enter just far enough to visibly confirm his chest was rising and falling. I just needed to verify for myself he was alive.

What a long and tiring night! I did not sleep a wink. Just by my recounting this story you can see I never forgot the incident. It took me quite some time to regain my confidence and realize I was still a good nurse. You know how some people say out of the bad you should look for the good? Well, if I was to look for the good in this experience I would have to say because of this incident I am extremely conscientious when administering medications. In the end, the man did not have any notable adverse effects from receiving the double dose. Each time I checked on him he was sleeping or lying quietly with his eyes closed, breathing regularly without any signs of distress. There were no nurses and doctors hovering over him administering CPR as I so dearly feared.

Actually, what I did not realize at the time was although he received the medications twice (at least we think he did), the combined amount he received for each drug still fell within the recommended therapeutic range. Most likely he was initially on lower doses because of his age and the renal clearance of the medication from his body. Thank goodness for strong functioning kidneys!

Transformation

I saw people in crisis, those permanently closing their eyes, people struggling to not take their last breath, and people gasping for air. I talked to people who were distressed, people who were angry, and people who were bewildered. I directed people who did not know which way to turn, and those who were distraught and confused. Such encounters change you; you learn, you reshape, you mature and evolve into someone different than the person you were.

You assume more responsibility. You have to think on your own and be accountable for the choices you make. Your actions impact the lives of others. You can no longer depend on others to make your decisions. Those individuals who previously shaped and guided your life are no longer by your side. You have to stand alone and make your own way; be your own boss. You have changed from a young adult to an adult, almost overnight in the eyes of some. You demand more and simply can't accept the explanation "this is the way it is." Now you ask why, why must it be? There is so much more; life is no longer so simplistic. Where once things were black and white, there now is gray.

You've changed. You are not the same person—the same young adult who left home. The change is hard for some to understand. You have evolved into a new person. The new you those who love you had not anticipated meeting so soon. They say the transformation was too quick. You just left and now the old you is hard to see. It is challenging for others to understand. There are struggles and battles, as well as tears and anger. Though change is hard, it is inevitable. For me, with my nursing school came personal growth. And, with my maturation emerged a new awareness and respect for who I was.

Assimilation

They became our teachers, not just about nursing but about their culture. The hospital needed additional nurses and as a solution hired nurses from the Philippines to fill the staffing voids. Some individuals had a problem with this solution. However, in reality the presence of these overseas nurses clearly eased the staffing crisis.

I am sure there were many political issues related to this decision. But, as students we were not enlightened on such details. Instead, what we saw were staffing crunches which seemed to improve. What was also evident was these nurses represented a group of healthcare professionals administering quality care and making conscious efforts to assimilate to the hospital and to America. Many of them started at the hospital before we enrolled as students, so were well acclimated by the time we assumed patient care roles. Some were head nurses on units, and some were staff nurses. Plus, there were those who worked as nurse's aides while waiting to take their nursing boards in the United States.

Some spoke English well, and some struggled with the language, but still managed to communicate effectively. Then, there were those who were hampered because they spoke almost no English. Despite cultural or language barriers, these Philippine nurses were well versed in the basics of human care and met the needs of their patients with respect and dignity. Care is care, and nursing is nursing; no matter the language or the culture.

They welcomed our help, even if we were "only" students. Several of us who worked as both nursing students and nurse's aides got to know some of these nurses on a personal level. Often the Filipino (English spelling) nurses took time to show us new techniques and act as our mentors. I believe the ultimate appreciation and trust was extended when several of us were invited to a house party in their community. It was a time to experience new foods, observe new customs, and to have a good time amongst friends and nursing colleagues.

Chapter Four

FACES

May the time never come when I will be above learning from the humblest person.

(NAPOLEON HILL)

As time goes on and nurses see more and more patients, new stories of patient encounters push old stories deeper to the back of one's mind. The old stories find a resting place where they are no longer thought of as frequently. But then, some passing image or event triggers an association. The connection causes one of those fond memories to once again find its way into the forefront of the brain, recreating itself so that the faces of those involved are once again illuminated. In this chapter, I tell the stories of some of those faces which float in and out of my consciousness and at the time of their acquaintance touched the core of my inner being.

Dignity

I believe our mouths hung open. We were too young and too inexperienced to know how to control our emotions, to mask our facial expressions. We were only freshmen, not yet having achieved even one of our three nursing cap stripes. We were truly neophytes, trying to find our way. I couldn't believe what our instructors had taken us to see. The man had no face on his left side.

We were speechless, awed at what we were seeing. As expected, we were mesmerized by the surgeon's renowned work. We fed into the surgeon's ego. Eight student nurses crammed into a small exam room to observe the surgical procedure performed by a highly skilled physician. All of our eyes were fixated on the man's face. I wanted to vomit.

We were encouraged to huddle around the exam table, on which the patient sat, to get an optimal view. As we gazed onto the man's face, at the surgeon's masterful work, the details of the surgery were explained. And as we gazed at him, the man who had undergone this horrific transformation, just sat there. I couldn't imagine what he must have been feeling. He probably felt like a freak on display.

How could our teachers be so insensitive? Didn't they think about the patient, and how we would react?

How did this man endure our stares, our looks of disbelief? Why didn't he scream? I would have understood if he had. What made him hold back? He was gone, vanished with the loss of his face. He was only a shell, no longer a being... I felt his sorrow for the loss of himself. But, I was to believe he had been saved, the cancerous growth cut away.

Instead, I saw a man deformed with a cavernous hole left where the side of his face and neck used to be. I could see his facial bones. I could see the anatomy of his neck. I felt sick, but I would not be sick for this man's sake. A student down—"quick get her out"—before he sees. Who are we fooling, before he sees? He already sees. He sees our faces, our shock and our ghastly stares.

I see his eyes, I see the anguish. He searches my eyes. I look away, afraid I will reveal my thoughts, afraid for him to see what he already knows. In my mind I struggle to comprehend what I was supposed to gain by seeing this man. I grapple with understanding just what our instructors felt was so beneficial to place before this man's self-esteem.

He had a radical neck procedure done, a surgical procedure we were supposedly lucky to see. We were told this was a teaching moment, a rare opportunity. A masterful procedure few would witness. That might have been true, but my mind asked the question whether it was right to be gawking at this man. Revealing our shock at what we saw? Eight stunned student nurses, and one out for the count. It was wrong. His eyes said it all. He taught me a lesson on lost dignity!

Roommates

Roommates—they're always good for adventurous stories! For us a story about two roommates sharing a room quickly evolved into a tale about four roommates sharing an apartment. To begin the story, let's go back to my first job and to the hospital I worked at following graduation. And also, before explaining how we went from "room" to apartment, I need to impart how two of us came about sharing a room.

Initially, at least while I was on the four-week orientation period of my first nursing job, I decided to stay at my parents and make the hour and a half drive each morning and afternoon. I figured once I received a few paychecks, made acquaintances, and became familiar with the apartment situation in the town, I would look for living quarters to rent. In the meantime, I thought I could handle the early morning drive. And by early morning, I mean leaving my parents' house before 5:15 a.m. to be assured I would not be late for the 7:00 a.m. patient report huddles. Being tardy for morning report is not something you want to do as a new graduate, or for that matter, as a new employee.

I was never an early morning person so getting up at 4:30 a.m. to leave by 5:15 a.m. did not sit well with my body. I lasted about two weeks going back and forth before I knew driving was not working. I felt like I was on a perpetual wheel. I would get up early, drive to the hospital and then work all day, usually not finishing until about 4:00 p.m. After my shift was over I would drive home, eat, go to bed early (so I could get up early), wake up, and start the routine all over again. I realized if I was going to survive this job then living closer to the hospital was a necessity.

Having the typical empty pockets of a new graduate, I needed to look for a roommate to split expenses. I knew being at a new job, and not knowing anyone other than the people at work would make finding a roommate difficult. But as fate would have it, another new graduate who selected the same hospital and same nursing unit for her first job was looking for an apartment as well!

The hospital we worked at was a rural tertiary center which despite being in the "country," was a busy place with lots of people coming and going. Frequently, people receiving outpatient treatments or who had a loved one in the hospital scouted around looking for places to stay. The hotel located on the hospital's property was often full or a little too costly for people needing rooms for extended periods. Thus, a wise woman, who was a clever entrepreneur, and owned a spacious house across from the hospital, offered a reasonable alternative.

This ingenious woman rented rooms and cot spaces in her house. No meals were provided, but tea was graciously served at various times. She reminded me of an adroit politician with a bit of Florence Nightingale thrown in. She would chat with her guests about how their day was going or how a hospitalized loved one was doing. I did wonder if maybe she walked a fine line between what some would call a "busybody" and what others would define as a truly caring person. Today, I am sure one could probably go on and on about how this lady violated the ethics of confidentiality. Nevertheless, at the time she provided a friendly ear for many needy people.

Years later, long after I had left the area, I heard this entrepreneur was still running the business. Now, with the advancing of time, this woman has most likely passed on and the business has either dissolved or transferred to new hands. I hope it is the latter because her house offered people gifts and personal touches that are not easily found.

Within a few days after starting her first job, my future friend was lucky and secured a small bedroom in this woman's house. Being the generous person this girl was, she offered to share her space with me when she learned the stress of my daily drives. So, I found myself splitting a room and gaining a true friend.

We had some fun times in our niche. I remember munching on handfuls of dry cereal (Cheerios) as snacks because no cooking or baking was allowed in the rooms. We ate two meals during the day at the hospital and typically went out to eat for dinner.

With the daily room expense, our eating out expenses, and the fact that our room deal was only temporary, we needed to find an alternative, more permanent, living arrangement. Therefore, each night after work we went apartment hunting. In our searches, we saw all kinds of apartments which were in various stages of living conditions. Sometimes we wondered how places could become so decrepit and how landlords could justify the rental price they quoted. After a few weeks of scouting we found an apartment not far from the hospital. It was in a somewhat remote area and a half mile from a state mental health institution.

The idea of our new apartment being fairly segregated from town, plus a mental health facility in the vicinity, initiated lessons on self-defense and a few karate tips from one of our boyfriends. We still reminisce about those karate lessons when we get together.

So, equipped with our new karate skills we made the transition to apartment living. We borrowed furnishings from our families, did without, or became very creative in making do with what we had. Eventually, with time, the apartment took on a personality and became "our place."

Within a couple months, two other nurses joined us in the apartment. One was a former high school classmate of mine, who also went to nursing school in Philadelphia, but not the same facility as me. The other person who joined us was an acquaintance of my new friend. The person she invited was one of her high school buddies who went to the same nursing school she did. Rather quickly our apartment grew from housing two to four. Crowding was never a problem because we pretty much worked different shifts and often one, two, or all of us would be off visiting families or boyfriends. It was rare for us all to be home at the same time.

One of the wonderful things coming out of sharing the apartment was our stories. To this day, we still laugh about the evening one of us cooked dinner and left a surprise in the main dish. Among the four of us, we had one skilled chef who taught each of us various cooking tips. But this night, the one who volunteered to cook was definitely not the talented cook.

She served us a whole chicken—and when I say a whole chicken, I mean the whole chicken. As we sat around the table ready to eat, we found out with the first carving she had not taken out the organ-filled bag inside the chicken. You know the bag, with the chicken gizzards and neck the butcher packs for one's dining pleasures! To our astonished faces, she merely declared in her sweet, soft voice that she never knew "they put those things in there."

I was the first of the four to move out of the apartment. After living in the apartment for about a year I got married and moved to another state. Sadly, and a story told elsewhere in this book, while I was on my honeymoon one of the remaining three roommates was killed coming home after working night shift at the hospital. That event made for a memory that will always be a marker of our roommate days. Her spirit and laughter will always be equated with our rented home. You can't think of the apartment without thinking about this girl or her gizzard mistake. She made us laugh, and she made us cry.

Thirst

Notoriously, when I stand up in front of a nursing class, trying to bestow the importance of monitoring a person's fluid and electrolyte balance, and explaining the significance of assessing a person's intake and output, the image of a particularly fragile, elderly woman comes to mind.

My first glimpse of her was on a home visit after I ascended a series of steps leading to an upper level room, a room which in all essence was an attic. She was lying in a metal-framed hospital bed with her gaze transfixed on my image emerging up the steps. I later wondered if she prayed the resounding steps she heard belonged to someone who would offer her a refreshing drink. Or, possibly, she laid there frightened the sounds she heard belonged to someone she feared. It was hard for me to tell her true thoughts because she never spoke. With each visit, I contemplated if she was indeed coherent and oriented to all spheres. The family assured me she was lucid, but I was never convinced their assessment was quite right.

On my first visit a note was tacked to the front door instructing me to come in and to "go right upstairs." Being left such a note was not one of my favorite ways to be received; however, it was not a novel greeting. I believe I may have made two home visits before I figured out exactly what this note really implied, and exactly what this woman's personal care arrangements were. When I entered the house, except for the resonating sound of a ticking hallway clock, I found utter silence and no traces of human sound. It was obvious no one was home except the elderly woman a floor above.

Now mind you, this house was not in the poorest of neighborhoods or the wealthiest of neighborhoods; but rather, what one would define as a community of "the working class." The house was maintained on the outside, even pleasing to the eye, and the inside was clean and neat, but quiet. A quick survey of the woman's room revealed all looked in order. There was a hospital-grade bed with all side rails in the up position, a clean sheet and blanket draped over her frail frame, her pillow behind her head, a bedside commode situated near the bed, and a small empty glass on the table placed alongside her bed. Artificial lighting provided a dim glow. This was a room I believe Florence Nightingale would find sufficient, but balk at the lack of sunshine and deficient environmental stimuli.

After two visits, without seeing anyone home other than the elderly lady, our agency called the relatives living in the house and made arrangements to visit with them to discuss the woman's care. During the meeting, the family voiced they had no one to sit with the woman during the day because the adults worked and the children were in school. They also volunteered they had no money to pay for someone to attend to her needs while they were gone. And, they pointed out she had no healthcare insurance to pay for care services. This was an interesting declaration since the information on the client's record clearly identified Social Security and Medicare benefits.

During our conversation the family shared information related to how they addressed their relative's hydration needs when she was home alone. They provided the woman only one eight ounce glass of water to drink for the ten or so hours they were gone to work or school. They feared if they left her more to drink she would wet the bed.

Several variables of concern surfaced. One related to compromising an elder's health for convenience, by restricting fluid intake. Another was use of care approaches which could be interpreted as negligence or abuse. And last but not least, potential misappropriation of the woman's finances by not employing a care provider.

Could this family's approach be written off as inexperience of a care provider's role and ignorance of principles of hydration and safety? Not likely, because whatever defense one would argue, the counter argument would be they were causing harm.

One has to wonder if they ever asked themselves how they would feel being allowed only one glass of water in a similar span of time. Not very well, I'm sure. And, unlike them, if this elderly woman did recognize her body's need for hydration, she still could not get out of bed by herself to satiate her thirst. Plus, with no other person home, there was no one around to even offer her a refreshing, thirst quenching beverage. She was at her family's mercy. So much explained those dark sunken eyes looking sadly back at me.

An Empty Cup

Opening the front door I sensed the stillness and calmness permeating the air. The hospital bed was positioned so when one entered the front door the withered face of the elderly man caught the eye. His head poked from the crisp white sheets, tucked securely around him, almost like a child tucked in by a parent for a good night's sleep. Only this was not the work of a parent, but rather a devoted wife.

His wife was expecting me. So she had left the clasp on the front door unbolted so I was free to let myself in. A quick nursing appraisal of what met my eyes instantly had my mental radar sounding. It was my instantaneous gut feeling which warned something was wrong. I sensed there was more to what was before me.

A quick visual sweep of the room told me the man was too still, much too still. No signs of the covers moving at chest level, no audible moans, gurgling or grunting, just quiet... and something else, something like an emptiness, almost like I was looking at something which was there; but not there. I knew immediately in my gut and wondered if she knew? Strange, but it was so quiet, too tranquil for what I sensed to be real. Where was the wailing, the shrill cries? No one was lying across the man crying, sobbing into his sheets. No, there was nothing, just heavy silence. How long had it been? There had been no greeting of hello when I entered the house, no one met me at the door to invite me in; no one except "Stillness" and "Emptiness."

There she was, just off to my side sitting at the kitchen table, hands clasping a ceramic mug. She was staring off somewhere beyond me and beyond where she physically was. She was far away, a place in the distance. Her eyes shifted and looked at me. With that empty look she informed me her husband was sleeping. She told me he was taking a nap and had been snoozing for quite some time. I knew she was in shock. She was just functioning; just going through the motions. She was seeing what she needed to see, what she could safely comprehend. I could see the shield. Her protective armor would be difficult to penetrate.

Deep down, though, she knew. All her senses told her he was dead. She could not deal with this reality. Instead, she ceased to think and did what was comfortable and what came naturally. She would protect herself; create a barrier so as to stop the pain from flowing in. She would stay where there was peace, where nothing was real. Her husband would be as he always had been.

It was better than dealing with what was happening. She had found her comfort zone, where she needed to be. She was a frail, elderly woman and her soulmate had just left her. In the blink of an eye she had become a widow. And now, an uncomfortable new companion had come to dwell: death.

She did as she normally did when her husband slept. She sat at her kitchen table and had a blissful cup of coffee with hopes of making all her troubles fade away. She could fantasize about the possibilities and relive the memories of their younger years, their carefree times. Times they shared which were void of suffering, without pain, and without old age. Their youth!

I knew to leave her be for the moment, to just let her sit while I confirmed what I already knew. There was not much I could do but remain composed to keep her calm. I sensed she would crumble easily. Hysteria might move in at any moment as her suppression lifted and reality surfaced. Or, when someone like me shocked her into validating what she already knew.

I sensed that cup of bliss must have been stone cold because my touch told me this man had been dead for quite some time. Rigor mortis had begun to creep in. He was stiff and his skin was cold to the touch, taut and hard. His chest was still, not one up and down movement, while his color was grey from no perfusion. His closed eyes appeared sunken above his now prominent nose. He had no palpable pulses, no resonating sound transmitted through my stethoscope, no beat and no flutter; absolutely no lub-dub.

I needed to pronounce him and make the appropriate calls. I had to tell her. But she knew. I saw it in her eyes when I told her what I had found. She simply nodded and quietly requested: "Please call my daughter."

Cinderella's Ball

It was St. Patrick's Day and people were out celebrating. Some began in the morning and continued into the evening. I do not know what time he got started but I do know when his green celebration ended. It was close to the moment when the clock would ring in a new day; the time when Cinderella lost her slipper, and when this St. Paddy's day celebration would fade into the past.

Just as Cinderella scurried from the ball, somewhat oblivious to her surroundings, this man too left his party to dash on home. He had decided it was time to depart. Maybe because he knew he had enough to drink, needed to meet someone elsewhere, or just decided it was time to return home. I did not see the man exit the bar and leave the other partiers. Nor did I see him laughing and smiling and having a good time. I only saw the aftermath of a tragic mistake, a mere second in time.

Whoever hit him in that one moment, ignored the thump of this man against their car. The person opted to continue on their way. They never stopped to see what caused the noise or to see what they had done. Later, I wondered if perhaps the hit and run offender was intoxicated from an evening of St. Paddy's celebration. Did the driver not comprehend the reality of what they had done? To think someone in their full faculties would knowingly opt to not stop after hitting someone, or something, seems cold-hearted.

Coming home from work after the 3-11 p.m. shift I took the exact road I had taken many times before. I arrived at this location about the same time I did most nights. But, this evening as I looked ahead into the dark, I could see a difference. I could depict some stopped cars and a few stationary headlights ahead. It was obvious something was wrong. A few people were out of their cars standing in the road looking down. I could not see clearly, but assumed, someone must have been hurt. No ambulances, no police cars…the accident must have just occurred.

Usually, I would be listening to music or driving in silence as I reflected on the night's events. I knew the road. Crossing from one side of the street to the other was risky; more so during the day then the evening. The roadway was a main thoroughfare during the day but sparsely populated with cars and traffic in the later evening and early morning hours. There were a few houses and businesses on one side of the road, and on the other side, ran a river. There was a parking lot along the river side that belonged to the tavern/restaurant across the street. Lighting was not bad on the business side, but as one crossed towards the river there was less illumination.

At this time of night, close to midnight, the road was usually less traveled. I always figured the few cars on the road belonged to people like me, happy to be heading home after a long night's work. Slowing my car, I pulled over to the side of the road and went over to those standing in a circle around the unconscious victim. How dangerous this scene was! There were certainly elements of concern: poor lighting, a fairly traveled road, and a victim lying in the middle of the road. This is not good, I thought. Another car could come along, not see us in the dark, and not be able to stop. But, the bystanders were following the cardinal rule of not moving an injured victim. They were doing the right thing by leaving this individual right where he was.

Of the few people who were on the scene, I was the one who could render care until paramedics arrived. No one else spoke up to say they had healthcare training. With only the faint light of some distant headlights and a glow from the moon, I could barely make out the man's face, let alone tell if he was breathing. I strained to see the natural rise and fall of his chest. I tried to determine if he needed resuscitation, but I could not tell in the dark. On palpation I found his pulse, which felt weak and thready. Head to chest, I could feel a faint rise of his chest and a wisp of nasal air along my cheek. He was breathing but very shallowly.

There was a bump on his forehead with a moderate sized cut. There was no active bleeding from his head or any other obvious body part. It seemed his injuries were predominantly internal. I stayed low with my head against his chest feeling for the exchange of air and praying for the quick response of paramedics. There was not much I could do.

Cell phones were not a common commodity as they are now, so emergency calls were typically made by someone running to a house or a business and using a telephone. Who or where someone made the call is unclear. More than likely the cry for assistance was dispatched from the bar/restaurant he had just left. At the time, it was just reassuring to hear someone yell, "Help is on the way!"

As we anxiously awaited the paramedics, the man woke up and tried to push himself up, flailing his arms and fighting against me to rise. His awakened state was short-lived and within a minute he fell back, unconscious again. Unconsciousness to agitation to unconsciousness had clinical bells ringing in my head. I knew such manifestations along with a head injury suggested he might have an intracranial bleed. I prayed even more for the rescue team's presence.

Finally, the paramedics arrived, probably in excellent time but what seemed like forever. With their appearance, I reported what I had observed, left my name and contact information and faded into the background. It was only a matter of minutes before the man was on the stretcher, the ambulance's rear doors closed, and with the siren blaring they sped off on their way. With the excitement gone, the onlookers slowly retreated to their cars, and one by one pulled away.

I had hoped for a telephone call from the paramedics or someone to hear how the man was doing, but I never heard. I wondered about his family. How were they enduring the trauma? Was the man dead or alive? I knew he was hurt badly and might not survive.

What I did come to find out about this man's condition, I read in the local newspaper. Simply, the police were looking for the person who committed a hit and run crime resulting in the death of another. I never learned the final outcome of whether the person who fatally injured this gentleman got away with the malicious crime. I would suspect, even if they were never prosecuted, the guilt of taking another person's life would be an unremitting nightmare to live.

Good Looking Guy

Fathers, new dads, somewhere along the way I became intrigued with the experiences of new fathers. There is always the initial excitement at birth, where everyone is supporting one another and enjoying being a part of the new experience, of the new life. Too often though, the excitement seems short-lived and the stressors of parenthood creep in. Some individuals can jump over the hurdles and keep going, others…Well they just tumble and actually crumble. Why can some men handle fatherhood and others not? Probably for the same reasons some women can handle motherhood and others cannot.

While working in obstetrics and pediatrics, I had the opportunity to interact with many new fathers. I found new fathers often just need to explore whether the emotions they are feeling are what other dads experience. Fathers question themselves if they find their reactions to the baby experiences are not altogether positive. A novel example is how some fathers experience a sense of isolation from the mother-infant dyad once the child is born. In such situations, informing new fathers this is a normal, common reaction is vital. Importantly, fathers should also be alerted having such feelings does not equate with being a bad father. Oftentimes, new dads just want to share their story, to talk about their fathering experiences and to seek approval. So, from working with new fathers, and talking with them, the phenomenon of what makes some fathers better parents intrigued me.

Around the time I was mulling over the differences in fathers in terms of their responses to fatherhood, I obtained certification as a board-certified lactation consultant. This new focus generated a unique area of interest for me. My new fascination would lead me down a path to complete my doctoral dissertation on a subject related to fathers and breastfeeding.

Talk about meeting fathers! In an attempt to gather information from fathers of breastfeeding infants, I met many fathers who were delighted and proud to share their experiences. I had fathers who wrote me their stories, who shared their fears and joys, and who sent me treasured pictures of their children.

I looked for new dads everywhere, e.g., restaurants, department stores, and amusement parks. When I caught sight of a male with a young child, who looked to be in a parent-child relationship, I would inquire if the male adult was indeed the father, and how old the infant was. Specifically, for my research, I was looking for dads who had infants between three to four months of age. If the father's answers fit my criteria, I then asked him if he would be willing to answer some father-related questions. I received numerous affirmative responses, as well as many negative ones. Despite the occasional refusal, I forged ahead. By the end of my information compilation, I had the opportunity to meet lots of new dads and had collected some rich father data.

In the course of gathering the statistics I also started collecting different novelties related to fathers: songs, books, jokes, stories, greeting cards, and statues. I have a storage chest full of father memorabilia. Some people collect stamps, some collect coins…and me… I collect "father" items. Strange, but that's me. Just so you don't think I am all that peculiar, I do need to point out the items are used. I link my father treasures into presentations I do for new dads on fatherhood topics.

I'm thinking you might be wondering why I am spending so much time going on about my interest in fathers and fatherhood. As you may have guessed, a story unfolds and quite an amusing one. This story, from my family's perspective would be tagged a classic. For them, the account is a favorite, which is not surprising since my husband and daughter are the scalawags who set the story in motion. As a matter of fact, they had a lot to do with its unfolding! So… what did these two beloved individuals do?

First though, I have to tell you what I did which caused my family to jump right in and run with the idea. You know how sometimes you get these whims, and sometimes, something is so farfetched you know there probably is not the slightest chance the event will ever transpire, yet on the other hand, you figure what the heck, no harm in trying. And then, there is the small part of you thinking "maybe it just might work." So you tell yourself, "If I don't try, I will never know." Well, I got one of those impulsive brainstorms.

My bright idea is related to my attending a national nursing convention where I was to do a poster presentation on father-infant attachment. And let me just add, this little brainchild I conjured up was not something I did in my early years as a novice nurse. No, instead we are talking an established, seasoned nurse—I had quite a few years under my belt. I was a veteran nurse and an adult, but I still enjoyed doing the unexpected.

I had been to this national convention several times so I was familiar with the enthusiasm and energy which flowed during the gathering. Annually, thousands of nurses come together to attend the various conference sessions, network, and share expertise. The enthusiasm and sense of excitement is contagious. The convention typically runs several days, with one of the evenings routinely reserved for some type of gala dinner party. Usually one or several of the convention sponsors host some type of entertainment which adds to the fun and provides participants an opportunity to unwind and socialize.

The particular summer this event transpired, the national convention was held in Utah. At the time, I was teaching so had time off during the summer. Typically, because my teaching loads are so tight during the academic year, I routinely save my summers to do presentations and attend continuing education programs. As for my family, summer is always linked with family time. For us, summer means road trips across country to explore national parks, visits to new places, chances to see distant friends and relatives, and opportunities for mom to attend conferences. With this convention being in Utah and rolling out in the summer, the event spelled road trip. So, the plans for a road trip began.

What we decided was to frontload the beginning of our trip. For us this meant we would do most of our sightseeing on the way to the convention, then, on the return trip when we were all tired with lots of road dirt we would drive back making just a few side-trips to tourist attractions. We calculated about three weeks to travel from the east to the west coast and one week to drive back. For us, such family excursions were the hallmark of fun.

So, about a week before we planned to leave for the trip and a month before the convention was due to start I got my inspiration. The idea surfaced from somewhere inside me as I asked myself, "Wouldn't it be terrific if I could get some famous male actor or singer (even two), who is also a father, to come to the convention; one who projected a positive father image?" I thought perhaps their presence would bring attention to fathers and fatherhood issues. Plus, I was sure my nursing colleagues would be beside themselves in having the unexpected opportunity to meet this person/s in the flesh and blood. I took my speculation one step further and contemplated how enthralling it would be if a celebrity attended the gala party.

Mind you, I did hear those inner voices saying "This is crazy… why would an entertainer do this…and for free no less." But, you know what my internal voice said to me? It said, "Because you are nurses" and "almost everyone"…"no matter how famous they are knows a nurse." More than likely there was also some member, even if a distant relative, of the celebrity's family who is a nurse. I figured if there was a nurse somehow associated with the star, it would be the actor's connection with the nurse which might lead him to think twice about his response.

That nurse, whoever she/he is (mother, grandmother, sister, cousin, friend) will be the voice behind the decision, for we are many. Thinking of "many," my thoughts darted in another direction. I reflected on the thousands of nurses who would attend the convention. And "thousands" translated into large fan exposure, which could be a definite plus for some star who just might appreciate the publicity. Attending might be a chance to be in the spotlight, and just maybe, he would find the possibility intriguing. What star wouldn't want to be wooed by a group of nurses!

So, without thinking too much about my brainstorm (because I knew I would talk myself out of it) I decided to just do it and put the wheels in motion. The first thing I did was to identify a few male actors, and at least one singer, whom I believed portrayed positive father images in the media. First, I came up with two male actors, one who at the time had a lead role in a sitcom family television show and the other an actor who played in several famous movies. Both men seemed to have potential. Next, I chose a country western vocalist to fit the singer category. Since the singer had recently become a first time dad, I figured he would be sensitive to the father theme.

But I wanted one other famous father since I figured four possibilities would increase my odds of receiving at least one "yes" response. To help pick the fourth member and also to obtain opinions from some of my peers about my other three choices, I asked a few of my faculty colleagues for their appraisals and recommendations. Since one male actor's name was mentioned by several of my friends he was selected as the fourth choice. In general, the overall consensus was if the agreed upon actor did accept the invitation, what a sensation his presence would be!

Of course, sharing my idea with some of my close colleagues made me think twice about the notion being ludicrous, but rather than abort the whim, I kept going. I swore my close friends to secrecy fearing if others heard what I had conjured up, they might begin to wonder about my sanity. I figured if a lot of people knew about the scheme and the idea flopped, those last famous words, "I told you so" would be uttered. The friends I did confide in were excited by the idea and were ones I could trust to keep the scheme in check. Just the possibility my crazy plan might work was exciting!

After consulting with my colleagues and coming up with the

fourth father, I decided to find addresses and/or contact numbers for the selected stars. I had no idea where to start. I could not pick up the telephone, call a friend, or say to a telephone operator, "Hey, can you tell me what ____'s telephone number is?" My only hope was to surf the Internet and find contact numbers for fan clubs. Finding legitimate fan clubs was also iffy. In the end, after checking out various websites, I managed to find at least one mailing address for each prospect. With this data in hand, it seemed a written letter of inquiry was my best option. My hope was a star's staff had to go through their fan mail, and forward at least some letters to the stars or to their mangers. I also knew there would need to be something intriguing about my letter to catch the eye of the opener, before it was tossed aside as junk mail. All I had to offer was that this was a professional request that represented fathers

There was another concern. This whole brainstorm came to me about a week before we were to leave on our trip. That meant by the time my letters got into the right hands (if they did at all), I would be on the road heading west. With us being on the road, getting in touch with me would be difficult. Sure, cell phones were the answer, but having strong connections and reception on the open highway was not always guaranteed. The only choice I saw was to include my cell phone number in the letter and hope if I received a call the tower connection would be sufficient.

Just before we were due to depart, an event transpired which took me by surprise, and at the same time, renewed my faith that maybe there was a chance this crazy scheme might work. The day before I was to leave on our cross-country tour, I had a telephone message from a person who identified themselves as a contact person for the country western singer/new dad. The recorded message stated this particular star, though interested, would be on tour at the time and therefore could not accept my invitation. Though the singer was not able to attend, I was appreciative of receiving a response. Receiving the response boosted my faith that someone at least sorts through this star's fan mail, and perhaps someone does the same with the other three's mail.

Well, we had a wonderful trip to the west coast with lots of sightseeing, lots of adventures and all around fun. The only thing missing was my cell phone did not ring with the voice of one of my chosen "fathers." In that respect, my phone remained silent. However, I did not give up trust in mankind. I thought possibly on our arrival at the hotel, where the conference was being held, a message might be waiting for me at the information desk. What a nice surprise that would be when I checked-in! But…no surprise messages awaited me. Basically, my hotel guest registration was uneventful. Instead, it was the next morning the antic would unravel and I would be the recipient of some family humor.

Unbeknownst to me, there was a maintenance man who worked for the hotel that bore a remarkable resemblance to one of the stars to whom I had sent an invitation. I had not seen him but my family did. As they later told me, when they saw him, his uncanny resemblance was too good an opportunity to pass up.

So what did they do? The day before the conference officially commenced there were a number of people about, but not an extraordinary amount. Those attendees who were presenting posters had the opportunity to set their posters up the day before the official ceremonies commenced. As I was busying myself setting up my poster, not tuning into much of the activity going on around me, but instead concentrating on what I was doing, my family was up to their shenanigans.

Some of the hotel's maintenance men were roaming about

making themselves available to assist conference participants and vendors with set-ups. I really did not need help setting up my poster, so I proceeded to independently work through the set-up process. My family, however, had a delightful conversation with one of the maintenance men who looked like one of my selected movie stars. They convinced this man to play the part of this movie star, come over to me to say he had received my letter, and then thank me for inviting him to be my guest at the convention. Yeah, really! Can you imagine?

When I saw this guy approaching it took me a few seconds to comprehend what I thought I was seeing. Naturally, about this time my family was off hiding, but certainly in clear vision to see their scheme play out. I can just picture the snickering those two must have been sharing, for I am sure they were proud of their skillful work, for clever it was.

As the pseudo-star advanced towards me, I looked and thought I was seeing what I was seeing, but I was not 100 percent sure. The guy approaching looked a lot like one of the movie stars, but, he appeared slightly older than what I thought the star would be. As I stared at the advancing person, contemplating his legitimacy, I erased the identity doubts in my mind by asking myself, "Who was I to know what he really looked like off screen." "Maybe he had a masterful make-up artist." "You know, maybe this was him without all his Hollywood make-up." "He could easily be the star he appeared to be." I continued to watch him as he closed the distance between us. I readjusted my thinking calculating if the man approaching was the star, he would be about the age of the advancing man, not the image of the younger star I had preset in my mind.

I could do nothing but stare dumbfounded at him as he came

nearer. He had this huge smile on his face as he came up to me, said hello, and commented on how happy he was to be at the convention and to have received my invitation. He gave me this big bear hug. Thank goodness, I never uttered his name as my mind raced with the question of ..."Is this who I think it is?" As he politely tried to make some vague conversation and I exchanged some generalized responses, my family suddenly appeared. I suppose "the clan" hiding off in the rafters couldn't take the humor anymore and decided they better intervene before the joke went too far.

I have to admit, I was quite embarrassed for almost falling for their joke, but this guy truly did possess an uncanny resemblance. We all laughed about my reaction and the pseudo-star assured me he was often mistaken for the real star. So, although none of the true stars did come, I at least got a hug from a very good looking pseudo-star!

Monkeys, Gorillas, and the Zoo

Why was she in the supply closet just standing there looking bewildered and unsure? How long had she been in there? I was afraid to ask. Something told me it had been a while. The students directed me to the supply closet. They knew something was wrong. I had simply come to ask her to join me for a morning break and to find a few tranquil moments away from the busy clinical units.

Yes, I had noticed she wasn't the most social person and had difficulty making conversation, but that was fine. The objective of a break was to get a breather, not necessarily to converse. We didn't need to talk much, but rather get away from the hustle and bustle.

She was new to teaching, had never taught before and seemed like she could use a friend. We were a few of the younger faculty (both in age and experience), the novices; a commonality which gave us a common bond. "Sure," she replied dully, "I could use a break."

I sensed I came just in time. For what, I was not sure. My gut said something was wrong. Hopefully, nothing was so erroneous that some time away would not cure. Maybe she was just overwhelmed with the demands of keeping pace with the learning needs of students and the stressors of overseeing the care of multiple patients. Being a nursing faculty member has its stressors, and challenges intensify if one is also new to clinical agencies where students are assigned. Sometimes, being the newbie I felt like hiding in the closet too. Subsequently, being familiar with this feeling I could understand her need to hide, but, I also know one needs to know when to come out of the closet.

But something was surely wrong. She was hard to talk to and difficult to draw out. As I interjected short comments here and there, I attempted to figure out if she was extremely shy or on the verge of tears. Despite misconceptions of teaching being a "cake" job, teaching is by no means easy. Teaching is both demanding and rewarding. Never would I say being a nurse educator is easy!

I wondered whether the expectations of teaching had already depleted her energy reserve. Had the pressures put her over the edge? Should I report my observations or watch her longer? Maybe the way she was acting was just her normal self. I did not know her well; hence I thought it unfair to judge her too quickly. I also rationalized since someone had recently hired her, they would have noticed during her interview if her affect did not seem to be on target.

But, I was perplexed as to why she suddenly started talking about peculiar things. My goodness, I was sitting in the cafeteria listening to her rattling on about something related to monkeys, gorillas, and the zoo. I half listened, only catching bits and pieces because I was trying to figure her out. I just couldn't understand her behavior. I was confused. I needed more time to think, to watch her, to talk to her, and to converse with her under different circumstances. I convinced myself she would be fine. She would make it through the clinical day. Once the immediate pressures were gone I figured she would level out. Break time was over, it was time to go back to our units, collect our thoughts, gather our students and wrap up the morning events.

You know, always go with your gut. I don't know what happened after we went off break and parted our ways, but something happened. By the resulting outcome, whatever transpired had been something substantial. The nursing administrators must have been watching her. They deemed her unsafe. Unsafe to whom, I am not sure. Were they concerned for her, students, patients....? The "higher ups" tracked me down. My presence was requested in the director's office. Someone knew we went on break. They asked "Did you notice anything peculiar about Carol today?" "Did she say anything odd or out of context?" Where did I start? Would I do an injustice to this girl by voicing my thoughts, or did I keep them to myself? How could I condemn her, before I even knew her?

Deep down I knew something was not right, I had the feeling she needed a mental health referral. Could I deny her this help? As I sat in the office, and they waited for my answer, I thought about the mental health world I have seen. On top of these thoughts, I reflected on how young she was, and how much of her career she still had ahead of her. I was not sure how to respond: support her or sentence her.

I recounted what I observed, only the facts. I was excused… behind me the doors closed. Time passed. The director's office remained sealed off, closed with "no interruptions." I speculated about her fate. I wondered if mercy would prevail. Would she continue with us or would this be her last day? Who else knew? I did not ask, and never knew. Down the hall I saw her leaving. Long coat on, handbag in hand...mother and father walking on both sides – escorting her to home or therapy, I was not sure. It was hushed, a secret. She had left...resigned we were told.

Short Term Mom

By the end, we all had silent tears streaming down our faces as we watched the mother hold and rock her dying newborn. Working in a neonatal intensive care unit, we had witnessed many newborns struggling to take their first breath, only to be followed shortly by their last breath. But, this pair stood out. There was more to their story. The mother would never again have a chance to carry a child. This pregnancy itself was considered a miracle. The infant was born early, just around the age of viability, so he struggled from the start.

The mother was a long time infertility patient challenged by advancing obstetrical age and health issues. Now, in terms of childbearing years, she was considered old to be having a baby. Her fertile years had ticked by and now her biological clock was against her.

Achieving pregnancy was a triumph in itself. She was ecstatic in becoming a mother after so many years of heartbreaking disappointment. Regrettable, with the wonderful news of pregnancy another overwhelming fact emerged. She not only carried her child, but her baby shared her uterus with a large cancerous tumor. She in turn was counseled against continuing the pregnancy and warned of risks to both her and the developing child.

In spite of her devastating news, her longing for motherhood was stronger than self-preservation. She chose to fight with all she had, and reluctantly agreed to the needed hysterectomy and chemotherapy after she delivered. She decided to sacrifice her body for her baby's birth. What she did not anticipate, nor we, was her precious child would contract an infection. Sadly, the organisms he acquired would prove too much for his delicate body to battle.

Whether he acquired the microbes coming through the birth canal or from our environment, no one would ever know. His time was limited. With each passing hour we watched him fail, knowing death was inevitable. There was nothing we could do but shower him with his mother's love. Bring her to the nursery and give her this time—time to say hello, and time to say goodbye. And so it was… a time to watch… and a time to cry… and a time for mother and baby to say goodbye.

A Small Imperfection

This little boy reinforced my thoughts of how sometimes people's paths are intended to cross. How certain people are put on this earth for each other and eventually their paths entwine. This child was meant to be with this family so they would provide him the love and security he would need to thrive. Their love and devotion would help this little boy live with, and maybe even overcome, his handicaps. It will be their hearts which break when their son comes to them because a classmate hurt his feelings, or made him cry. Their smiles will change to frowns when they see people sneaking looks, or staring at their son. Most of all, they will raise this child as their own. There will be no delineation of bio-genetics. Instead, he will be one of them; a part of their heart and soul.

To bring this child and family together certain events needed to transpire if fate was to unravel. The child had to be born to a young, single mother who painstakingly decided to put her baby up for adoption. She dreamed her child would have a better life than what she felt she was prepared to offer.

The adoption process was in place, the potential new family was anxiously awaiting the birth. His young biological mother had begun the legal process of relinquishing her child. But unanticipated, when the child was born there were imperfections. His anomalies were notable enough that the intended adoptive family waived and decided against becoming his new parents. Thus, instead of the typical two day post delivery discharge for normal newborns, he remained our guest in the nursery. He became our surrogate child. We looked out for him and cuddled him. We gave him the love we knew he deserved and at the same time prayed a couple would come forward to say, "Yes, please allow him to be our son."

He was a beautiful baby, but for whatever reason his arms and legs ended at the wrists and ankles. Essentially, his hands and feet had failed to develop. Instead of regular hands and feet, he had small buds where these anatomical parts normally would be. Reconstructive surgeries and prosthetic devices could be interventions in his future, but not without emotional and financial commitments. He would need a family with lots of patience and one who had the healthcare resources to see these options become realities. Consequently, he stayed with us while "feelers" went out for the perfect family who could meet his needs.

Finally, after about three weeks of our loving him we heard his new parents were coming to take him home. He was going to a well-established family where he would have lots of new brothers and sisters. His new father and mother had heard of our nursery boarder through someone in their congregation and knew their family would graciously welcome the child. Though it has been a long time since I held and rocked this baby in the nursery, I like to think our short-term boarder flourished and grew into the handsome, healthy young man I envisioned he would.

Anesthesia Tears

She cried, I cried inside. She was old, I felt old. Old from sharing the burden she revealed. She was anesthetized, enough to control the pain for a wound debridement but not enough to render her totally unconscious. Somewhere her brain was alert; but losing control. Secrets and regrets found their way to the surface. She was revealing things she normally held in check, but like any monster, those inner terrors unleashed when opportunity struck. For this elderly woman the anesthesia she received served as the demon's opportunity. The nitrous gas administered opened the restraining gates.

I had learned in my obstetrical career that women always remember their miscarriages. I recall learning it does not matter how many years lapse, a mother-to-be always remembers her lost child. The sense of grief never dissipates. From this woman I saw the reality of that truth. She was in her 80s, a nullipara, which meant she had no children. She had never carried a pregnancy beyond the point of fetal viability. For most women in their 80s, one's childbearing times are tucked away as memories of the past. This was not the case for this woman.

Currently, she lived in a nursing home and had no surviving relatives. She was virtually alone, brought to the hospital on a stretcher by an ambulance crew. No relative was at her side to hold her hand and offer her comfort. She was simply alone.

That day, as I stood at her bedside after she was anesthetized and waited for the procedure to begin, she began to sob. Not from pain, but instead, for the baby she had lost so long ago. She had named the baby and was calling her lost child by name. She mumbled about her loss, her guilt and displaced personal blame. She believed the miscarriage was her fault; a self-reproach she obviously had harbored for years.

She touched my heart. To think of all the years this woman concealed her inner torment. Did anyone ever provide her the opportunity to share? Did anyone even care? Did her spouse, now deceased, ever know the extent of her pain? Did they talk together of their lost child? Was she a victim of infertility and all its emotional drains?

So anesthesia allowed her to talk and unveil her secrets, and I was there. There to listen to a woman who would never know her secrets were shared, and that someone had listened and felt her pain. Someone had simply been there.

Mascot

I think she was there throughout our senior year. We all knew her by name and many of us cared for her either as nurse's aides or as student nurses. I wasn't around the first night of her admission. She was a victim of a tragic fire, merely three years old and on the verge of death when transported to us. Our burn unit was not pediatric specific, but the staff routinely cared for victims of all ages. Age did not denote one's admission, burns did. With so many children injured through fires or electrical accidents, our burn center staff was well versed in caring for children. Burns were their specialty.

She was a victim of a fire intentionally set by one of her parents.

As a result of her family situation, her assigned counselor stressed there would be no visits by relatives. She would only be visited by county caseworkers.

Over time she became the amulet of the center. Everyone greeted her and said hello when coming onto the unit. You couldn't miss her. Despite several touches with death, she eventually rounded the corner and began to improve. As she progressed, the rambunctious child in her returned. One could often find her running, or I would be more correct in saying, "hobbling" down the hall. Her hobbling gait was the result of a limp caused by a partially amputated leg. Part of her extremity was removed, along with parts of both arms, as a result of burn complications. The constructed stumps, we were told, could one day be revised, cosmetically corrected and concealed with prosthetics. But for now, we were instructed "let her go, let her play in the halls, the physical exercise was good for her."

She would need to adapt. Her life would surely be different from others; she was scarred over 75 percent of her body. I often wondered what her future would be like as she matured and would be faced with the reality of her situation: no parents, no relatives who unconditionally loved her, no one claiming her as their child, disabled, and living in a distorted body with years of reconstructive surgery ahead.

SIDS – Simply Meant to Be?

This incident happened on a night when one of our nurses graciously agreed to stay as an extra for the 11-7 a.m. shift because the prior shift was overflowing with laboring and delivering women. Sadly, while she stayed and helped bring other women's children into the world her own newborn, home with other family members, left our world. Her child died in his sleep. He was a victim of SIDS (Sudden Infant Death Syndrome). How badly we all felt. Of course, we could not help but wonder: "Would the night's events have been different if she had not stayed? Or, was the night just fated to play out as it did?"

Blue Hue Birth

She was a colleague, an obstetrical nurse, one who witnessed numerous births and many healthy babies born. But when it was her child's birth, the tables turned. The all familiar outcome changed. The baby was beautiful, picture perfect, yet by his color something was obviously wrong. There was a distinct blue hue to the baby's skin. Her child's heart had failed to develop. Essentially, part of the left side of the heart had not matured. Most of the ventricle simply was not there.

Skilled hands tried to reconstruct his heart, while other hands were clasped in prayer. In the end, surgery proved too much for her son to endure. Sadly, before his surgeons had time to complete their repair, her son left this world.

Returning to work as a grieving mom and continuing to help new mothers bring their newborns into the world must have been hard. But she continued to open her heart to laboring soon-to-be moms. Eventually as time moved on, and she once again gave birth, her tears of sadness were replaced. Now she had tears of joy, as she welcomed her second child into the world, a perfect baby girl!

Misplaced Doll

There was a doll. She was a toy cherished by a young child who was only five years old. The doll was the ticket in caring for the little girl. Incorporate the doll into the little girl's treatment plan and one could care for the preschooler. This was what the student nurse came to realize.

He was in his first weeks of pediatrics, however, not a specialty in which he really wanted to be. His assignment of caring for the little girl was uncharted waters for him. Pediatrics was not within his comfort zone; instead he would have preferred to care for adults. As his clinical day evolved, and with the help of the doll, he formed a bond with the little girl which led to her finding a place in his heart.

He left at the end of his clinical day feeling good about his new found friend, anticipating seeing her again in a few days. The unit nurses projected she would still be a patient when he returned in two short days. He would be able to care for her again.

Sure enough when he returned the young girl was still there. One look at her face and he knew something was wrong. In tears, she told him her beloved doll was gone. She related her doll had been missing since he had last been there and inquired if perhaps he knew what happened to her. The little girl's words pierced his heart. Her beloved dolly was missing and she thought he might know where it had gone. Not a good way to start his day! He had no idea where the girly figurine could be.

Even worse, the little girl's mother and the pediatric nursing staff believed it was possible he had mistakenly misplaced the doll. They suggested he may have wrapped the doll up in the bed sheets and inadvertently tossed the toy down the laundry chute. Was it possible? Could he have lost her doll? He needed help…he needed advice.

Talk about feeling crushed and disheartened! The student felt so bad he went on a quest to find the missing toy. A thorough search of the girl's room and a visit to the laundry room yielded no doll. He enlisted his student peers to help in the search, but no one came up with the prize. It seemed the toy had truly vanished.

Despite no one being sure who definitely lost the doll, he assumed the blame, and decided he needed to replace the little girl's possession. Pooling funds amongst his friends, he collected enough money to purchase a new dolly from the hospital's hospitality shop. There he selected the "perfect" doll to become a new security toy for the little girl to hug and love. She was absolutely thrilled and provided her "student" friend with an immense smile and a tight bear hug. Overall, I would say a pretty simple story, but a genuine memory.

Quick as a Flash

This was one of those incidents that happened so fast I never expected it, never saw it coming. But I have to say losing my nursing licenses flashed through my mind. I was working with a student nurse who was giving her first intramuscular injection. Giving one's first injection to a human is often an unnerving experience. First, because you have the fear you might hurt the person, and second, because an instructor is typically standing by your side throughout the whole process.

Yes, I was nervous when I gave my first injection. Ironically, it wasn't until I withdrew the needle from the patient's skin my hands began to shake. For me and the patient, having post shakes instead of quivering hands throughout the procedure was a good thing. Non-shaking hands allowed me to inject into the patient's skin without a problem.

I have seen the hands of students quivering so badly I've had to steady their hand with my hands so they could inject. Thank goodness, when students inject into someone's buttocks, the patient can't see behind themselves to spot a student's trembling hands or sometimes the non-verbal guidance of an instructor.

Before their first experience of injecting into human subjects, students practice giving injections in simulation labs on mannequins or into practice pads. As faculty we cannot stress enough the importance of practicing. The old saying of "practice makes perfect" holds true. Nurses who become proficient at procedures through practice project confidence when applying the learned skills in the clinical setting. Patients pick up on the nurse's self-assurance and in turn are comforted feeling the nurse knows what he/she is doing.

Think how you would feel if a student nurse, who has been your primary nurse for the day, announces just before he/she is about to administer your pain shot, "This is my first injection on a human being...I hope it goes well." More than likely, you would want to jump out of the bed and run up the hall, fleeing to put as much distance as possible between you and the shot.

Think no nurse would be so brainless as to knowingly make such a declaration? Foolishly, they do! I am not sure if their affirmation is due to a need to be honest or because they are so nervous. But I find students, and sometimes RNs in some situations say things they know are not therapeutic, and utter statements they normally would not make.

She knew her injection sites, having shown them to me on a peer before we entered the patient's room. She correctly elected to administer the medication into the gluteal maximus muscle, a muscle on the patient's buttocks. At the bedside, while her client was rolled on his side so as to expose the injection area, she showed me the proper landmarks along the hip. The landmarks identified the correct site for the needle to puncture. Once locating an injection site, the standing rule is to hold one's hand on the skin, with fingers spread in a half circle fashion so as to frame the injection spot. She had the steps right: locate one's landmarks, position one's hand to mark the spot, keep hand in place marking the spot, wipe the skin with alcohol, pick up the syringe, and inject. But quick as a flash, on the drawback of the hand, she changed the rules. She moved her placement hand, the hand that referenced her exact spot, and essentially darted blindly into the skin of the patient's buttock.

I could not believe how quickly she altered her technique. The hand release happened so fast, I couldn't have stopped her approach. I never anticipated her lifting her hand.

There are certain spots along the buttock if hit by a penetrating needle could cause irreversible leg paralysis. To accidently hit the sciatic nerve while giving an injection is one of those unforgiving spots. Mistakenly hitting the sciatic nerve is what dropping a baby is to a nursery nurse, an accident which most likely won't happen, but still a daunting trepidation.

I am not sure which of us had an angel on our shoulder, me or the student. Some miracle happened, because when the needle came down and slipped into the skin, it was in the exact spot where it should have been. Unbelievable! And, what a relief! I could breathe…the patient was not paralyzed, he could move his leg, and the site was right. It was a jolting experience – one leaving me with an acid stomach and ever so grateful for a positive outcome.

Third-Spacing

A small boy just a little over two years old lying unconscious in an ICU bed caught my eye. His little body was so distorted from extensive swelling. He looked like an over-sized balloon. His small frame was puffy and blown out of proportion from shifting body fluids. Third-spacing was the correct term. They were waiting for him to die. He would say goodbye.

He was a toddler, curious about his world. He had gotten into something lethal. It was the time when fuel prices had skyrocketed, and many families were using kerosene burners as supplemental heating systems. His parents had not foreseen what could evolve by implementing their simple solution to collect leaking fuel. They had placed a drip pan against the base of the heater where some kerosene leaked from the device. Unknowingly they created a makeshift contraption their inquisitive child would find interesting. Being a child and not anticipating the harm, the child drank the drippings. How much? Who knows? But it was enough kerosene to permanently shut his puny little body down.

Senseless

I remember this patient, a fairly young woman of childbearing years. She had not listened. She failed to have her intrauterine device (IUD) changed within the five years stipulated by the manufacturers of the device. She did her own thing. She left it in place for over ten years. Now she lied in an ICU bed oblivious to her surroundings, a blown up version of herself. She was septic; an overwhelming infection had taken over her body. Sorrowfully, she would succumb to the insult: a senseless death.

Ethics

Working in Obstetrics I saw many less than perfect children come into this world. There were children with too large heads, too small heads, extra fingers, missing fingers, cleft lips, cleft palates… familiar syndromes, unfamiliar syndromes…some loved, some not loved. Some were like Joey, and some were not. He would live, but then he would die.

Joey, a fragile newborn, was born prematurely with a chromosomal abnormality. Joey had Trisomy 18, a syndrome marked by multiple body anomalies, typically incompatible with life. Most children do not survive beyond several months of age. Joey's parents decided they did not want extraordinary measures performed on him. This they defined as surgery and cardiopulmonary resuscitation. They also decided when the time came for Joey's discharge they would not take Joey home. Instead, his parents opted to place Joey in a pediatric long-term care facility. They made their decision for fear their other children would become too attached to Joey and suffer attachment-separation consequences when his premature death occurred.

I had learned a lot about ethics and ethical perplexities in nursing school and in practice, but Joey's whole existence seemed to open a Pandora's Box of ethical dilemmas. There were questions about the right to live versus the right to die, to resuscitate or not resuscitate, quality of life, acute versus long term care and whether to treat aggressively or pull back. From Joey, I learned the uniqueness of each situation. This small, fragile little boy innocently challenged the values of an entire neonatal staff, and truly rocked our unit to its core. As a matter of fact, the ethical dilemmas related to Joey's care touched me in such a way I decided to share the experience with fellow nurses. Joey's story became my first professional publication.

Joey spent several months with us in our transitional nursery while he awaited placement in a long term care facility. It seemed his parents could not agree on his new home. What they wanted was to keep Joey where he was. Their wish of keeping him with us was contrary to the hospital's need for placement. Joey had crossed the line from acute to chronic care, which meant he needed to be transferred to another facility so his bed could be freed for an acutely ill newborn. Although Joey was born a few years before controlling the length of stays of patients became key operational strategies to control healthcare dollars, the hospital where Joey was a patient pushed to have him placed. Ironically, after several months with us, and after several ups and downs, the night before Joey was to leave our unit and be transported to his new home, he died peacefully in his sleep. In a way, I guess he did go to the ideal long-term care facility.

Grays

What do you say when a person with a terminal illness with nine months to a year to live, says he/she wants to die? He/she would rather overdose on some of their medications rather than continue living as they are. They're tired, their hope is gone, and they can no longer live with pain. Prayers, thoughts of hope, and beliefs that perhaps a cure may soon be found no longer seem real; only lurking death is authentic. What do you say? You can't say, "You'll be fine." Such words would truly be farce.

Could one now say that this person is a threat to his or her self? Does this open the door for relatives to admit this person to a mental health facility because he or she shared thoughts of taking control of their death? What would be the point of therapy if psychoanalysis were suggested? What would the outcome be? Would it be to give hope to the person? Or would it be to find meaning in their life, and in their death?

What do you say when he or she asks if there is dignity in losing control of one's body? How do you reply? Do you answer as a nurse; a palliative care provider? Or do you answer from your heart, or from the philosophical teachings of some great scholar? Do you keep your emotions in check, and deal with the facts and truths that waiver in the realm of death?

Oh, but the gray side of nursing. The questions you frame, the answers you seek......never to find an exact truth...you forever ponder, and always ask, what is right? It is hard to say. There are no guarantees. You're on your own... you need to respond...yet, do no harm! Ethics!

The Champion

Inevitably, I am asked if I ever cared for someone famous. You know, I really don't know. Those who truly know me realize I rarely pay attention to who's who in social networks. To me, there are so many other things to address. Now, give me an individual who is extremely intelligent, or who has developed some invention, won the Nobel Prize, or found some cure for mankind and I have the utmost respect for them. They are the people I believe are noteworthy and whom I hold in awe. Those are the individuals I think should be brought together to solve world problems and lead nations.

So I could have cared for someone famous; say maybe, a movie star or sport celebrity. Though more than likely, I would never have realized unless someone clued me, or I associated the person with some interest of mine. That sense of connection is how I know I met a world-famous champion boxer (Stay tuned for this story!); one of the legendary figures amongst the names George Foreman, Joe Frazier, Muhammad Ali....

Were there others? Not that I can name, except, I did care for the owner of a leading potato chip company. We had bags of thank you chips delivered to our nursing unit for quite some time afterwards—appreciation for all we had done. Could I have cared for other individuals who were famous in some way? Probably, since I worked in enough different states to have come across a wide variety of people. But in the end, people are people, and even with illness we all act the same; we all want the same, and we all have to look to others for help. Illness brings us all to the same level. Cancer is cancer, no matter who has it, or who you are. It consumes us all; there are no social classes, no prestigious names, and no fame.

The Boxer

Growing up, my father would tell us stories of how he used to box while in the military. So in our house watching boxing matches on television was commonplace, particularly championship games. Like most homes during my youth one television in the house was all our family had. You either watched the boxing match or found something else to do.

The sport was so popular in our family we had a punching bag set up in our basement. The bag naturally came with a pair of boxing gloves, which meant we could practice the sport whenever we wanted. My brother and I practiced punches and thought we were hot stuff since none of our friends were as lucky to have their own punching bag. We fabricated some fancy moves as we danced around punching the bag. We were definitely cool!

As a result of our childhood exposure, I had a respectable handle on who was who amongst boxing champions. We were familiar with names and faces. Imagine my surprise when several years later in my nursing career, I walked into a patient's room and realized one of the then popular heavyweight champions was visiting a family member.

I had been working as a nurse's aide when I went into a room to answer the patient's call bell. The patient who rang the buzzer was the mother of this legendary boxer. He was visiting along with his brothers and sisters. Looking at the name listed on the vital sign clipboard clasped in my hand confirmed who I thought he was. The name fit the face! "That's right." I thought. "They said he was from Philadelphia!"

There were no bells and whistles announcing his presence because he was merely a visitor, someone who had come to see his ailing mom. He slipped in and out, no big deal, just a guy visiting his mother. No reporters, no cameras; just family.

One distinct impression I walked away with that evening was the demonstration of respect this family exhibited towards their mother. You could sense the mother's position of esteem within the family unit. Things seemed to revolve around the mother's presence. Portrayal of such refined family values earned the champion even greater respect from me. He had my vote, not because of his boxing skill, but because of how he treated his mom. So in the end, I got bragging rights to say I met one of the heavyweight champions of the world, and he was a decent guy who knew how to treat a lady…his mama!

Oh, and my dad did think it was pretty awesome I had the opportunity to meet this heavyweight champion. And you know what? I thought so too!

Young Moms

She was sixteen and giving birth to twins, so much excitement, and so much fear. The delight over the anticipated birth was contagious, manifested by relatives and friends. For her, the motto was calmness and control. By the end of the day, she would leave girlhood behind and shift into womanhood. Adolescence would be in the past, and motherhood on the horizon. Today would not be easy, nor would the next eighteen or so years.

She seemed older than her mere sixteen years; projecting a

maturity beyond her years. It was her demeanor. She did not cry, nor yell with labor pains, but instead focused on her breathing and being in control. She had plans. She knew just how the babies would be cared for, how she would finish school and continue on. She was confident, and had parents who cared and supported her. They loved her and would see her through this unanticipated and premature path.

Her mother was there to coach, to offer advice and support, but clearly not to prescribe the way. The family support was present, yet clearly this sixteen year old recognized herself as the twins' mother. She would prove she possessed the skills to be their mom. Years later, I heard she had raised two loving sons, mature young men who had grown and left home to serve our country; to support their nation in time of conflict.

There is another teen mother I speculate about. I wonder how she fared. Did she make it, and did she finish school? How did the child turn out? Did her mother continue to support her? She started out with so much less than the mother having twins. They were both so young; still girls in high school.

I met her during a postpartum home visit in her mother's house. The teen's mother had accommodated her daughter, and her new grandchild, with their own room in her cottage-like house. Each was alone: no husband, no father, and no grandfather. They were on their own with little funds, little education, and dependent on the state's welfare system. This girl was extremely quiet and hard to draw out, only answering questions directed at her. Her words were few but in fortitude she was strong. She too, but so very different from the other girl, had a strong inner grit. She was determined to raise her child and return to school. So many others, so like her would become mothers before what would seem a reasonable time.

Some would succeed with needed support, and others would falter, adversely impacting so many lives.

CCU Friends

I was admitted to our cardiac intensive care unit, a surprise to us all. My heart was beating its own rhythm, faster than it should. It deviated from the familiar lub-dub. It was in command, and I was along for the ride. Its new rhythm put my head to spinning, and turned my legs to rubber. I felt foreign, strange to myself. I needed control, someone to stop the tempo's flow. My colleagues knew they could gain control—take over for me and restore what I could not. So with rest, expertise, medications and tender care—they gained control and gave me back my old friend, my familiar tempo. They were my friends, my professional colleagues who stepped in and cared for me; one of their own!

Conserving Water

Nurses new to home care nursing, particularly those who come from inpatient care settings often fail to realize it is the client and his/her family who dictate care. They plan meals, make diet selections, set daily schedules of care, carry out (or not) recommended treatments, and either take or fail to ingest prescribed medications. Directing care takes on a new dimension. There is a change in power, and of who calls the shots.

I learned early on as a visiting nurse I was the guest. Equally vital, I also discovered depending on how one presents oneself on initial intake visits sets the stage for future relationships with clients and their families. During my years practicing as a home care nurse I aided many individuals and families, but this assistance was not a one-way street. I, too, grew by gaining new perspectives from my numerous home-based patients and their families.

I have many tales from my home care days. Talk to any visiting nurse and he/she will have intriguing stories to tell. Typically stories relate to such themes as getting lost trying to find someone's home, animal attacks, peculiar family members and potential injuries from poorly maintained homes. And of course, amongst all the similar stories are threaded the unique tales, sometimes only the patient, family and nurse involved can truly appreciate.

For me, there are several unique stories quantifying my visiting nurse days. Some of the stories reflect lessons I learned, some describe the unfolding of some of my strongest therapeutic nurse-client/family relationships, and some convey concerns for my own safety. But overall, what I learned from these diverse encounters I used to make myself a worthier nurse.

First a story with a lesson, an incident that may not seem profound for you as the reader, but for the patient and for me, was genuinely troubling. Me, I never forgot my reprimand.

Growing up I typically lived in the city or the suburbs. I never really lived in the country or ever received my water from a private well. Obtaining a water source simple meant turning the faucet on and city water coursed through the pipes. From my world view tap water was synonymous with utility companies. In the youth of my nursing profession and limited worldly perspective, I was not aware some people had their own wells dug and their own septic systems installed. I thought utility companies managed all these services.

I had lived through droughts and even a devastating flood in which stringent water conservation policies were imposed, but I never had the experience of being deprived of some source of water. In the end, my ignorance of the finer points related to well water usage would teach me a valuable lesson.

It was during the summer and the weather had been hot and humid with little rain. Not enough drought to threaten the city's water supply, yet enough to have the city recommend people refrain from using their garden hoses for washing their cars. Since the drought was minimal, conserving water was not at the forefront of my mind. I knew there were conservation directives, but because I did not wash my car with city water, I only half paid attention to the restrictions.

My day started out like a typical workday. One of the clients on my visit list was an elderly woman who needed a wound cleansed and redressed, nothing major. Though she was actively being seen by other staff through our agency, she was a new client for me (someone I had never visited before). When I arrived at her country home, I introduced myself and told her what I planned to do. Next, I set out my visiting nurse's bag to retrieve my hand washing supplies, washed my hands at her kitchen sink and proceeded to lay out the supplies I would need to manage her dressings.

She sat on a chair in the kitchen not saying much but watching me as I went through this typical arrival ritual. Once I had all my dressing supplies gathered, I needed to wet some gauze to clean around her wound. Not thinking about well water versus city water, and the drought warning, I set out to make the water warm so the gauze would not be cold against her skin. So with the intent of warming the water, I mechanically flicked the hot water spigot on. At the point of my turning the water on at a steady flow the lady lost her patience and chided me.

Maybe she lashed out because she perceived I used to much water when I washed my hands, and then, wasted even more water when I turned the hot water faucet on at a steady stream.

She informed me I was inconsiderate for wasting her water, and had no appreciation for what it meant to have one's own well.

I have to say I felt put in my place and at the same time remorseful I had made this mistake. Her comment and my natural need to shield myself from her annoyance caused me to proceed with her dressing change in a cautious, subdued manner. This transformation in rapport made the atmosphere in the house somewhat tense. I think I was stunned because I had never had a patient react quite like her. I was so taken aback and preoccupied with controlling my emotions, I finished changing and redressing the woman's wound in silence.

My silence was not a reaction of anger, but was rather my attempt to control the tears I felt welling up inside of me. I was embarrassed by my lack of awareness of this woman's water plight. No doubt my face turned crimson when she angrily voiced her dissatisfaction. Whether it was the lack of conversation, my red face or the woman's realization I had not intentionally set out to deplete her well supply, she did apologize for her harsh outburst. Maybe she was afraid I would not finish her dressings properly if she were not hospitable. I do not really know, but I do know despite her attempt at reconciliation, I still felt at fault.

I managed to leave her home with some dignity restored, but I knew deep down the woman was right. I took water for granted and never considered her personal predicament. I learned a lesson the hard way, a country lesson which I never forgot. This lady taught me about conserving, being frugal, eco-friendliness, and respecting someone else's property: valuable home care lessons.

Cup of Tea

Ah… a cup of tea, a time to share and a time to relate. This story revolves around a dying man, his wife, niece, and many cups of tea. Sipping tea with this man's family provided opportunities for them to reflect on the man's story. He was failing; his organs were calling it quits, they had lived out their years. During the weeks of my visits before all functioning would cease, I came to know this man through the eyes of his family.

They marveled over what a handsome and self-confident gentleman he was, a self-established businessman who built a flourishing family enterprise. He had started his own company and managed to run the business until his current illness. And now, over a cup of tea, his wife and niece contemplated whether the grandchildren would take over the business legacy, or would the business close; surely it would be a family tragedy they agreed, if the business should cease to be.

I didn't know the man they described and loved. I only knew the frail man I saw in the bed who no longer overtly responded to words or touch. In the first few weeks of my visits he would look at you, and sometimes follow your movements with his eyes. But in a short time even this tracking ended, and he only stared ahead with a glazed-over look. What he saw or comprehended was merely a guess.

I watched this man's family step right in and address his every need. Family members developed a turning schedule, bathing regime, visiting times...he became their lives. They were a close family, from immediate to extended members. Family unity was a symbol of their ethnicity. He was truly the patriarch of the family, the confidante of all. It was common and acceptable for family members to frequently drop by or call on the telephone to check on him. Their family cohesiveness impressed me. So few patient families I encountered had this sense of connection. Much of the elderly I visited were alone, ignored or forgotten by their children and grandchildren. Others were victims of children who only called or visited only when the monthly income check was expected, rightfully a pathetic symbol of family. But this man's relatives were different. Their caring nature seemed sincere. Relatives really cared and supported each other.

I visited this household for a number of months. Time passed and seasons changed as I continued to visit. Each encounter was marked with a tea session. Tea provided a time to converse, a time for stories, a time for comfort and a time for laughter. Eventually, as life would have it, his heart failed and ceased to beat. Oddly, on a mystical level, I have wondered if perhaps our tea sessions really served another purpose. Maybe they served as the avenue to allow the women to grieve, and for this dear man to recognize when his family was ready for him to leave an empty cup of tea at the table.

On one of my visits his wife and niece presented me with a gold and brown afghan they had stitched, piece-by-piece just for me. Now, sometimes, as I sip a cup of tea wrapped in my afghan, I continue to remember a man, a family and many cups of tea.

I attended his large funeral to support the family and to say good-bye. It had been a long and sincere road.

Pacing New Mom

We did not catch on at first. I remember thinking the new mother's behavior was odd but at first I did not understand her true purpose. It never occurred to me there was another motive besides boredom explaining why she kept cruising by the nurse's station.

Her walking started after dinner on our 3-11 p.m. shift when most of the babies were back in the nursery, bedded down for the evening. For those new mothers doing physically well following their labor and delivery experience, the return of their babies to the nursery made for a long evening; particularly after visitors departed. Once babies were returned to the nursery many of the mothers would take walks in the halls or spend time conversing with one another. Knowing this, I figured the walking mom was just bored. Perhaps she decided to take a stroll to spend time outside her room and explore the environment.

To see this new mother reading while ambling was different, but not so peculiar we thought twice about her actions. I did think the novel must have been one which was so intriguing she could not bear to put the book down.

In the early part of the evening we commented on her repeated trips down the halls and around the nurses' station, but then we became distracted from her behavior as we were slammed with admissions. Several hours passed, and our focus left this woman as we rushed about working to survive the post-delivery chaos whirling around us.

When shift change was transpiring, one of the oncoming nurses waiting for the start of "report" noticed the walking postpartum mom. After observing her circling behavior for a few minutes the night nurse inquired how long the woman had been walking and reading a book. Refocusing our attention back on this woman we deduced she had been strolling for several hours. Unknowingly, quite a bit of time had flown by while we were rushing about attending to new deliveries. When we responded she had been walking several hours, our colleague simply and explicitly clarified what the new mother was obviously doing. Hearing the nurse's explanation I had one of those "aha" moments.

The revelation of the true meaning behind this woman's walking was so apparent I wondered if we hadn't been so busy attending to the needs of the fresh deliveries whether we would have figured out what she was really doing. We all took psych courses, we all passed our state boards, and we were all smart; we were nurses. I like to think we would have eventually figured out her underlying motive. With our focus on new deliveries, we saw what we wanted to see. Here was a woman walking and reading a book. We missed the link she was so very thin. She still had a small postpartum bulge in her abdomen, but other than this pregnancy residual, the rest of her torso and extremities were exceptionally slender. What we came to realize was this woman was attempting to ward off any extra weight she perceived she still possessed after the birth of her baby. She walked, or should I now say paced, so as to lose the pregnancy weight and any accumulated calories she gained. She was wasting no time exercising to achieve her self-defined weight goal. Walking and reading, two acceptable social behaviors employed to mask her attempt at calorie burning. Walk and burn, walk and burn; we missed it! She was an anorexic, preoccupied with weight control!

Mattresses and Rabbits

I was overseeing a group of nursing students on a surgical unit where students were in various areas observing procedures and assisting with pre- and post- operative care. Several staff members and I stopped at the nurses' station to check on aspects of patient care. While at the station a conversation surfaced about retiring. One of the nurses present had only a few days left before she would be enjoying the start of this blissful phase of life. After we spent a few minutes talking about how nice it would be to retire, and how we could not wait for our day to come, the conversation shifted to the telling of a few stories about the "good old days."

Some of the anecdotes surprised me. I never thought of nurses assuming some of the roles described, but I could understand how the related responsibilities fell on the laps of nurses. The particular hospital that was the focus of their stories was the one we were standing in. The hospital, which was originally a neighborhood house, had grown to a modern medical facility. Over a hundred years before a nursing school was established within the system. After the graduation of many classes, the nursing school eventually closed, although the hospital remained opened. Despite the school's closing many of the program's alumni continued to show their loyalty by remaining at the institution.

The retiring nurse and some of the others talking at the nurse's station were former graduates of the hospital's nursing school. Those alumni present began to recount stories and experiences which personally happened to them, or ones they recalled having been told by other alumni. Here are two reflections they shared. Of course, each account began with "remember when…" Well, here goes!

"Remember when after patients were discharged we had to drag the mattresses up to the roof to air them out and beat them with a broom?" Can you picture former nurses doing this? I never witnessed this action, or even heard of this task before; definitely an expectation before my time. You know what? I could picture it happening. When you think about it, nurses are very concerned with the spread of germs, organisms and "bugs." And of course "way back then," bed bugs and lice were common mattress and body companions. Reflecting on this expectation, I could easily see a policy in place mandating "all nurses are to air mattresses between patients to eliminate risk of cross contamination." Of course, the policy probably contained a detailed outline of precisely how the task was to be carried out, including a part describing exactly what type brooms were to be used. Though I find it hard to picture myself lugging a mattress up a set of steps and onto a rooftop, I know if I was a nurse when such a policy was in place, I would have been up on the roof with broom in hand.

"Remember when the rabbits were kept in cages on the roof and we had to go up and feed them. And, "remember when they all got loose on Mary Jane." Whether the puzzled look on my face revealed I was wondering "Why in the world would rabbits be at a hospital," or the nurse telling the story just felt the need to explain, my self-reflected question was immediately answered. She informed her audience rabbits were used for pregnancy tests. Therefore, to have available specimens the needed rabbits were housed on the hospital's rooftop, instead of inside the diagnostic laboratory. "Okay" I thought "that's interesting." From my mental image of rabbits caged on the roof I could easily visualize a young student nurse frantically scurrying about on the shingled roof attempting to capture loose rabbits hopping about. Actually, I could almost picture something similar happening to me, or one of my peers, if we had been in school at the time. As students, we always seemed to find ourselves in some comical situation. Truly, the joys of nursing!

Black Eyes

There was a middle aged nurse's aide who would come to work a day or two after we received our paychecks with black eyes, and other impact markings on her face. She lived with her significant other who apparently felt entitled to her wages. We tried to convince her to leave him, but he gave her promises. She always believed his "good intentions" would materialize and never seemed to recognize his assurances were never kept. Over and over, she would tell us how he promised to change.

She caused us heartache, but we couldn't persuade her to leave him or seek professional help. Eventually I left for new opportunities, but I often wondered if she ever found the strength to move on and leave her abuser, or if in the end he caused her demise.

Faceless but Memorable

I recall the room, the unique bed. I can visualize her lying there, but can no longer put a face to the body. Not being able to recall her face bothers me. I wonder when I lost her vivid memory. Instead, I now remember her by her condition, a quantifier as nurses we are taught should never be the sole definer of a person. So I am breaking a cardinal rule by referring to this woman, not by who she was, but rather by what disease state she bore. So regretfully, I define her in this account as the woman with extensive decubitus ulcers. An individual with the deepest, ugliest "bed sores" I have ever seen.

I recall the malodorous odor when entering her room, the distinct scent of pathogen infected wounds. An odor once smelled, would never be forgotten; pungent to the point of inducing bouts of nausea. I encountered her during one of the times I worked as a nurse's aide.

Being a student nurse and working as a nurse's aide basically meant you were capable of doing a little more than the typical healthcare aide. I never minded the extra responsibilities because sometimes I had the opportunity to participate in situations, which might not come around again. Usually I did not see the same patients each time I worked, since I only worked on weekends and not each one. Also, as student aides we were not assigned to specific nursing floors but to whatever unit needed the extra help.

Sometimes additional hands were needed because a regular nurse called out sick, there was a full patient census, increased levels of patient acuity, or a particular patient needed someone to sit with them because of confusion, suicidal tendencies or some other issue necessitating one-on-one supervision.

I do not remember specifically why I was scheduled to work on this particular unit the evening I was to encounter this woman. Most likely my placement had something to do with her acuity level and the fact her care was extremely time consuming. Just prepping to go into her room involved gowning, gloving and masking, since she was on strict isolation precautions.

Infected wounds, offensive odors, isolation precautions, time-consuming dressing changes and emotionally taxing care were all variables that made this a rather challenging and demanding patient assignment. Over time such assignments can often overwhelm the regular staff. What takes its toll is the mental and physical exhaustion encompassed with caring 24/7 for someone with such extensive needs. Recognizing care burnout does not reflect insensitivity of nurses, but rather is a reminder nurses have human qualities. Nurses, too, have limitations.

I am sure, such exhaustion of the regular staff had something to do with my being assigned to the unit where this woman was a patient. I was respite for the staff, and as a double bonus, I was a senior level nursing student. This meant I could be assigned the woman's dressing changes—a big part of what consumed the staff's time. The nurses were thrilled with the extra help, and I was glad I could assist and learn.

Having not worked for a fair number of days meant I had not met the patient before. When I was briefed on the woman's history I learned she was an elderly woman, who several days before had been brought to our facility by ambulance from a local nursing home. She was extremely weak and debilitated with pressure ulcers, or bed sores, on her hips, buttocks, heels and elbows. She had no corresponding family, which meant the nursing home was her home. Only the transport team had accompanied her to the hospital, and no one had come to visit her since.

I was provided with detailed instructions on how to treat the various, bone-deep bed sores. The dressing procedure consisted of removing the old dressings and wound packing, flushing the wounds, applying specific creams/ointments, repacking the wounds and applying new dressings. Clearly, by no means was this a simple dressing change procedure.

None of my previous patient experiences prepared me for the moment I laid eyes on this woman. I think one could be a nurse for many years and never see a case of bedsores quite this severe. With the isolation mask and goggles on it would have been difficult for someone to see my stunned expression. However, if they looked deep into my eyes they would have seen the dismay. I was shocked by what I saw, but was quick to cover any outward signs of my concern. The disbelief was immediately replaced with a sense of sadness that anyone had to endure such a life. All I could think of was how inhumane it all seemed, and when I did her dressing changes or even touched her I was going to cause her more pain, a care paradox.

Though I knew before entering her room her sores were infected, I would have known the minute I opened her door. The defining odor was there, a stench a nurse only needs to get a whiff of once, and will never forget. The smell permeated my nostrils even with a mask shielding my nose. Were the organisms infecting the wounds eradicated? Certainly not, my senses shouted.

What else did I know about her? I knew she was on a special type of circular electric bed that was called a Circo-Lectric Bed. I had heard of such a bed frame, but never saw one. She needed this type of circular frame because she could not lie flat on her back due to the size and location of her ulcers. Certainly her positioning on this type of bed was vital to her care. When I looked at her suspended on the circular frame, lying on her abdomen, with her arms and legs extended outward and most of her back and lower areas exposed, I had a fleeting depiction of Jesus Christ on the cross. I could not help but wonder if she would be better off in some celestial place as well.

She was semiconscious, probably from the sedation she was given, or from the overwhelming toxins invading her body. But still, above the faint mechanical sounds of the equipment, were the faint sounds of her moans. Basically she was skin and bones; a poster person for anorexia or some other debilitating, malnourished condition.

I was fortunate the unit's charge nurse gave me a limited assignment. Because I was delegated only this woman, I had time to spend with her. My aspiration was to try not to cause her any further discomfort and perhaps even ease a fraction of her anguish. Being so new to nursing, and quite idealistic, I wondered about the nursing home staff that let this happen. I found it hard to comprehend how anyone could let another person's body advance to this state. In my view, this was pure neglect. For this woman to be in this state, I perceived she could not possibly have been turned every two hours, principles learned in Nursing 101. Simple, I perceived some nurses had not done their jobs!

At that point in my career, I never thought about other variables such as poor protein intake, poor nutritional status, and immune compromised conditions that could have contributed to skin breakdown in this woman. For me, this was a case of poor nursing care by the nursing home staff. I failed to give credence to the fact that possibly she came to the nursing home with bedsores, and the decubitus were really a result of poor home care. No, to me the nurses were to blame because as students it was preached to us that good nursing care, adherence to turning schedules, sheep skin protectors, and routine skin inspections helped to prevent skin breakdown.

So what went wrong? There could have been one variable or multiple variables. The result could have been someone's fault or nobody's fault. Today though, I know there are many factors that could have predisposed this woman to having these ulcers, but I still wonder at times, if any preventative skin measures were ever implemented.

Advancing into her room I did not anticipate problems completing her wound care. In class I had learned to do dressing changes, pack wounds, and redress wounds. No big deal, piece of cake, I thought. I could handle it. But I was wrong, this woman needed so much more than any of us could provide for her. It was obvious to me her care was out of our hands.

That night I did all I could but knew it was not enough. I recognized as everyone else that we could not make this go away. Her condition was beyond our expertise. It was only a matter of days after I met her that she passed away....I always hoped she found the peace she truly deserved.

Tired

We were four new graduates who converged, shared an apartment and became best friends. The tragedy happened while

I was away at a tropical island having a wonderful time on my honeymoon. When I returned I found she had already been buried and my two remaining friends felt our now departed friend would have wanted it that way, to not spoil my honeymoon by her death. So I returned and found our foursome had become a threesome.

We often cautioned her not to drive the hour and a half to her parent's house after working all night. "Stay at the apartment, take a nap," we encouraged. We knew working from 11-7 a.m., and then challenging oneself to stay awake to complete a task was difficult; weariness creeps in. I could not do it, stay awake all night and drive a distance home without feeling like I needed to put my head down to take a nap.

We knew she shouldn't attempt the trip without first stopping at the apartment and sleeping. We cringed when she told us she sometimes caught herself dozing while driving. But the desire to go home and see her boyfriend, who lived near her parents, enticed her more than sleep. "Roll down the windows, play the radio, drink strong coffee; do whatever it takes to stay awake," we pleaded.

Smack...a demolished car, an undamaged truck and a departing soul. She was rushed back to work in a speeding ambulance, coded by our colleagues who gave it their all. But life was not to be; she never returned. I was told she remained beautiful without one visible mark or external scrape. All her life-taking injuries were internal.

What happened to cause the accident remained unknown; one could only surmise. Her car crossed the divider and went head on into a large eighteen-wheeler truck. They said when she departed she looked asleep. Her much needed nap.

Starched

I can still hear the swish of her white nylons rubbing together when she walked the halls. She was the perfect picture of an angelic nurse, from the white cap atop her head to the whitest "spit polished" leather nursing shoes I had ever seen. She looked like she stepped out of one of those antique pictures depicting a bunch of straight-laced nurses standing together wearing similar white, tailored dresses looking as if a bottle of starch had been used to stiffen their uniform from collars to hems.

She was a bit stout, and had one of those endowed bosoms that filled out her uniform. One's eyes naturally traveled up her chest, starting from the white center button at her waist, straight up to the protruding point of her chin. She was buttoned straight up, almost military style, with nothing out of place, not even a wisp of hair tumbling free from under her cap. Sometimes it seemed all that was missing was a click of the heels and a morning salute. She was our head nurse, our leader. She kept us in line.

Our director had this look; the one you dreaded. The stare you knew meant you were about to be called out on the carpet. Being called out on the carpet in this part of our career happened a lot. Several of the new staff members like me were new graduates. And try as diligently as we could to be perfect, we were novices. We were not proficient in organizational skills, weren't seasoned time managers, or familiar with all aspects of patient care. We were fresh out of school and had lots to learn. We might have been smart, but not a hundred percent there yet. Like any new graduate we needed transition time. Our "newness" and "awkwardness" is probably why we rarely saw her smiling. Occasionally she would flash us a grin, but most times she was straight-faced serious. I suppose she had a lot on her mind, wanting to see "her" unit function impeccably.

She was in command. She was the sergeant and we were new recruits. We learned fast, and made mistakes, but we learned from our mistakes. In the end, she taught us well and introduced us to the everyday realities of nursing. She showed us the way. She was our first career mentor.

Angels

This was a peculiar day. I am not sure if the day was linked somehow to a bigger meaning, or was made up of a number of isolated events with no relevance to one another. I guess the beginning of the events started with a trip to the public library. We were planning to leave on a family trip, so my daughter wanted to get some books to take along. Before we went into the library, I promised myself I would just look and resist the urge to check out any books. I knew I already had work-related reading to do.

I have enough personal insight to know, I am one of those individuals who has a hard time putting a good book down. I would rather read than sleep. So I know when I have things which need to be done, particularly related to teaching, I have to limit my pleasure reading.

So this time I was in the library to just wander around and browse the shelves while my daughter selected her books. I even left my library card in the car so I would not be tempted to leave with some intriguing novels. As I moseyed around just looking, the new book section caught my eye. I wandered over to see what authors were writing about, and what some of the hot topics were. Who knows I contemplated, I just might obtain some ideas from other authors, or perhaps identify a gap in the literature, which someone needs to write about.

Anyway I figured I would peruse through the new books. As

my eyes skimmed titles on the binders I mentally passed over those books with titles of little interest to me. There were a variety of subjects covering topics such as politics, exercise (e.g., Pilates), and cooking. All topics I found interesting, but which did not spark enough curiosity in me to send a signal from my brain to my arm, tempting me to extend my hand and pluck the book from the shelf. That is, not until I came across a title called something like "Angels 101." For some reason, at that moment, in that space of time, the title intrigued me and I retrieved the book from the shelf. Standing there flipping through the text I paused and read some short passages. My curiosity of what might be said caused me to walk over to a circular table while still reading, sit down and continue scanning the text.

The volume was not very thick, and an easy read, so it did not take me long to come across some informative data. One of the sections I found interesting was a discussion of the clues people should be aware of which could signify angels are attempting to communicate with them. There was mention of clues such as having strong feelings of a presence, seeing images, luminous lights, and hearing angels speak softly into one's ear.

My last thought as I re-shelved the book when my daughter came over to tell me she was ready to leave was, "Interesting…I guess the author is right, you need to keep an open mind."

Maybe my mind was just focused on angels, but for the rest of the evening it seemed like symbols of angels floated before my eyes. Driving home over the same route we drove many, many times I seemed to notice the Blessed Virgin Mary statues some people had displayed in their front yards. You know, the painted ceramic statues about three feet high set within a grotto. Figurines I probably passed a thousand times, but really did not take notice with such acuteness as I did that evening.

Later in the evening, I went to a free clinic where I volunteered as a nurse practitioner. I had been working at the center for a number of months, but since I was relocating to another state, this evening was to be my last. The free clinic was started by parishioners of a Catholic church and was housed in a former Catholic high school. To express their appreciation for my help, the other clinic volunteers had a little party after all the clients had been seen, to say goodbye and wish me luck in my new ventures. My friends presented me with an angel statue inscribed as the angel of healing. Was this perhaps, another angel sign?

Once home after my family enjoyed a piece of cake left over from my farewell event, I dimmed the kitchen lights and went to put our plates into the kitchen sink. Darkness had already fallen. As I put the plates in the sink, I happened to look up and into the window just above the sink. A bright white light shone back at me. For a second or two I just stared at the illumination, the brilliance of the light awed me.

As I stared at the light, the realization processed through my mind I was looking at a reflection in the window of the nightlight I had on in the kitchen. Though leaving a nightlight on is a nightly ritual in our house, I swore as many times as I had seen the light's reflection in the window, it was never as radiant as it was this night.

Lastly, my husband typically puts a radio on at night as he falls asleep. Rather than music, he prefers to listen to talk programs. Most of the time he falls asleep fairly fast, but not me. Now, unlike my earlier dorm days, when I could sleep in a bright room and with commotion about, I can't advance into a final slumber until there is utter silence. So, I usually just give him a few listening minutes, knowing he will soon doze off and then I can turn the radio off. This night, like clockwork he fell asleep within a matter of minutes as I half daydreamed and half listened to the commentator. But what do I hear tonight? There is a caller calling to talk about angels. He proceeds to talk about the "Lost Book of Enoks" (something I never heard of before) as the language of angels. Then, as the commentator and caller conversed, the discussion moved on to discussing the topic of angels versus archangels, and angels and archangels as spiritual beings. More angels I think. Could all this focus on angels be a coincidence? Maybe I reflect, but it still seems mighty peculiar. This was a strange day I conclude as I turn off the radio and succumbed to sleep.

Can't You See What I See!

At the time, I did not recognize his widening pulse pressure (top blood pressure number widely separated from the bottom number) of 208/60, his heart rate of 48 and his irregular respirations displaying on the cardio-respiratory monitor above his head, told the true story. Neurology was not my specialty, and I had forgotten Cushing's Triad, three signs of rising intracranial pressure (ICP).

It seemed the ER staff also forgot Cushing's Triad because concerns of increased intracranial pressure were never discussed with the man's family. Despite this cluster of symptoms there was no mention his intracranial pressure was increasing, nor any attempt by the staff to measure the pressure within his head. He had been brought into the trauma center unresponsive, a state perceived to be caused by an injury sustained when striking his head on the cemented ground. Evidence suggested he lost consciousness and then fell out of the open door of his parked postal truck.

The ER team proposed several possible diagnoses for his condition. Some providers surmised he had food poisoning because in a conversation with his wife, shortly before the unconscious incident occurred he remarked on purchasing coffee from a convenient store which he stated tasted "funny" and made him vomit. Another physician, a cardiac specialist, felt with such a low heart rate he more than likely had some type of cardiac dysfunction, which was yet to be determined. There were also postulations he had thrown a blood clot. Bottom line, there was no definitive answer; it was too soon to tell exactly what had hold of him.

But he was there, lying unconscious on a stretcher in one of the cubicles in the ER, heavily sedated because he had been combative when he started to arouse during flight to the ER. So there he lay completely restrained on the narrow bed he had been transferred to from the helicopter's stretcher. His arms and legs extended outward with cloth restraints anchoring him to the bed. He was intubated with a tube taped to the side of his mouth, hooked to the extended arm of a respirator. His almost naked body was exposed to the cool air as he laid spread eagle in nothing but his male briefs. A putrid grayish blue color around his mouth matched the ashen-blue coloring around his eyes and nail beds. Dried blood was caked in his hair and in the auricle of his ear, old blood which had originally seeped from a head contusion. And overall, his skin reflected this ghastly whitish-grey color.

He had involuntary twitching, leading me to question whether the patient was having seizures. "No," I was told forthright, "He's moving like that from the medication we gave… to keep him calm." What medication, I thought. What medication used to calm someone would also make them twitch like this; like having a seizure? Mentally I questioned the care provider's explanation and pondered, "Is this how they respond to everyone?" Are people's questions so commonly dismissed? No wonder providers are often perceived as insensitive. I, too, am feeling as if I am bothering them.

I touch his arm, and take his hand, so there is a connection when I speak to him. I am shocked at how cold he feels. I do not feel the warmth of life, he seems so empty to me. I know in my gut he's off somewhere. I might be seeing him, but he is really not here. He is somewhere between here and there. I speak to him, but there is no response, no tightening of the hand, no eyelid flicker, no change in his heart rate and no sign of recognition. There is nothing, absolutely, nothing. His prognosis hits me hard, and I know I am helpless. I can't help him through.

Can he fight? Does he have a morsel of energy to give life a try? I sure hope so. But what if he does give it his all, and manages to come around? What happens then? Will he be cured? Will he be permanently scarred by whatever this is? What will be left? Will there remain any resemblance of who he was?

He looks so bad, I wonder about the health of his brain. Is it getting the nutrients it needs to survive, to allow him to speak and think? What if the higher faculties of his brain have ceased, should these heroics be stopped? Has he gone too far beyond our reach? What has happened? His present state seems unreal. I want to shake the providers and say "can't you see, can't you see how bad this man is." Nurses mosey in and out, check a tube, check a chart, check a reading and then slip out. I feel like a bystander watching a slow moving parade; a lone figure, fading away.

"Can't they do something? Where are the physicians? They should be here. This patient is critical. Can't they see this man, surely he needs their help...No, don't leave...help! Make him warm, stop the seizures...talk to him...touch him and reassure him. Please, don't just leave. Don't just turn and go. Don't you care? Deep down I know it's bad. All my medical wisdom is triggering in my mind and telling me everything I see is nearly incompatible with life. I tell myself I can't think about such things; instead I need to help him fight. I need to send him positive vibes, nothing negative. He needs the energy if he is to survive. He needs more time to be a dad, a husband and the brother he is to me.

Toenails

I was sent on a home visit to check on a middle-aged man and his elderly mother. Age-wise I would say the son was about fifty and the mother in her eighties. Both were to be our clients. I was the first to visit their home and to do an intake evaluation to assess their needs. They had the bare necessities in their sparse living quarters. A dim light emitted from the sole light bulb, which dangled by a single wire from the center of the ceiling in their one room flat; the only evidence of electricity flowing through the home. A table, two twin beds, and a few wooden chairs pretty much made up the contents of their home. All of the household items were well-worn and structurally weak. There was no television or radio blaring and no visible sink, instead buckets of water served their needs.

I felt like I had stepped back in time to a period in our history when massive numbers of immigrants first settled within our nation and were forced to stay in deplorable, one room shelters. These two people and their setting belonged in those black and white immigrant photographs where groups of very thin, poorly dressed people looked back at you with solemn expressions and sunken, hollow eyes. Those familiar pictures where images of despair, loneliness and isolation dominated the photos.

Neither the man nor the woman was thin, but they both still had that weary, somewhat washed out look. And as for their house, well, their one-room home looked about as shabby as any tenant house portrayed in those dated snapshots.

One look in the door, and I knew this was not going to be a short visit. I did not have a portable telephone to call our home office and request additional help. So I had to work alone. Consequently, I ended up spending several hours at the house trying to deal with the situation at hand. And, even then, when I left their home I knew they needed so much more. Ideally the mother and son needed to be taken from their home and literally cared for.

The mother, now elderly, could no longer maintain her own personal needs. The son had some evident mental deficits which compromised his ability to care for himself and his mother. He could follow simple instructions, but was by no means self-reliant. He did not have a grasp of basic care needs for himself or his mother. Like so many others, this failing team lacked healthcare insurance, money, and family resources to help them with their circumstances. Basically, as I understood their situation, they only had each other.

Though addressing the mother's needs took time, there really was nothing out of the ordinary about her care. It was when I got to the son, I would be shocked. He had long pants on and wore a pair of high-top black canvas sneakers, well worn of course. Above his sneakers his legs were quite swollen and edematous. The fluid had settled into the tissues and now caused his lower legs to have a brownish discoloration with a brawny appearance. To touch the skin on both legs felt taut and hard.

As I assessed his legs, and asked him about the condition of his feet concealed beneath his sneakers, he told me he did not know. He proceeded to tell me because of the difficulty he had in removing his sneakers, and because of the condition of his feet, he had not taken his sneakers off for about a year. "For a year" my brain resonated. How could someone not take their shoes off for a year, I questioned myself? He must be confused, or not comprehending what I just said to him... I'll need to look!

Surprise, the sneaker cloth is adhered to his skin. The sneaker fabric had embedded into the oozing ulcers. Down close I catch a stench which offends my nose, but even worse than the smell, is the effort needed to diligently dislodge the shoe cloth from the ulcer beds.

Maybe I should not have removed his shoes, but left the noisome task for someone else, in another time and place. But I appreciated neither the mother nor the son would leave their home for someone else to care for them, and more than likely with no money, no one else would freely take on the monumental task.

I knew removing his shoes would reveal something bad, but was I in for a surprise! I could handle the smell and the look of the wounds, but it was the appearance of his toes. I never anticipate what I saw! With my first glimpse all I could think of was a ram's head. He had these really thick, yellowish toenails on every toe which lifted up, curled forward and wrapped up and around towards his ankle. The front of the shoe prevented the nails from growing forward so the nails grew where they could: up and over the top of his foot. I had never seen such a sight! Truly another first for me!

What could one do to address such feet with meager household and medical supplies? My inner voice said "Where do I begin" and "look what I've gone and done…by checking his feet." The odor, the oozing wounds, the discolored skin, the gruesome toenails and the organisms which I knew lurked about made me think he was right... surely he had not removed his sneakers in over a year!

I spent hours assisting this man and his elderly mother. Since I had made the visit on the evening shift, it wasn't until I came on my shift the next day that I was informed our agency administrative staff were working to place both mother and son in personal care centers. We would not be making further home visits. I never saw him or her again. I was just left with the memory of a little old lady, and a son with some pretty horrific toenails.

Deep Scars

Boarding the plane I made my way past those passengers who had already occupied their seats in the first several rows. I traveled down the narrow aisle, waiting patiently as people ahead stood at their seats attempting to push and shove their "small" carry-on items into the overhead compartments. Everyone knew the drill, remain cool and wait one's turn. Besides, we all knew the rule. The plane would not begin to move until everyone was seated.

I was flying to join my family for a few days in Florida where they had already started their vacation. Since I had such a short time off from nursing school, not even a week my parents had purchased an airline ticket for me. By flying to join them, I would not have to waste part of my break by driving. Prior to this flight, I had always flown with someone else, so because I was flying alone this time, I knew I would be sitting next to someone I did not know. There was the possibility the person might be pleasant and strike up a conversation, be someone who liked to sleep, or be an individual preferring to engross themselves in a book. Whatever transpired, I was prepared. I would welcome a nap or read a book if my unknown seat partner preferred to be silent, or I would welcome a chat if conversation was initiated.

The idea of having to sit next to someone I did not know really did not bother me. Because I had the window seat, if my seat partner proved to be even slightly offensive, I could look out at the passing clouds and minuscule objects dotting the ground. Conversely, since I had the window seat, my flying partner had the aisle seat. This meant I would have to crawl over him/her if I had to use the bathroom; clearly a disadvantage of a window seat. But maybe not so bad, if one were interested in meeting the person sitting next to them.

As I proceeded down the narrow aisle to descend on my spot, I looked ahead to approximately where my seat number might be. From where I was, it appeared my flight partner was already seated. As I got closer I could see my seat companion was indeed a "he" and was comfortably settled into his aisle seat next to my vacant window seat.

What I saw intrigued me, particularly from an anatomy perspective. I was curious of what I saw on his face, but being polite I did not want to stare. There was no doubt this man must have had his share of people gawking at him. His voice was pleasant. He greeted me with a friendly hello and politely rose so I could squeeze by and plop into my cushioned seat.

Sitting side by side, as one typically does on an airplane, had its advantages in this case. Because of the changes I glimpsed in his face when advancing down the aisle, I could see where some people might find it difficult not to stare at him. This would be particularly hard if someone were sitting directly across from him. For me, glaring at him was not a problem, since we sat side by side.

We sat in silence as the plane ascended and leveled out. I flipped through the provided magazine while he put his head back and appeared to rest. After we were cruising for a bit, he opened his eyes and initiated conversation. As we conversed, I disclosed I was in nursing school. My association with something medical seemed to provide the stimulus for him to share. He revealed he was traveling to Florida from another state for plastic surgery, one of many surgeries he had already endured.

His story was one of those where a matter of seconds can change the whole course of one's life. He unveiled the story of his ordeal. At the time of the incident, he was driving in not-so-good weather, maybe a little faster than he should have been, when his car hydroplaned, spun off the road and hit a telephone pole at high speed. As his car spun around he was ejected from the automobile. What happened next he recounted, transformed his life. From the impact of the car some telephone wires came loose. One of the snapped and dangling wires whipping about swung across his face in a cutting motion. In that very instant both his face and being were totally altered.

From his description, I can only imagine how disfigured his face must have been immediately after the injury, when the wounds were fresh and the skin was grossly lacerated. Even as I conversed with him his face was markedly distorted, yet he described the scars as better.

I listened intently to the man's story, only commenting here and there. Obviously, I provided him with a therapeutic opportunity to share his story with someone who might understand. And he was right. I felt empathy for him knowing from a healthcare perspective what he must have gone through physically and emotionally. Just his being strong enough to be in public and enduring the many stares, I felt was commendable.

Though our paths only crossed for several hours while on the plane, I figured we were destined to meet. I was there to hear this person's personal account of a terrible misfortune and he was given the opportunity to share his story with a stranger who could understand. That day he may have revealed more of his inner thoughts to me, a stranger, than he had to his closest family and friends.

Really, Iced Tea?

Sometimes as a friend you no longer see in your friend what others clearly see. A number of us missed her telltale signs. Almost embarrassing to admit, since we were all nurses, and had studied the classic behaviors people typically exhibited with this type of history.

As nurses we had been working together for a couple of years and knew each others' strengths and weaknesses. We knew which one to call when we couldn't get an intravenous (IV) line started, who responded the best when a patient was crashing, and who always seemed to be on top of their game. We relied on each other and collaborated with each other. We had a solid team, until things began to change.

First came a new boyfriend, then came the behavior of just making it to shift report, and next came the behavior of completely missing change of shift report. There were always explanations. Initially we accepted her stories because they seemed plausible and the resulting behaviors were so unlike her. She had a flat tire, she was caught in traffic, or she had a minor accident... lots of believable excuses. Then, she started to miss work because she was ill or she came into work saying she felt sick and needed to lie down or go home. One time she convinced us she had to lie down because she was having a miscarriage, but later we found she even fabricated that story.

We, as her friends missed a telltale clue of her true problem. We did not question her when she told us she was trying to lose weight and was forcing fluids so she would feel full and therefore would eat less. To be able to drink frequently she kept a tall, dark-colored beverage container with her which she frequently sipped from. It was her "unsweetened iced tea." Her sipping of fluids, lateness, and excuses went on for a couple of months until one day, despite her name being on the staffing schedule she did not show up for work. At first we figured she was late, but then much to our surprise we were informed she had resigned.

We knew her nursing job was her main source of income so to hear she had resigned so unexpectedly came as a surprise. However, within a matter of hours through the rumor mill (which was typically correct) we learned the true reason for her leaving. We had been totally naïve. She was not drinking "unsweetened iced tea" but rather sipping vodka. All the excuses, change in personality and lateness were related to her addiction. Our friend had resigned, but not for self-selected reasons, but instead to undergo substance abuse therapy. Now with hindsight, all of her erratic behaviors had a different meaning.

Devotion

I was awed at both this man and woman. She was remarkable for the care she gave. And the man, her husband, I found to be extraordinary. I had learned numerous facts about rheumatoid arthritis and seen a number of individuals suffering from different forms of arthritis, but I had never seen someone's body so crippled, contracted or debilitated from the disease. He was dying from the arthritis which invaded his body. He could no longer rise out of bed or even stand. His thin, bony, rigid legs were contracted into bent positions; his arms the same. Lying flat was impossible because his spine was fixed and bent. Even eating was an effort. All his energy went to fighting the constant pain his medication no longer relieved. Every hour was a struggle, but he fought to be with his devoted wife.

She had learned the fundamentals of nursing care through trial and error. Now though skilled in basic care, her husband's care had become too complex for her to manage. Instead we were called in to see how we might assist her. It was evident by his present state she soon would be free from her husband's care. But then, what was time without her husband? And, what would her day be like without addressing his needs?

Our agency staff made a few visits before we were no longer needed. He soon expired. Hopefully, he moved onto a pain-free place. She, I am sure with all her devotion, lost part of herself with the death of her husband. I recall this couple not because of the man's pain and suffering, but because they exemplified love. This couple truly embraced the marriage vows of "for better or for worse, until death do we part."

Sweet Corn

It was a piece of trivia I learned about corn. I would not have discovered the plant's fact if I did not work in the geographic area I did.

He was school age by lay standards but had never seen the inside of our public schools. The young lad had gone to school, yet his education was different than most students. His school building was a one room structure with all grades taught within.

Schooling had its place in his world, but was not one of the true virtues of his life. Religion, family and work were strong values within his faith. He was a member of the "plain people." His name was Amos. Typically, he wore simple black clothes, a brimmed hat, and spoke in a distinct German dialect. He was a true contrast to the other clients who populated the tertiary center; a distinction between the past and the present. Many of his faith lived in the hospital's surrounding communities. Consequently, they were familiar with the center's healthcare system and commonly used the entity. His family did not come to visit by car, but instead, would arrive by a horse driven black buggy; an image of days gone by.

Amos was a patient in the intensive care unit. He had been in a farming accident. His arm had been almost completed severed by a piece of agricultural machinery used in the processing of corn. Microsurgery and some extremely skilled physicians reconnected his arm. They did an impressive job. But despite their crafty work, the surgeons still had to be cautious. Their work could be in vain if the known bacterium and/or fungi which often inhabited the corn crop and machinery lurked about. Corn, a colorful fall crop which tastes so good with a pat of butter, and a pinch of salt, now affected whether this boy's arm would remain or be lost. As he lay in the bed, in and out of sleep, I could not help contrasting his life with the lives of non-Amish kids. Surely, a marked difference!

In the end, Amos was lucky. Medication given preventively to ward off suspected pathogens did the trick, at least while our paths crossed. Working with Amos drove home to me the point that illness and disease know no cultural and religious barriers; basically we are all the same.

Mother-Daughter: Cat and Mouse

They had a unique relationship. Theirs was not the typical mother-daughter rapport. They did not help each other, but instead verbally insulted each other. They had no other family members, no significant other, no husband and no siblings. Basically, they had each other.

I often arrived at their home in the midst of a bickering session. The mother would be declaring her frustration at what she perceived was a lack of concern and respect on the daughter's behalf. The daughter had convinced the mother caring for her was burdensome. In a loud condescending voice she would remind her mother she had more urgent things to do in her twenties then be straddled with a crippled, arthritic parent. She rebelled by staying out late, coming home intoxicated and exhibiting what the mother defined as immoral behavior.

From frustration, the daughter in so many words informed her mother the only reason she lived at home was because the mother could not survive without her. On the other hand, from the mother's accounts it was revealed the daughter made no contributions towards maintaining the household, had no job and did not offer money towards the monthly rent. She essentially depended on her mother for almost everything.

In terms of their home, their apartment did not omit a sense of hominess, nor did the household seem to be a place one would feel good about. Instead, their home seemed to be merely a dwelling which provided a roof over their heads and convenient lodging. Because of mobility problems, the mother spent little time outside the apartment. Not having the freedom to come and go as her daughter did, further frustrated the mother.

The mother's main income came from disability funds. The wrath of the arthritis had taken its toll to the point where walking without assistive devices was difficult. She was at the point of care where she was receiving gold injections (a therapy for rheumatoid arthritis) to see if perhaps her body would respond to the therapeutic effects of the medication, and at the same time, provide some relief from the discomfort of painful, swollen joints.

The dynamics between the pair saddened me. They only had each other and their current relationship was hanging by a thread. Perhaps, both mother and daughter had valid points; however, they needed to work their issues out in a healthier way. It was obvious their hurt went deeper than unkind words. It seemed living with chronic illness had taken its toll and both mother and daughter were victims. I wondered if the mother could survive without the daughter, or whether the daughter was the catalyst that gave the mother her fight.

Relief

We always kept extra medical supplies in our cars just in case we would need them. Naturally, before we ventured out for the day we gathered what supplies would be needed from the agency's stock. As a visiting nurse, having one's supplies was always critical to save unnecessary trips back to the office which could prolong one's day.

We were often called to pick up emergency cases because someone was having an urgent problem. An example of an urgent need might be an issue with a urinary catheter. The catheter could have become blocked, fallen out, or been pulled out. In my role as a visiting nurse, I had responded to a number of such calls. Re-inserting a urinary catheter was no big deal. I had inserted many, although most I had done were primarily female catheterizations. Those I had inserted into males were all done in hospital settings, not in homes. In most home settings one does not have the typical hospital bed which can be adjusted for positioning, peers are not readily available to assist, and an assortment of catheters are not stocked on shelves just in case insertions do not go smoothly.

Since cell phones were not something we carried as visiting nurses, it was customary before leaving the main office to provide one of the agency's supervisors with the telephone numbers of the patients we would be visiting. If we were needed when out making our rounds, an agency coordinator would call the client's home where we would likely be. So this particular day, while I was out and about completing my visits, I was notified I needed to add this man to my schedule. He needed a urinary catheter inserted because he was having difficulty urinating post hospital discharge. When I agreed to see this man, I did not know he would make history with me as my most difficult catheterization.

Inserting urinary catheters into elderly men can be a challenge if there are issues of enlarged prostates. A short history from the man revealed, like other older gentlemen, catheterizations were difficult because his prostate was enlarged. Because previous catheterizations had been uncomfortable, he voiced his apprehension in having the procedure done. Now, I was a little concerned. Apprehension meant tension, tension meant tightened muscles, and tightened muscles could make insertion problematic; and these were only the physical barriers. A home setting, poor positioning due to rigid bones, low bed, no assistance, one catheter, a female care provider and my limited experience in male catheterization made for a potentially disastrous procedure.

I knew I would need to proceed slowly if we were both to be successful. One variable in my favor was the man had not voided in many hours. This meant his bladder would be full so if the catheter was inserted properly, I could instantly see urine course down the tubing connected to the urinary bag. Seeing urine would signify "yes," the catheter was in the bladder, just where it needed to be.

It was a summer day. He had no blowing fans and there was no country breeze coming through the open windows. I knew we both would be sweating by the end of our ordeal. As I suspected might happen, the insertion did not go easily despite my implementing all the tricks I knew. I had him first drink fluids, advanced the catheter slowly, waited several minutes between advancements, talked with him, incorporated deep breathing exercises, and tried different body positions. Finally, after an hour and slow advancement of the catheter urine flashed and coursed down the tubing. I wanted to dance about and shout "Yes, we did it... there's urine!" Seeing the dark yellow fluid flowing down the tubing allowed us both to let out our breaths. We had miraculously done it!

Late Night Call

Finally in the early morning hours the telephone rang. It was a relief to hear the ring, but on the other hand, it was a sound that provoked anxiety right to the pit of my stomach. The caller either would be bearing exceptionally good news, announcing everything was fine and his symptoms were a residual of a prior illness; or the news would be the stimulus which instantly alters a number of lives. Certainly, it was not like the last few weeks had not shaken his family.

His life had been advancing along on a normal course. There were the everyday ups and downs of family life and the physical aches and pains from some old high school and military knee injuries. Life coursed along pretty routinely until two weeks before this early morning call.

For many years his day consisted of delivering mail as a postal carrier. Within the last few years, thanks to seniority he was transferred to a delivery route which was a little more knee-friendly. He now had the good fortune to deliver letters and packages to businesses by driving a mail delivery truck instead of the usual walking route. Mail recipients on his route referred to him as the "friendly" mailman, because he always bore a smile and had a pleasant greeting for everyone. The day his smile was missing, and he was "not his usual friendly self," is the day the corporate receptionists grew concerned.

The office workers later described his behavior as odd. They stated on this day, unlike him he just came in, handed them the mail, and quietly left with very little interaction. He seemed almost dazed, they reported. From their large office window they noted when he exited the corporate building he got in his vehicle, but did not pull away. Instead, he remained parked and sat in his truck for quite some time. Just as they decided to go out and check on him, some man walking across the parking lot went over to his vehicle. Later the man shared when he inquired as to whether or not anything was wrong, the postal carrier curtly stated all was fine and to leave him alone. As the gentleman turned to leave a receptionist looking out the window reported observing the postal carrier falling out of the open door of the mail truck and hitting the ground.

The events that followed were what one would expect in such a situation. CPR was initiated when he was found to be in cardiac arrest. He was transported via helicopter to a medical trauma center, received in the emergency room and then transferred to intensive care where he remained unconscious for several days. The medical team tried their best to come up with a plausible explanation for his unexplained behavior and condition. Like detectives, the doctors examined each clue and tested its practicality through assessment and testing. Each team of specialists had a different take on the situation.

Even after he regained consciousness, and could speak to

describe what he recalled happened, no definite diagnosis was made. Instead, several possibilities were ruled out, but no answer surfaced for why he lost consciousness and fell from the truck.

Following whatever body insult he had endured, his speech now had a slight slur and he had some right-sided weakness. One could almost suspect he had a stroke, but this was never stated as a final diagnosis. With time his overall physical status improved and he was stable enough to be transferred to a rehab center to work on his speech impediment and right-sided weakness.

By the time he reached the rehab center he was tired of being in hospitals and wanted to go home to be with his family. From his repeated request to be discharged, and by promising to complete outpatient rehab, he was allowed to go home. Unfortunately, he was only home for a few hours when he started having chest pain. His discharge instructions clearly stated if he had any problems, including chest pain, he was to go to the nearest emergency department. Since he had been airlifted to the hospital where he received treatment after falling from the mail truck, the hospital closest to his home was a different facility. The trip to this different hospital would be the beginning of the end. At this second facility, he would be given a timeline; a ticking clock which came preset.

He later told the story of what transpired the night he went to the emergency room for the chest pain. Apparently upon hearing the story of his previous ordeal and intensive care stay, the physician working in the emergency room felt all the pieces of the story did not fit. He felt something was missed. As a result of his hunch, the physician ordered a stat MRI scan of the head.

When the preliminary MRI report came back the findings were grave. Despite the early morning hour, a specialist came in to review his case. A team of two, the emergency room physician and the neurosurgeon came to him and his wife to break the news. The bomb was dropped. He had a lethal problem that was originally missed. A large ugly tumor resided on the right side of his head in the temporal lobe. Unlike some people, his diagnosis was not followed with words of hope. The neurosurgeon had enough expertise to have seen the results of similar tumors and to predict the course of the malignancy. The image bore a typical pattern that gave little hope. In response to the postal man's question of "how long," the surgeon quoted six to nine months.

Now, so early in the morning, confused and functioning on automatic pilot he made the telephone calls to tell his family the news. When my phone rang at 2:00 A.M., I held my breath and answered the call....

In the end, the neurosurgeon and the ER doctor were right. My brother had an ugly, progressive tumor which ended his life in exactly nine short months.

Perched

Because the practice of this woman was so unique, she belongs in my recollection of faces. This middle-aged woman had come to our free clinic to inquire what we could do about the irritated, itchy skin that circumvented her ears. The skin truly was excoriated and looked uncomfortable. When asked what was causing the skin changes she explained how her small pet parrot loved to hang out on top of both her ears and would peck at her scalp. Yes, this is one of those times when as a healthcare provider you have to refrain from blurting out "you do what?" I controlled my dismay, but still was inwardly shocked anyone would allow a pet to do such a thing. But as typical in cases like these, she did not seem to think there was anything wrong with this behavior. I was amazed the discomfort from the irritation and pecking sensation did not cause her to remove the perched bird. Though it was my first encounter with this lady, I found this was not her first visit for the same issue. When the skin around her ears became excessively uncomfortable she would come seeking medicine to heal the raw skin.

Given the woman was a diabetic as well, the open skin areas were a critical concern. Other providers at the clinic had tried to convince her to stop the practice with the bird, but their preaching made no difference. The parrot continued to perch on her ears and peck at her scalp, and contaminate the area with excrement droppings.

No wonder her scalp itched and looked so nasty. Truly our preaching to change her ways went in one ear and out the other. I do not know the outcome of this woman or if her parrot still perches atop her ears. However, I would feel pretty safe in predicting "yes" the bird probably does.

Heavy Burdens

From this man I learned the true depths of depression. How deeply depression can consume the entire being of a person. His wife knew better than me how difficult motivating a depressed person can be. She tried so many times to encourage her husband to just do something, to eat, to change his clothes or to just venture to the porch and take in a breath of fresh air. She was concerned. Once again he would not eat.

Only about a day had lapsed since he had been discharged from an inpatient mental health unit. His family was not convinced he was well enough to come home but his discharge was really about healthcare dollars. The benefits of his healthcare plan provided mental health coverage for a specific duration of time. Then, as per the coverage guidelines there would have to be a lapse of care expenditures before the inpatient payment cycle was reactivated. So he was discharged home, with everyone hoping he would be fine, and would continue the progress he had made as an inpatient resident. But that was not to be.

Seeing someone with a primary diagnosis of depression as a community nurse wasn't typically the clientele I encountered. Most of the people I saw were individuals with medical-surgical problems. So, although I knew this man had a history of depression, I was mainly seeing him to evaluate his nutritional status and determine how our agency might be able to help him. I never expected to find a person so deflated and with such a flat affect. As a result, any amount of encouragement I offered seemed to fall on deaf ears. I could not penetrate his emptiness with any reasons for why he should eat or even live. He rarely spoke, did not look at me, and most of the time did not acknowledge he heard me.

Some say as nurses we have this innate need to fix everyone. Sometimes we forget we are not always right, nor in control. We often have to remember patients have to want to do what we suggest; care cannot be planned in isolation.

In a client's house, he or she is in charge. After the nurse leaves, the individual decides whether or not to follow the regime recommended. People make their choices. It is so easy to forget the home is not the hospital. If nurses want to control something in the hospital, like a diet plan, they can simply call the dietary department and have the client's daily food menu changed. In this case, I knew despite all my encouragement, and regardless of the wife's pleas for him to eat, consuming food was not going to happen. This man desperately needed emotional and physical help beyond what I or his family could offer.

I left this man's house feeling completely deflated. It was hard to accept after an hour of trying to convince him to eat and the value of life, I had not made any gains. My words did not seem to touch him or offer a glimmer of hope to himself or his wife. I felt mentally exhausted, but nothing in comparison to what he and his wife must have felt. I could see the weight this man carried with him. Existing had become a burden, and he slouched with the weight of life on his shoulders. He could barely stand up!

Within twenty-four hours of my visit, he was re-admitted to the mental health unit, this time almost catatonic. What eventually happened is another mystery. I do believe, however, it would have taken a miracle for this man to find a glimmer of hope in life.

Victims

The television news and other media typically keep these people in the spotlight. It was not until I found myself as one of them that I saw these people differently. Before my personal experience the people affected caught my attention and stood out, but I really did not grasp the true impact of what they had endured. I saw their predicament as sad, but it had happened to "them" and not to me. I just didn't have the depth of experience to truly appreciate what they were experiencing.

Surely in our psychology classes we learned about the emotional crisis such people undergo, but what we learned and understood was quoted in textbooks; words and wisdoms of authors. Within the textbook are lists of interventions which speak to conveying empathy, balance and developing emotional connections with such individuals. Our readings gave us at least enough understanding to know we would never restore them to who they were before the incident. Rightfully, nobody could go through such life altering experiences and remain unchanged. The reactions commonly displayed by these grieving individuals are ones many know: grief, shock and denial, anger, bargaining, depression and hopefully then acceptance; all stages of grief. But the piece which is the most difficult to convey in a book, is what the experience truly feels like for those victims moving through such moments in time. And maybe, unless a similar experience touches your life, in some defining way, you will never have the level of empathy to really reach out to these people, these victims.

My new empathy emerged from the type of early morning telephone call, which triggers an instant awareness. Even before you pick up the receiver you know the caller is not telephoning with good news. No, pleasant news could wait until morning. Only this is the time when the news can't wait. When seconds mean life or death, and in this instant, a second meant death. In the early morning amongst tears of anguish we were informed a young relative who was the victim of a senseless crime, had lost his short battle with the devastating aftermath of a gunshot wound.

He was gone...one minute here and smiling... and the next moment lost forever. No time for siblings to poke fun at him one last time, and for family to say good bye. Instead, he was swept right from under our feet in a matter of seconds, passed back to the hands of his creator.

But like so many other things, not until this personal experience hit home did I finally gain a true perspective of something I had learned in my professional education. Despite my textbook knowledge, I lacked the depth of understanding I needed to fully comprehend how homicide victims grieve. I learned surviving the homicide of a loved one is uniquely different than surviving the death of a loved one in general. When illness or disease takes a life the sense of loss is not any easier, just different. However, when the death is because of homicide the surviving family goes through an even more complex grieving process. From the time they hear the devastating news, through the zombie like burial services, and through the agonizing court drama, where unexpected and new emotions may surface, homicide survivors are on a long, lonely journey.

I now know the sorrow will never end. Survivors will have to find a deep inner space to plant some of the unknowns related to their loved one's death. Lingering questions will never be answered, only surmised. Within this personal place they will have to put their loved one to rest, yet preserve them in their hearts. And because it is about them they have to reach even deeper, maybe in the smallest, deepest part of themselves for the inner strength to realize their own life is still worth living. And sometimes, this takes guidance and patience from those around them. Some seem to transition with little support, yet others may become so consumed in grief everyday tasks are overwhelming. But hopefully for everyone, with time comes healing.

Breast Pump Rental

As a partner in our lactation consulting business, I made many home visits to help new families struggling with achieving positive breastfeeding experiences. Most times I walked off the porch of a family's home with an optimistic feeling because I had truly made a difference and had helped a family become a breastfeeding success story.

With this teenage mom, I did not have this type of feeling. Instead, after visiting her I left feeling frustrated with our country's support systems for indigent individuals. This new mother appeared lost and stuck in a poor situation which was perpetuating faster and faster out of control. And unfortunately, she did not seem to know how to get off the merry-go-round. Totally impoverished, she had absolutely nothing from what I could tell. She was having difficulty caring for herself, and now she had a newborn to love and support.

Our company received a referral to make a home visit to check on the breastfeeding status of both mother and baby. When I arrived at the dilapidated looking house I noticed sheets had been haphazardly placed over the front porch windows to shield anyone from looking in. The doorbell did not work and hung loosely by a wire. So, if I hoped to alert someone of my presence I had to knock. I rapped several times with no answer. Just as I was about to turn away, I saw one of the makeshift curtains move. Then I heard audible footsteps approaching and a frail looking girl opened the door, apparently the young lady I was looking for. As I stepped into the barren room I could see how destitute this girl's situation truly was. There were absolutely no furnishings in the house. She had a small hospital baby blanket spread out on the wooden floor where the baby was lying. There were a few complimentary baby care gifts on the floor. Items from the newborn discharge gift pack provided by the hospital.

This mother told me she had no money, nowhere to go, and the house belonged to someone else. There was no significant other and no friends. Despite all of these social issues swarming about her, we were only allocated to evaluate the mother-baby breastfeeding dynamics. Our job was vital. If this mother did not breastfeed her child, she might not have access to synthetic "milk" which meant the baby could potentially go without food. At least with breastfeeding, she wouldn't have to worry about finding free formula, transportation to get formula or money to buy formula.

In working with the mother and baby, I knew a hospital grade electric breast pump was needed until mother and baby were over their breastfeeding latch-on hurdles. Getting the young mom started on a breast pump was a problem since she had no insurance, and no funds to purchase or rent the grade of breast pump needed. I had to do some quick thinking and some shuffling. In the end, I was able to provide her with a new breast pump our company had received as a sample.

I spent quite a bit of time assisting this new mom and baby so they could work in unison. Since our referral only allocated one postpartum visit we needed to accomplish as much as we could in the one approved visit. When I eventually left, I felt I might have made a difference in their mother-baby breastfeeding situation, but on the other hand I was saddened by the long road I envisioned for the pair.

The reason I remember this case is because when I checked back to see how this new mom was doing, I learned from the postpartum home care nurses she was no longer at the house. Where she and the baby went we do not know. I hope our breast pump and her acquired breastfeeding skills were sufficient to provide her child with the nutrients he needed to grow into a healthy young boy. I still can feel the sense of loneliness and despair projected by this mom and baby in the barren room. I hope she found her way and they did not become a homeless pair.

Testosterone

Testosterone can be a good thing and a bad thing. A little too much pumping through the veins at one time can transform a man into someone he normally might not be, in this case an embarrassment to himself. Add a problem of genital-urinary nature to testosterone and there becomes this innate need for a male to defend his manhood, to wave his masculinity about as a symbol of vitality. In this story, hormones and an embarrassing situation turned what seemed to be a generally nice guy, into a nit wit.

My routine after receiving a change of shift report is to prioritize the patients on my care list and then begin to make rounds to check on each person. He was on my list, not a person with priority needs, but one needing a postoperative assessment. His having had surgery earlier in the day meant I needed to observe his surgical site. Therein lay the challenge. This man's surgical site was his genitals, and in terms of age he was in his prime, somewhere in his early forties. Me, I was in my early twenties, definitely young enough to be this man's daughter.

At this point in my career, seeing a patient's "privates" equated to listening to someone's lungs; it was just part of the human body needing evaluation or treatment. The best approach I had been taught, with matters of the genitals, was to be professional and respectful of the person's sensitivity. My explanation of my need to examine his surgical site sparked this man to begin making crude gender jokes about the state of his manhood. He also found it important to express how the surgical swelling of his genitals accentuated his manliness.

I am sure he was deflecting his anxiety and embarrassment by attempting to be humorous. If what happened next did not transpire, I probably would not have remembered this incident. As I was examining this man, and after deflecting several of his inappropriate comments, he happened to take note of my name tag. At the time I was unmarried and still had my father's last name. Our family name is one of those names, if someone has the same last name, they must somehow be related. No two unrelated people could possibly have the same name; our surname was that unique.

There it was printed boldly on my tag, a name he recognized and one he had a connection with. I was the daughter of an old navy buddy, an associate he had played cards and watched boxing matches with. A man he had not seen in many years, but who had been an acquaintance at one time. They were two former shipmates who had gone their separate ways.

I am sure with the recognition of my name and confirmation of the connection with my father, this man wanted to die a thousand deaths. If there was a hole to crawl in, I think he might have slipped in. He was beside himself with embarrassment, and I'm sure would have given anything to retrieve his previous remarks. He obviously no longer thought his puns were cute, and his words seemed to linger in the air. I remember he could not apologize enough for his behavior, his face crimson. He knew he had put his foot in his mouth and could do nothing to take it out gracefully. The damage was done.

As for me, I had let the wisecracks roll off my back, chalking his behavior up to someone coping with an embarrassing situation. I did not feed into his attempts at jest. As I left his room, I chuckled to myself and thought what a splendid lesson this man had learned. Without revealing his name and leaving certain parts of the story out, I ragged my father about meeting one of his former "navy buddies."

Chapter Five

BUGS, NITS, AND CRAWLERS

❧❧

Some days you are the bug, and some days you are the windshield.

(INSTITUTE FOR THE ADVANCEMENT OF HUMAN BEHAVIOR (IAHB))

❧❧

Imagine having to call a person to ask him/her to put their pet boa away before you arrive. Or feeling the sense of alarm one might experience when driving over the crest of a hill on a country road and seeing a cow meandering across the path of your car? Or, ascending the front steps of someone's house and being greeted by two large barking dogs coming towards you from both sides of the structure. These images mirror the larger mammals of nature one might be surprised by as a visiting nurse, but, these creatures are nothing compared to the even smaller, creepy crawler specimens sometimes encountered.

Cockroaches

There were ugly cockroaches on her pillow, and others crawling on the food in her bed. The room was fairly dark despite the midday hour. As we advanced into the room my eyes caught sight of the scurrying critters. We startled the pests by the sound of the opening door and our movements. However, my surprise to see the cockroaches was nothing compared to the alarm I felt in seeing someone lying on the floor. The lifeless body was jammed between the door and the bed in a room so small, the sparse furnishings made the entire enclosure look cramped.

This room was her home. What she lived for and what she called her own. And here she was alone, lying dead-still on the floor with cockroaches crawling on her, and a bloody gash on her swollen forehead. At first glimpse, I had no idea if she was dead or alive, nor how long she had been lying there. Because the blood that once oozed from her head was now dried, and the cockroach-infested food looked desiccated, I figured she must have been unconscious for quite some time. Hours, days…who knew.

And just before, when she had not answered our knock, I had

to convince the agency driver not to leave her meal tray outside her door. I had been concerned about the unanswered knock. The driver, on the other hand, was anxious that the time he spent waiting for someone to respond would disrupt his delivery pace. He was so focused on delivering trays, finishing the task, and staying on schedule he forgot the true purpose of his job. He forgot about the people who were the reasons for the trays. No people, no trays. No trays, no reason for deliveries. He no longer thought of the plights of the elderly. Instead, his sensitivity to their issues seemed to have gone by the wayside. Now his job was just a job, a weekly paycheck.

With some persuasion to wait while we inquired about the tray's recipient, he directed us to the manager's office. A student nurse's uniform and the familiarity of the agency's driver was enough to convince the manager to unlock the woman's door. What an unexpected scene! This was not a scenario I had anticipated on my first day of community health nursing in the city.

Our assignment was to ride on the community van and help deliver food trays to the homebound. Basically, we were assigned a fairly simple and straightforward task. We anticipated an easy day. No complex responsibilities, no paperwork, no homework… pretty laid back. A no frills clinical day riding on the community van!

Entering the room, our immediate response was to check the woman for a pulse. There was a pulse; a weak one, but a pulse, nonetheless. Taking a closer look and applying a hand to her chest, I could see and feel her breathing. "Thank heavens," I thought. "No need for CPR!"

We called for an ambulance to whisk her away. No time to dilly-dally; we also needed to be on our way. The driver graciously reminded us, "There were more trays to be delivered, and we had done all we could."

Did she survive? Perhaps she did, or possible not. We went our separate ways. She went in the ambulance, and we departed in the community van trying to rid our minds of the unfortunate scene.

Queen for the Day

"Let me see, let me see" was the reaction of the nurses. I could not believe their responses in front of the little girl. Their shocked exclamations and the child's look of fear made me regret I had reported my findings. She had head lice. Not just nits, but the actual louses.

I saw the roaming critters when I split her hair to make the braids I promised to weave. I had heard of head lice, but I had never actually seen them. The image I had of head lice was the little white specks that resembled fine dandruff. I did not realize the white dusting particles were eggs, and they hatched into real live crawling bugs. There they were though: bugs the size of large sesame seeds meandering about on her hair follicles and on her scalp.

As a student, I was expected to report any abnormal findings to the staff nurses who worked in the pediatric unit. They knew best. I was merely a student nurse and they the RNs. I trusted they knew what they were doing. Every nursing curriculum is immersed with communication strategies to incorporate when handling delicate matters, particularly those situations involving children. I think because the nurses were so shocked in seeing those feasting parasites, all sense of what was therapeutic in terms of communication went by the wayside.

The little girl was only six years old. And because her family lived a distance away she spent much of her hospital time alone. I was her pal and surrogate mom for the day. Some friend, when I was the one who brought the "mean" nurses to see the "ugly bugs." She started to cry because of everyone's need to see. I didn't blame her for weeping. Surely, she did not want bugs in her hair. She was in the hospital because of her appendix, not for head lice. Plus, being only six years old, she didn't quite comprehend what the nurses meant by her "having bugs."

A pretend game was in order. I would dress her like a queen, wash her hair and make her pretty. A medicinal pediculicide shampooing, a hair brushing with a fine tooth comb and a saloon pampering treatment were the indulgences bestowed on her. With my dress-up theme, I managed to gain her trust, washed the bugs away, combed her hair, and saw her smile once again.

After departing and returning to my dorm, I diligently washed my long hair. Despite having my hair swept up in the traditional chignon, I worried I might have taken some of the creepy-crawlies home with me. Of course, thanks to a touch of imagination, my scalp had the sensation of being itchy and tingly…its way of convincing me I indeed had hitchhikers going home with me.

Thankfully, there was no problem. I did not have any louse in my hair. If I had transported the parasites back, what a nightmare a dorm infestation would have been. Perhaps it was the wise person who mandated nursing students with hair longer than shoulder length to securely tie their hair up off their shoulders.

The look of fear on this little girl's face when everyone came to see "the bugs" will always be ingrained in my mind. When I think of this story, I recall she was several days into her post operative recovery. Since the nits and louse were present in the postoperative period, that meant she had gone to the Operating Room (OR) and through the surgical procedure with the head lice problem. This made me wonder if the OR was contaminated, and whether the surgical patients who followed her to the OR later complained of itchy scalps. No wonder, we now put OR scrub caps on patients when they go for surgery!

Infestation

At first he looked angry, but with closer inspection, I could see this was the face of weariness and sheer exhaustion. He could not sleep and could not rest. The itching consumed him. He spent every minute scratching at his body in response to the disturbing mites that irritated his skin. They caused him to scratch as he reacted to their presence and the excrement left behind. His skin was their home. A blood-enriched place to mate, hatch and burrow. Scratch marks from persistent pruritus caused his skin to be excoriated and opened, clearly disrupting his body's natural line of defense.

He was an elderly man who lived by himself in a small one bedroom house. A room now infested with these microscopic pests. So much so, I dared not take my coat off or place my nurse's bag down in his home without first draping a protective covering. At least I was fortunate, only one individual was infested and not a household.

I had been sent to his house to help him gain control of his scabies and to kill the mites ruling his world. We would meet many times, and he would apply numerous layers of treatment cream from head to toe before my visits could cease. Eventually, I saw him smile and report he was once again able to sleep through the night without being disturbed.

White Threads

It was summer and the weather was hot and muggy. I was covering someone else's territory which meant I would be seeing new patients in a different geographic area. Before I left the office, I was given the low down on each of my assigned clients. Through this report exchange I learned this woman would be my challenge for the day. A sweet aged lady, "You'll like her" they told me. But, they added… We're having a problem with her keeping the leg dressings on…she just takes them off, probably, right after we leave.

With this introductory warning, my colleagues went on to describe the appearance of the woman's ulcers. Their preferred adjectives were nasty, infected, and gross. All real medical terms! Clearly, their choice words created a vivid image for me, and one which caused my inner voice to predict there was going to be some type of challenge.

Knowing just how healthcare people delight in getting a rise out of one another, I can imagine the joy my peers felt when they described what I could expect. Sick humor, but sometimes this is the way providers cope with stress. "Oh… by the way," they added, with a chuckle, "She'll probably be sitting in her chair on the front porch, feet up on the railing, waiting for you." Then, their last caution came. "Oh…, and don't be surprised by what the ulcers look like!"

Were they right? Was I taken back by what I saw? You betcha! There she sat, on her front porch, with her legs up and open wounds exposed to the warm summer air, just as predicted. Absolutely no dressings were on her legs!

She watched me pull up across the street from her house, park my car along the curb, get my navy leather nurse's bag out of my car trunk and head up her sidewalk. "Hot day," she said as I approached her porch. And, as I ascended the steps she continued, "Where's June today, you're not one of the usual nurses?" "No, I'm not, my name's Brenda. June could not come today. I'm here instead…I'll be doing your dressings."

It is a wonder, I did not stop in mid-sentence when I got closer and noticed what my peers knew I would see. There wiggling within the reddened tissue of her exposed leg ulcers were tiny crawling maggots. They had hatched from the larva left behind by the flies landing in her open wounds, while she sunned her legs on the front porch railing.

You know, as wicked as the maggot-infested ulcers looked, the little buggers were doing their job. They were helping to keep the wound clean. Perhaps, I had just stepped back into the dark ages. Or maybe on a positive note, there was some unconventional care measure at work. Truly, alternative medicine at its finest!

Bed Bugs

The seniors were enthused. The time had finally come and graduation was approaching. There was talk of continued friendships, interviewing for jobs, and moving out of the dorms. As lower classmen, what caught our interest was the talk focused on exiting the dorms. Moving out meant vacant rooms, which for us, was the invitation to put in requests for room transfers.

I had my eye on a corner room, slightly larger than my present unit, and on a nicer end of the hall. It was a single room, but then most of our dorm rooms were. Luck was with me. The resident housemother informed me once the seniors officially vacated, I could have my desired room. Naturally I was thrilled, but unfortunately, neither the housemother nor I knew other inhabitants already occupied my chosen room.

I fixed my new room up so it defined me; a reflection of my personality. I used the same mattress which came with the bed frame, just added my new sheets, pillow and comforter. My room was all set for a good night's sleep.

    The first night passed uneventful. I did not notice any itching or swelling upon awakening. I had a restful night's sleep. Nothing surfaced until the second morning. When I awoke that morning my face felt tight and puffy. One glance in the mirror caused me to gasp!

    My eyelids were swollen almost shut. From the fluid trapped under my skin, my face was puffed out like an inflated balloon. On my arms were what looked like bug bite marks and red irritated lines. Obviously, I must have been scratching in my sleep. From past experiences, I knew exaggerated skin reactions following an insect feast were typical for me, particularly after mosquito attacks. Where the average person might have a little swelling at the site of a bite, my swelling would quickly rise to a large puffy mound. But this time, it appeared all the mounds had run together, so now I looked like one large puff ball.

    Like me, our housemother flipped when I presented myself to her. She feared I was having an allergic reaction to whatever had bitten me. As a result, she had me taken to the Emergency Room, in the adjacent building. There I was treated with the necessary medications so as to ward off further systemic reactions, and to calm what had already flared. Once it was deemed I was not likely to have an anaphylactic reaction, I was sent on my way.

    Later, back in my dorm and feeling better, I inspected my room from top to bottom, including my bed. At the conclusion of my search, I was convinced there were no visible pests lurking about. Having no discernible evidence, I deduced either a crawling or flying bug must have seized the moment and then gone away.

    Just to be sure no crawlers or flyers were hiding I got some bug repellent and sprayed my entire room. Then, I closed off the space and slept on the floor in my friend's quarters for the night. The next day, once my room had aired, I changed my bed linens and rechecked my room. With no evidence of lingering bugs, and the belief my problem was resolved, I anticipated once again achieving a full night's sleep.

To my frustration, in the middle of the night I awoke once more to itching. Upset I was under attack, I got out of the bed and went down the hall; again to my friend's welcoming room. The next morning, I presented myself to the house mother to reveal my newly acquired bites. She was quite upset, and immediately put into motion what needed to be done to have a professional exterminator fumigate my room.

I never had bedbugs. The possibility of being the owner of such tiny pest was not something I thought remotely possible. You see, like most people, I mistakenly believed having bed bugs equated with being grimy and unhygienic. I was totally on the meticulous side. And as far as the girl who lived in the room before me, she also seemed painstakingly clean. So the possibility of bedbugs living in my mattress and pillow and coming to feast at night never crossed my mind. Rather, I kept thinking some small bug had crawled into my sheets, or some flying insect was trapped in my room.

If my house mother was thinking bedbugs she never mentioned the critters to me. At the housemother's request the exterminator came. He thoroughly embalmed my room. Following the debugging ritual, I was given instructions to keep the room closed for two days, and of course not to sleep in the room. The exterminator was to be the one to re-open my room and conduct an inspection.

I was not in the dorm when the walk-through happened. Instead, I was at the hospital caring for patients. However, when I returned the housemother took me into my room. There, on my pillowcase laid one dead bedbug. A bedbug, and there was only one? Instead, it felt like a whole army occupied my bunk!

Only one tiny critter was ever discovered. Despite my hesitancy to return to my room, when I did go back, I never was bitten again. If the bugs were in my mattress when I inherited the room, imagine what my big sister must have silently endured. I suspected although only one parasite was revealed, there had to have been more. But thankfully, they seemed to be in check!

Thousands

They were everywhere, and if I did not soon get out of the room, they would be on me! Hundreds were walking up every wall and screen. They were on top of one another, ambling over one another and manically swarming about. They were dive bombing at me. They were on the ceiling and layering the floor, above my head and at my feet.

Where had they come from? Too many were about to have been let in by an open door or window. There had to be nests and we were in the midst of a hatching frenzy. We had only been gone a short time, just to the mess hall to dine and sing. We had fun singing all those happy-go-lucky Girl Scout songs, and were feeling uplifted and somewhat jubilant. Never did we expect to come back to such a disaster.

Truly at camp, bugs are to be expected, but not to take over. We humans were now the invaders, the ones that did not belong. The occupancy of the cabin was no longer our domain. We had to leave, in a hurry, I might add, or feel the wrath of retaliation. We were the unwanted guests disturbing their tranquility.

Of course, when else would the hatching occur? It was a holiday weekend and a humid, smoldering one at that. It was great weather for a hatching party. Our sleeping corridors had already been taken over, and the intruders were fast infiltrating the connecting infirmary. "Quick, everything off the shelves...just toss the items into the draws and cabinets...get out...or you will be attacked!"

A rescue call was made to an exterminator. Yeah, right, an exterminator on a holiday weekend, and at a late night hour. Not likely to happen. Their response: "We'll be there in the morning. For tonight, find makeshift quarters." We had to split up and find available spaces elsewhere in other cabins. There were five of us, head counselors and me who needed new sleeping quarters. Call me "Band-Aid," the now homeless camp nurse.

With sleeping essentials and emergency care supplies in tow, I trucked down the dark, tree laden path to the very edge of camp. Tonight the cook's cabin would be transformed into the makeshift infirmary. The health center followed me; I was the center. Thank goodness, no human catastrophes occurred that night.

The next day the exterminators came and "bombed" the cabin; our beloved health center. The concluding diagnosis: Infestation related to the rapid hatching of ants under the cabin's floor boards during hot, humid weather conditions.

History at the Camp

I could see them running across the green grassy field flaring their arms and yelling. At first I could not discern what they were saying. Intently watching as they advanced, I soon realized they were yelling to me. Clearly their shouts sounded urgent. This was major, something was truly afoot. I caught pieces of their hollering. A "girl," "pool," "unconscious," "come quickly!" With comprehension, it was now my turn to run across the field towards the direction from where they were coming.

At the pool the water was now still and devoid of the once playing young campers. All the juvenile swimmers were directed away from the pool area in hopes of shielding them from the scene. Left behind was a school age camper lying dead still on her back along the pool's edge. Several young adult counselors were standing in a circle looking down at her. From the looks on their faces, it was obvious they were unsure what to do. They trusted me, and thought I would know exactly what was wrong.

I found no clue to help pinpoint why this girl might have been found unconscious floating in the pool. At first the lifeguard, Dolphin, thought the girl was playing a floating game. Keeping an eye on the girl, the lifeguard soon realized there was more to the inactivity. A plunge into the water and a rescue from the pool did not reveal even a response. No choking, no coughing and no audible sound. The scout remained limp and unconscious. No response to light touch. And, even worse, not even a flinch in response to my deeper touch.

No flinch, no "ouch," no flicker of the eyes, not even a withdrawal. She remained perfectly still. There were no giggles or controlled expressions. I had no doubt this girl was not playing a game, something was truly wrong!

A 9-1-1 rescue call was activated. Never before in their fifty years had such a call for help been made. But, we were about to make camp history and break the record, maybe not so complimentary an accolade. Hard to image no other true emergencies in fifty years!

The team arrived and went about the task of attempting to arouse the girl. She did not react. Immediate actions were taken to stabilize and transport. Unconscious, she was transferred onto a stretcher and placed behind the ambulance's closed doors. The transport vehicle sat for several minutes as the response team worked on the girl while in the mobile unit. Just as the ambulance circled to leave, a transport member announced the young girl had come around and was now verbally responding.

I wish I could say there was some great medical marvel over what happened to this young lady, but that was not the case. Instead, I was told when she arrived in the emergency room of the local rural hospital she was alert and talking. Assessment findings and her ER workup revealed she was in no acute distress and could be discharged home. Unfortunately, the story does not end here, at least not for me, or for the youngster!

You see, what happened is the girl's mother was a single parent. Since the mother worked, one of the benefits of sending her child to camp meant she would not need a summer babysitter. This meant if the girl did not go back to camp, babysitting would become an issue. So based on the ER report, the mother's babysitting predicament and some administrator's decision, the girl was returned to our haven. This time I was the one who was not the happy camper. I knew what the girl looked like by the pool, and unlike some others, I was not convinced this was a one time, freak incident. I was not comfortable having her return. Particularly to a facility where there was no oxygen, no defibrillator and very few supplies besides basic Band-Aids, dressings, sprays and ointments.

Well, as my gut predicted, an alarming call came out to me once again. This time just before sunset while most of us were still in bed sleeping, a pounding on the health center's door echoed through the cool night air. Awaking abruptly to the sound, jumping out of bed and opening the bolted door I saw the same young girl with a frantic, distress look etched across her face. She stood alongside her counselor who looked about as frightened as the child. Both were alarmed by the youngster's obvious need to breathe in more air than her lungs were exchanging. The girl was in some type of respiratory distress, extremely frightened and distraught by her inability to ventilate. Realizing the graveness of the situation, I was frustrated by my lack of emergency equipment. I really had no medical supplies that would assist this girl's breathing until help arrived. What was even more frustrating was the fact that in my mind, the girl should not have been discharged from the hospital. If this happened in an acute care facility, they would have had the appropriate equipment to support her. Instead, I had nothing but myself!

Once again we needed 9-1-1... and some ingenuity until they arrived. What could I do? I needed to maintain her airway, and perhaps, soothe and bronchodilate her narrowed passageways. All I had was a teakettle and water.

With teakettle in hand, my goal was to bronchodilate her airway. I hoped by opening her passageways, I would prevent further deterioration and support her respiratory efforts until the better equipped team arrived. I had to try. So we set to work having her breathe in warm misty air, applied heated moist compresses to her chest and directed her on deep, breathing exercises. Every minute was vital. It was obvious this girl's airway could totally occlude. Once again, I escaped even greater havoc, since thankfully the paramedics arrived before the situation worsened.

This time the little girl did not come back to camp. Her final diagnosis was never shared but I suspect either she had some viral respiratory bug, or the camp's wet, moldy environment triggered a full blown asthma attack. Truly, when I opened the door that early morning, there was one very distraught and frightened young child looking up at me!

Chapter Six

SITUATIONS

All the world's a stage, and all the men and women merely players: they have their exits and their entrances; and one man in his time plays many parts, his acts being seven ages.

(WILLIAM SHAKESPEARE)

"The State Boards!"

Ask any nurse if he/she remembers taking their state licensure exam. More than likely you will receive an affirmative answer followed by a request to tell a story related to their experience. I remember my hallmark day well. I took my state boards before computerized testing so I did the old paper and pencil format. What was unique about my experience was where I took my examination. Most graduates completed their tests in buildings on high school or college campuses, but I was scheduled at a fairground where the town's annual state fair was held. This meant there were no permanently structured buildings that could accommodate the quantity of testers, so an enormous carnival tent was erected. To appreciate this, visualize hundreds of graduate nurses inside a non-air conditioned circus-like tent on a warm summer day seated in collapsible wooden chairs at long tables.

Though the setting was not ideal, testing security was at a premium. Each table lined with testers was patrolled by strategically placed proctors. You didn't dare lift your eyes off your paper, or take a second to lean back and take a deep breath. One knew to do so might cause a proctor to think you were attempting to see another's paper. So there we sat in a tent, taking a test which could "yay" or "nay" the start of our professional career.

There were several sections to the test divided by clinical specialty, each section to be completed within a specified time frame. Allocated time frames helped to move the test along, but also caused some underlying apprehension to complete each section before the "pencils down" time was called.

Another memory related to my state board examination was how disappointed I felt in not being scheduled at the same testing center where most my former classmates were assigned. When we sent in our registration forms we assumed everyone from our school would be assigned at the same location. Counting on this detail, we planned to meet at a particular hotel near the testing site a day earlier. Since there were only about twenty of us, trying to have everyone converge on one site was not impractical. We reckoned the extra day would give us time to catch up on what transpired in our lives during the short weeks following graduation. We did not realize until receiving our confirmation letters that sites were determined by our home mailing addresses. Most of my classmates had lived in the suburbs of Philadelphia, but my hometown was about two and half hours north of Philadelphia. So unlike most of my peers, I was scheduled in an area midway between my home and my alma mater.

It would have been nice to drive to the testing center with friends. Or, just as encouraging to know there would be some familiar faces when I arrived. Unfortunately, such novelties were not to be. Instead, although we were all there for the same reason, and everyone had just graduated from some school of nursing, I did not encounter anyone I knew. I suppose not being distracted spending time with friends, and not staying up late to reminisce had testing advantages.

When the examination was finally over and I was leaving, I remember passing by clusters of people conversing about how they thought they did on the test. For the most part, I heard people saying they were not sure; my sentiments exactly! I could not predict whether I passed or failed. My score could go either way. But, just hearing others voice similar reactions was reassuring.

By the time we sat for our state boards most of us were already employed as graduate nurses (GNs). This meant, if one did not pass their boards, professional embarrassment was inevitable. Even if one did not tell colleagues he or she was unsuccessful, word got out.

Since everyone in the state took their boards on the same day, results were received within a few days of one another. Therefore, it was easy to tell who passed and who did not. No rocket science. One simply watched to see whose credentials on their name tag drum rolled over from GN to RN.

Waiting for results was the worst. We waited weeks before receiving letters notifying us of our pass or fail status. Nowadays, graduates obtain their results much quicker, no longer by "snail mail," thanks to computer technology. In my day, checking the mail became an obsession. Some of my friends forbade family members to open "the letter" and some even blessed or kissed the envelope before opening the seal. Others, due to a lack of courage, assigned someone else the special task of opening the envelope and breaking the news. Me, I wanted to open the seal myself. I wanted to know the results before anyone else.

In the end, because of where the letter was sent, and because I never forbade anyone to open the letter, I was not the first person to see my results. The envelope went to my parents' residence (my permanent home address). Recognizing how anxious I was about the envelope's content, my mother decided to open the letter. Knowing my mother, if the letter came and the content was not good, she probably would not have notified me while I was at work (which I was). Instead, she would have saved the news for when I got home.

But…. all was perfect. I passed the NCLEX boards on my first attempt! Talk about grinning from ear to ear. I'm sure I had this huge smile on my face when I got off the telephone and announced with a little yell, "I passed my boards!" First I was thrilled, but then I felt slightly cheated. I missed the moment of heart-stopping excitement by not opening the envelope. But being so relieved I passed, my disappointment was short lived. Later, my mother did fess up she had engaged a little superstitious charm before unveiling my score. Her selected magic was to have my younger sister kiss the envelope as ceremonial good luck. I guess having a "lucky" sister is a good thing (just kidding). All the hard work was done long before the generated envelope.

Once Again

I had no college credits when I graduated from my diploma nursing program, so in a sense when I decided to go back for my bachelor's degree, I started college as a freshman. The four-year college I transferred to advertised a special program for registered nurses returning for their BSN. The concept of a RN to BSN program was fairly new. However, despite publicizing having a unique curriculum for this population of nurses, the approach turned out to be very much like a traditional undergraduate nursing program.

We had very little opportunity to challenge nursing courses and few credits allotted for prior learning. Overall, I would go to school part time for eight years before earning a bachelor's in nursing. I completed the bulk of my credits at two community colleges. Later, I transferred to a four-year college where I finished the nursing specific credits.

The credit cost of community colleges, compared to four-year colleges, is why I first chipped away at transferable courses on the associate degree level. The financial piece was an important variable, but location was another reason I attended the community colleges first. Both community colleges were located closer to where I lived. While working full-time, and going to school, I needed a program of study geographically close by.

While attending the community colleges, I never tapped into the employee tuition reimbursement programs at the hospitals where I worked. Once I transferred to the four-year college, I did use the tuition reimbursement programs to help with cost. For most of my remaining nursing education, I utilized employee tuition programs. Using this approach saved me from taking out student loans and accumulating financial debt. You see, with age does come maturity, particularly pertaining to one's future investments. Needless to say, such wisdom typically does not proliferate at age seventeen.

So, I did not take eight years to earn my bachelor degree in nursing because I was a slow learner, rather, because I chipped away slowly at credits because of life's responsibilities and financial constraints. Another reason I took eight years to complete my bachelor's was related to restrictions of the employee tuition assistance programs. Most benefit programs limited the number of credits (usually about six) employees would reimburse per semester. Probably a wise stipulation on their part since a qualifying variable for most tuition benefit programs is the person needs to be a full-time employee. So that means you work full-time, go to school, and in most cases have family responsibilities. And for me, I fit the profile: student, full-time employee, wife and later mother.

Anyone who has kept such a schedule knows taking on all of these roles simultaneously is challenging and often overwhelming. If only I had a crystal ball back when I was making my first nursing school selection, I would have gone first for my BSN as encouraged. But, back then, I probably would not have listened to the wisdom of the crystal ball either.

Three Strikes

I can think of three times it almost happened, but in the end did not. Three times I was moving towards the same goal, but something precluded me from seeing my ambition fulfilled. I wonder why it never came to be. In thinking about why, I have to figure it was simply not in the grand scheme of things laid out for me. It wasn't part of my destiny. No, I wasn't meant to be a flight nurse or a Navy nurse, an Air Force nurse or an Army nurse.

Originally, when I had finally decided on nursing school, entering the military following graduation was the direction I planned to pursue. I hoped to become a flight nurse and during the course of my military career become a nurse-midwife. Since the military had been my father's career, I was aware of various aspects of military life and family experiences.

From my view, I figured becoming a flight nurse would increase my chances of seeing different parts of the world; an opportunity often too financially taxing in civilian life. So, when classmates and I talked about our ambitions following nursing school, the plans I described related to entering one of our armed forces and becoming a nurse midwife.

It turned out my best friend in nursing school was also thinking about a military career. Together we approached an armed forces recruiter. The representative we spoke with encouraged us to think about entering under what was known then as "the buddy system." We were told this meant we would be guaranteed placement together in the same geographic location for our first tour of duty. You can be sure friends and relatives cautioned us about believing everything the recruiter promised, particularly about guarantees such as "the buddy system." Though we were forewarned, we still leaned towards signing on the line. In the end, despite everyone's cautionary words, do you think our signatures flowed across the dotted lines? For the answer, I guess you'll have to read on....

Something happened in my senior year that changed the career plans I had neatly laid out. I met that special guy and ironically, he was in the service. I suppose with Philadelphia being a seaport there was always the chance I would meet someone in the military.

He had a year left of his four-year term when I met him. At the time, his plans were to finish his tour of duty, then exit the military to pursue educational goals. Prior to enlisting he postponed his educational goals for ambitions to serve his country. With him about to finish his military commitment and our relationship showing future promise, my going into one of the armed forces seemed counterproductive. Instead, I contemplated other ways to pursue career aspirations as a non-military nurse.

Certainly there were midwifery schools outside the military which I could attend. One of the pioneer schools was located in Philadelphia. As far as my dream of traveling, I had met someone who enjoyed global travel as much as I did. Subsequently being able to travel was not an issue. As for my best friend who was also considering enlisting, well, she never joined either. Instead, we both took different civilian career paths. I pursued a career in obstetrical nursing and she specialized in coronary care nursing.

The next time I contemplated enlisting, I was a bit older and more established in the profession. I had just finished my second master's degree. Now I had a master's of science degree with a certification in early childhood education and a second masters in nursing. I was in the midst of compiling data to once again begin the enlistment process when an immediate family member became ill and needed family support. There was no doubt the best decision at the time was to defer the opportunity until my family's needs changed.

So, several years later, when I finished my doctorate, the time seemed right. This would be my third attempt. At the doctoral level and with my years of professional experience, I figured I would be an asset to our military healthcare system. I also saw enlisting as a great opportunity for personal growth. It would be a mutually beneficial enterprise. So, I felt prepared to make the career change and my husband and daughter were ready and supportive as well. We saw it as a great opportunity for all of us to grow and try something new. But, there would be a glitch. By putting off enlisting for so many years, I was one year over the eligibility age. I did not feel like I had left my youth, but I guess by military standards I was perceived as "old." So the recruiters went to work and completed the necessary process to seek an age-related waiver. We received the go-ahead, but in the end despite this clearance, I would not be inducted. This time I was at the point of completing the physical entrance exam when events took an interesting turn.

Several years before reactivating my military enlistment dreams, I was hospitalized for a cardiac arrhythmia episode while ill with influenza. Not sure if the dysrhythmia had been a complication of the illness, or whether I had an undiagnosed chronic arrhythmia problem, I opted to stay on a cardiac medication to curtail further occurrences. However, I did not realize being on a cardiac medication would be the concern it was. As a result of being on the medication and my arrhythmia history, I was disqualified from entering the military. That was my third and last strike. This time I was officially out! A military career was not meant to be. Why? I can only surmise there were other plans for me.

Horrific Night

Usually when there was a downcast mood or a sense of

anxiety lurking in the OB unit, something had gone drastically wrong. Possible an infant did not survive, a mother gave birth to a stillborn, a child was born with a congenital defect, or overall it was just a horrific night. In my many years working in obstetrics, I lived through many such horrendous nights. But there is one which stands out as the bad night of all bad nights. We lost a baby after heroic efforts to save the child.

As we foresaw, the nightmare did not end that night. About a year later we found ourselves called to give depositions about what had happened. We were called to do depositions on the 23rd of December, just before Christmas. Not exactly a jolly way to embark on the holiday. Luckily, for us as staff, the case never went beyond the deposition phase. However, the experience and implications of a potential malpractice suit caused all of us excessive levels of stress.

Unnerved as we were at the time of the depositions, I saw some positives emerge from the experience. For one, I gained the lived experience of giving a deposition. This meant I would have the knowledge to explain what to expect to peers who might find themselves in similar predicaments. And secondly, from the experience teaching/consulting opportunities surfaced for me.

One outcome from the deposition voiced amongst those interviewed in the process was feeling intimidated with the degree of questioning centered on interpretations of fetal monitor strips. Fetal monitoring strips are visual tracings of a baby's heart rate and mother's contraction patterns recorded by a machine while the mother is in labor. The tracings are interpreted, and findings used to guide care of the mother and baby during the labor process. By no means are interpretations used in isolation or considered diagnostic. Instead, fetal monitoring is looked upon as a screening tool. Since fetal monitoring skills are vital for obstetrical nurses those working in labor and delivery are trained to interpret tracings and expected to attend annual educational updates. All of us who gave depositions in this case were skilled in reading fetal monitor strips. However, despite our knowledge there was self-doubt when our decisions were challenged and contradicted. It was during the deposition interrogation I vowed I would heighten my fetal monitoring knowledge to the level I would be comfortable teaching the skill to other nurses. So despite a horrific night, some good did come out of the ordeal. And true to my word, I later taught fetal monitoring classes to other nurses.

A Remembered Delivery of Care

She remembered, but I did not distinctly recall the incident she recollected. What she mentioned sparked a distant memory, though facts were not clear. Time had gone by. As a matter of fact, I would say a number of years had transpired. At least enough years had passed for both of us to have moved on to new employment and for our recognition of one another to be slightly blurred.

A social gathering, groups of friends, introductions and recognition of names…all ingredients which lead to the "I remember you" and "I remember the time" accounts. You know, one of those incidents where you run into someone who was more of an acquaintance than a friend, and they start to share "I remember…." stories. That was my position in this encounter. I felt my gut nose-dive when this former colleague opened with the "I remember the time" phrase. It was one of those moments where you have no idea what the person is about to say. I had no clue to whether the story was going to be positive or embarrassing. Worst of all, she chose to share the story amongst my circle of friends. Now, this introduction caused me some unrest!

Apparently, I had done something she admired. Clearly, something impressed her enough to remember the occurrence years later. As she retraced the story, I tried to imagine the time, but vaguely recalled the event she reiterated. Since the account revolved around a child, it surprised me I did not immediately recollect the incident. Later, reflecting on her words, I could call to mind some of the events she was saying but not enough for me to say, "Oh yeah, I remember that day!"

So what did she remember? She related we had been working together one evening when I was sent to Labor and Delivery to assist in the care of a newborn that was anticipated to have distress at birth. In imminent deliveries when fetal distress was a concern, if a pediatrician was not "in house" our role as "special care neonatal nurses" was to attend the delivery and assist the obstetrician with the child until a pediatrician arrived.

This nurse shared her memory of the caring way I handled a particular baby who was born with imperfections. She reiterated to our circle of friends how before I brought the baby into the nursery, where anxiously awaiting relatives peered through the large nursery windows in hopes of catching a glimpse of their offspring, I took time to create a makeshift hat for the newborn. Today, labor and delivery nurses routinely apply caps to newborns for thermoregulation reasons, however at the time, applying head coverings was not as common a practice.

You see, she explained, where the newborn's ears should have been there were only tiny tabs. The baby's ears had failed to develop in utero. What she admired were my efforts to downplay the child's defects and cover the missing ears. As I paraded the baby by the glass windows, my attempt at applying a hat allowed the viewing family's first glimpse to be one of a beautiful, perfect child.

Reflecting back, I thought perhaps I had only a vague memory of the incident because I viewed the child as simply a newborn. I saw beyond the child's ears and saw the child for the lovely being he/she was. This nurse's memory brought home to me the importance of always doing what is in one's heart. And the reminder...you never know who around you is watching!

One Discharged Little Girl

This is one of those stories which made me whisper softly to myself, "And this too shall pass." The actual incident was not something I took part in. However, being a manager I had to address the outcome. One of those staff dilemmas a mid-level manager can easily find themselves in, merely because of association.

At the time, I was the director of several nursing units, one of which happened to be Pediatrics. To this day, I truly do not know the exact account of how the event transpired. Though, from the post-event investigation I did learn a number of people were involved and a series of events unraveled before the culminating act transpired. Kind of like the expression "too many hands in the pot."

Here's what happened: a preschooler was discharged home with her sister, who herself was not yet a teen. How could the two have been permitted to walk home, "just down the street from the hospital," without the guardianship of a parent?

I recall when the incident hit the local television news, I felt like time was standing still and we were reliving and reliving the story in slow motion. As I stood there watching and comprehending the impact of the news clip, I wished we could turn the media off and go back in time to erase the mistake. Of course I knew we couldn't. That day I was off from working at the hospital, and got a telephone call to turn on my television, watch the news, and come in ASAP. Even before I could put the telephone down and turn on the television, I felt the pit of my stomach take a millisecond plummet with the remnants of a sick feeling left behind.

The finger pointing was terrible. Lots of people tried to defend their part in the scenario. Nobody wanted to be the key person held accountable for the incident. How do you pick one person as the sole culprit in a scenario manifested by a string of errors? At the time, I felt like I was caught in a never-ending drama. Nursing defended nursing, and medicine defended medicine. No discipline wanted to be blamed. Nevertheless, the hospital board insisted someone was to be held responsible because the media wanted answers. So, how do you pick one discipline, or one person to account for the bulk of the blame when the blame was not so easily isolated? When really, in the scheme of things, not one person was to blame? Too many checks and balances had failed.

We were lucky. The young child got from point A to point B without harm thanks to her responsible sibling.

There was the breaking story for viewing by all our local communities. The chronicle included an interview with a parent, clear identification of the hospital by name, and a picture of our pediatric unit. Of course, the remarks were less than flattering. The hospital's fine repetition was taking a hit, and my unit was responsible. Oh, God…I knew our administrators were not going to be happy. Actually, I knew they would be livid!

I asked myself how could this happen? I wondered how many parents and people would vow never to use our hospital again, if this was the degree of care they could expect. The news flash was not good. The publicity was a black mark against the hospital's name. And, understandably, the hospital's board of directors would not take the news lightly.

Quite simply, the hospital officials would be fuming, and rightfully so. The values and standards of the establishment were at stake. How was I going to undo this? I wondered about the discharge instructions. Were they given to the older sister, or to a parent via the telephone? Who signed the discharge sheet...did the sister? What transpired to make the normal discharge process go askew? These were needed answers.

It just so happened, as the girls were walking down the street heading home from the hospital, one of their parents came along in the family car and saw them. The parent picked them up, went home and then called the local television news station. Recognizing a story with an impact, the media gave the parent air time to tell their version of "the discharge" mistake.

I was reminded over and over by the hospital's administrators just how lucky we were no harm came to the girls. We all knew this, and silently counted our blessings, but we could not go back in time. We could not erase what occurred. We had to do what we could to ensure the incident never happened again. Our peds unit needed to regain a positive public image and begin to pick up the pieces.

Pediatrics was certainly in the spotlight and we knew we would be there for quite some time. We had a reputation to rebuild and could not afford to make further mistakes, which would put us back in the watchful public eye. We needed to shine. We needed to turn our image around and flick the dark light of doom off. We had to rebuild our trust in one another. The finger pointing and blaming, now ramped, needed to cease.

First, administration and our public relations department took matters in hand and dealt with the family and community pieces. We in nursing tightened up our discharge policy to guard against similar occurrences, and began the long road of rebuilding trust. Truthfully, despite progression of time and trying to move ahead, I do not believe everyone was able to build a new sense of trust. There would always be an element of skepticism for those who lived through the television news and who recalled the story of one discharged little girl.

The organizational push was to pinpoint the error to one person. As a result, some held onto their jobs by a thread. As for me, I almost lost my management position for defending the actions of one of the nursing staff. However, in the end, after much clarification and piecing together of stories, no one person shouldered the blame. Nobody lost his/her job including myself. However, from knowledge of how our system failed, many new policies and procedures evolved.

Holiday Shift

Holidays have their stories. Most people would prefer not to work them to have the time off to be with family and/or friends. The unselfish part of each of us knows someone has to work. People need to be cared for, and with the job comes working holidays.

For the unit director who might shoulder the responsibility of overseeing or developing the monthly work schedule, upcoming holidays can be a nightmare. It is always a balancing act to be equitable to everyone and still have enough bodies to cover the unit's demands.

Typically, more seasoned nurses know the routine. They get holiday time off requests in early. Often long before the novice nurses realize, if they want time off near the holidays, they best take early measures. Some unit supervisors control holiday time by utilizing an on/off scheduling pattern. Thus, everyone works every other holiday.

Not until I became a manager and had the responsibility of doing monthly time schedules, did I come to realize that in the geographic area where I was living, not only were December holiday dates big ticket items, but so was the Fourth of July. The hankering to have the Fourth off was certainly not something I predicted. The holiday was an extravaganza of fireworks and fun! So everyone wanted to go. Picnics, fireworks, warm weather, and a good time. Who'd want to miss this?

But holiday time in December is different. The overall sentiment of departments even changes. Typically there is the push, when working with children, to try and get them home for family celebrations. Usually discharges start early Christmas Eve so by the time Christmas Day rolls around, only the sickest kids remain with the nurses and doctors.

As nurses, we typically always try to make December holidays just a little special for patients who can't go home. Units are decorated in festive décor, carolers often visit and Kris Kringle with his elves comes to cheer patients and distribute donated gifts. Menorahs are set about, nurses bedeck their uniforms with holiday trimmings (often just tasteful enough to bring a smile) and the hospital's dietitians plan special festive meals.

Sadly, because of illness, injury or disease, for some families and patients the holidays come and go without the realization the days are special, or have even arrived. And for some parents, one day melts into another, and their child's needs continue exactly as they had hours to days before.

During the holiday seasons we tried to focus on the families of the children in our units. We made special efforts to do something special for immediate relatives of sick neonates. This could have been taking a photograph of their child wearing a red stocking hat and mounting the photograph in a holiday card. The infant's nurse would also record a message, written in the child's voice, wishing his/her parents happy holidays. Along with the holiday greeting would be a personal message from the child to the family they could share and cherish. An insightful exchange meant to inspire bonding between the infant and family. A simple gift!

Kudos to mom or dad was always sure success. A tribute as simple as, "Thanks, Mom, I really enjoyed your milk today. I sucked down 15 milliliters and kept it all down...can't wait for more." Signed, "Love Katie" was sure to melt their hearts. That simple note, attached to the infant's isolette/warmer, in clear view so as not to be missed, would take on a new life. It might bring a tear of joy, a smile of elation, a deep sigh of relief, a cherished kiss, or a spark of hope. Whatever it did, the message was meant to provide struggling parents with a treasured keepsake, even if the token was merely a messaged picture that could be saved and pulled out in future years to relive their child's first holiday. As for this moment, the memento provided a current picture of their lovely newborn to allay Grandma's and/or Grandpa's worries.

And for us, our reward was catching sight of the joy spreading across the faces of parents when looking up from their children's notes. It was these tiny glimpses and looks of fulfillment which motivated us to come in and work our holiday shifts.

Hometown Politics

People in the area where I grew up often talked about how nepotism seemed to correlate with certain jobs. Not only did family members seem to naturally inherit certain positions whether they were qualified or not, but there was also the assumption obtaining secure employment depended on who you knew. For many, getting a good job translated to, "You must have known someone."

My family was an ordinary hard working middle class family. We had no connections, nor did we "know the right people." My Italian father was not connected despite living in an area whispered to be mob-affiliated. We were who we were. No familiar last name and no old money.

Growing up amidst this mentality and tainted societal values, I swore I would never depend on anyone to secure me a job. I would be my own person. If I got a job, it would be because I was qualified, and I was the best applicant. I would procure the position because I was the one with the suited credentials. My hiring would not be based on what my father had, or who my mother was, or who I knew, but rather, because of me.

A part of me wanted to hold on to ignorance. I wanted to believe those who complained of nepotism and unfair hiring practices were exaggerating. Knowing something about human nature from the various psychology courses I had taken, I could believe such unfairness and human tendencies did exist. On a certain level, how could it not, when humans are humans?

Everyone knows some individuals acquire a so-called "birthright" entitling them to certain things in life such as jobs, personal possessions, and status. We all have met such individuals. I wanted to believe the majority of people in our neighborhoods were not part of these practices, nor stooped to such levels. But many were convinced one could not get a decent job in our valley if not associated with "the right people." And, if one wanted a teaching position, and did not know somebody, they were destined for the unemployment line if they weren't willing to relocate out of the area.

I tried not to pay too much attention to such accusations, but instead believed my employment would be based solely on qualifications. I also never figured I would return to the valley of Northeastern Pennsylvania to work. Instead, I saw distant workplaces in my future. I planned to take flight after nursing school. I never saw myself returning home and working in the geographic area I was raised. I did not see myself even returning for a short stent of time. But, how many of us eventually find ourselves returning to our roots, even if we convince ourselves the stop is only temporary?

If I was to describe my relationship with my hometown after graduation from high school, I would have to equate it to a swinging door, or maybe a bouncing ball. I would return for a while, then in time swing out again. In our family, we joked about this itchy feeling. We attributed this family trait as being a throwback from my dad's Navy days. Our family just never seemed to get comfortable in one place for long. For us, boredom sets in easily. We seem to possess a need to get up and go; a need to seek out new adventures. As you can imagine, such a sense of unsettledness can have good points, and yet, at the same time have drawbacks.

Okay, okay… I need to get to the point of all this explanation. So what do you think? Despite all my inner rationalizations that people had to be exaggerating about the prevalence of the valley's unfair job market, especially in education, I experienced it firsthand. In this instance, for me at least, not getting the job was about who I did not know, and who my husband was not. Essentially, the outcome played out because we were not politically connected. Or, as some might say, we did not travel in the right circles.

I had been gone from the valley for a number of years. Enough time had passed for me to have earned two master's degrees. Which, when I returned to the valley qualified me to be a nurse and/or a school teacher. I had often thought of combining my nursing expertise in pediatrics and my early childhood education degree to work with children in a school setting. A school nurse seemed the perfect fit. Thus, you can imagine how an advertisement in the newspaper for a registered nurse to work in a private school's healthcare center and teach health classes jumped out at me. It was a perfect fit. I could have the best of both worlds!

Since this job was at a private school, having a school nurse certification was a nice complement for the position, but not a mandatory credential. I applied for the position and did well in the initial interview process. The position came down to me and another person. Whether intentional or a slip of confidentiality, I learned my competing candidate also did not have a formal school nurse certification, had not held a prior school nurse position and did not hold the combined academic degrees I possessed.

Apparently, there were debates between members of the search committee on which of us two to hire. I was later told, I had the stronger academic credentials but I could not bring socially, politically, or financially to the table what the other candidate could. Remember, this was a private academic school that relied heavily on donors and philanthropists. From the start, my surname was wrong. My name had no familiar ring to those sitting around the decision table. I was up against tradition, money and politics.

When I was informed of the committee's decision, the principal of the school in a one-to-one meeting shared with me the variables which drove the final selection. I know he took a risk in sharing the information he did, but I believe he felt compelled to explain why I had not been chosen. On the other hand, perhaps he was supplying me with the information because he wanted me to challenge the decision. He certainly alluded to the fact he had reservations about the search committee's final decision.

As I began telling this story, I shared the person who I was up against lacked comparable academic qualifications, but was politically connected. After the selection was made, I learned through a public announcement just how politically linked to the community and state she was.

Sure I was disappointed, and yeah, some people thought I should have made a fuss about the inequity. However, I believed if the outcome reflected the school's ethical and political standards, then most likely the school and I would not have been a good fit. With such a mindset, I probably would have found myself on opposing ends on many of their philosophical positions.

At the time, as I mentioned, I figured there must have been a reason for this situation to play out as it did. Years later, when time passed and feelings healed, the school did come back into my life. But by that time my career had taken off in another direction.

Well, about eighteen years later, our valley would hit national news as the FBI disclosed the many counts of corruption committed by my hometown's politicians and educational systems. I guess in the end, there was some truth to the valley's residents declaring it was who you knew, or did not know, which got you the job!

"Gross" at the Dinner Table

I suppose the habit took root when I lived in a house with three other nurses. It was not unusual for us to share our experiences or recap to each other what we perceived were interesting stories.

Typically we were around the dinner table when we finally had the chance to converse about our day. For us, sharing seemed natural, so we just told our stories. We did not think of our stories as "gross" or "unsettling," but rather just illustrations of our days.

My family, however, had a different perspective of my storytelling. They soon learned what I perceived as interesting was not necessarily what they would call captivating. Instead, what I thought of as fascinating was often interpreted by them as "gross." As a result, I learned when recounting a work related story to tell them the "not so bad," abridged version.

Whenever, I lapsed into telling a story they sensed was going to be "disgusting" or really medical, they'd interject with "this isn't going to be one of those nursing stories again, is it?" In response, I'd pause and then add animated, "just let me tell you this one piece… it's not so bad." Sometimes with such a prelude, I could continue my story, but often their bellyaching would win. Hence, I would just tuck the story aside, and save the telling for a colleague who I knew would appreciate the account.

In a way, for nurses I guess telling stories serves as a therapeutic outlet. So our best listeners are each other. If a peer is not available, I believe many of us unconsciously turn to our families.

Comedians have picked up on this nursing tendency of telling gross stories and portray the behaviors in their skits when showcasing nurses. Typically the scene selection is a group of friends or family members conversing at a table. In the comedy scene, nurses lapse into a conversation with each other about what they perceive as an unbelievable patient story. In their enthusiasm to share with one another, the nurses become totally oblivious to those seated around them. The other members seated at the table could undress down to nudity and the chattering nurses would simply continue with their accounts.

Or, one nurse at a table is depicted as recounting a story which no other non-nursing person at the table "interprets" as normal conversation. Despite looks of disbelief on the faces of the non-nursing people, the nurse continues to recount his/her amazing story, totally unmindful to the astonished expressions of the others. It's the open mouth looks and disbelieving stares comedians capture so well. Sometimes comedians will have family or friends sneaking away from the table while the nurse continues to share his/her story, totally unaware of the dwindling guests. Of course, the humorous side of all this or the moral of the story is: be cautious of how many nurses you have at your table, you might hear more than you bargained for!

Vacation—The Right Way

What a great feeling. I walked out of the computer testing center and gave my family a high five—that universal "yes" symbol. It felt so good to be done, to be able to close another education chapter in my life's book. I could now relax. I passed the nurse practitioner certification exam after three and half years of schooling. Another challenging and rewarding endeavor achieved.

Many of my friends assumed since I had my Ph.D., becoming a nurse practitioner would require little effort and minimal studying. But my perception was quite different. I realized there was a lot I needed to learn. I would need to change some of my practice approaches and think somewhat differently. I would need to put on a new set of lens. Though I knew a lot about nursing from years of practice, my nurse practitioner credentialing added a new dimension to my scope of knowledge. This new role would surely take me out of my comfort zone.

There was plenty to learn and lots to study. However, I knew passing the nurse practitioner certification examination did not mean the end of studying. I knew to maintain certification and provide clients with the best possible care; I would need to continue to stay updated on current treatments, standards and evidence-based practice protocols. Though passing the certification test signified success, studying and learning would continue as lifelong pursuits.

What a challenging test! Before I went into the testing center I told my family, despite three hours being allotted for the test, I would probably be done in two to two and a half hours. I must have been feeling pretty smug when I quoted those times because in reality, I only had five minutes left when I finished the exam. I found, particularly in the beginning of the exam, I was second-guessing myself. Not a good thing. One needs to feel good about a test. I found myself marking several questions which I wanted to come back to. You know those questions you rehash in your mind. The ones you want to mull over despite knowing test experts tell you to go with your first answer.

When I finished the test I honestly wondered if I had passed. Many said to me, "Oh, you'll pass." Unfortunately, I did not possess the same degree of self-confidence. How embarrassing would it be if I did not pass? Very! It was a test and I was a teacher. Teachers are not supposed to fail tests. Especially, a test in their discipline! The personal pressure was high.

As I pushed the finish button, I prayed, "Please, please… let me have done this," "let me have passed." "Don't ruin my upcoming summer vacation." "Don't make it hard for me to kick back and enjoy the beach, to delight in reading an entertaining, no pressure novel."

I was looking forward to reading an engrossing novel. I had a pretty good stash tucked away in my suitcase. So as I closed my eyes, prayed, and clicked the submit button, I watched as the screen page "processed" my answers. And thank goodness—Hallelujah! A message printed declaring I had passed. What a relief! This was the right way to start a vacation!

Chocolate Cherry

Tenure, academic freedom and lifelong learning are not quantifiers which come to mind when I think of my first teaching experience. Instead, I have aroma visions of chocolate cherry, vanilla, and hazelnut. These delicacies, were the sensational smells greeting me most mornings when I arrived at an office I shared with a fellow faculty member. She loved gourmet coffee!

Those pungent, spicy coffee scents permeated the air as she brewed a fresh pot of coffee most mornings for us to share. A cup of coffee became our ritual for the start of a day. At least, on lecture days while we were both together at the school. Other mornings, at the crack of dawn, we were off mingling amongst the hospital staff as we oversaw students on clinical units. No time on clinical days to share an inspiring morning coffee.

Like most rookie nurse educators, I found my first two years of teaching quite challenging. I was not unlike other nurses who come into teaching. Most beginning nurse educators have strong clinical backgrounds and weaker teaching credentials. Few have had formal education related to teaching learning strategies and nursing curriculums.

During my first two years as an educator most of what I learned about teaching came from other nurse educators. Educators who like me, mostly learned what worked and didn't work through trial and error, from colleagues, and by attending seminars and workshops. I put in hours of prep time for both classroom and clinical settings. For the first year, I felt as if I was only one step ahead in my lesson plans. Often I found myself prepping right up to the last minute before class.

Truly teaching can be exhausting, yet rewarding. The biggest return comes when you see the light bulb go on. When you realize they "got it." That gleam is what outshines the tedious hours of preparation and sacrificed sleep.

My office mate and I taught the same specialty. Since she had been at the school teaching before I arrived, she was assigned as my mentor and instructed to introduce me to academia. She taught me many things and certainly helped me through those years.

As I studied education principles and philosophies, I came to value self-learning, creativity, and self-reflection as key variables in student learning. With my hands-on knowledge, I refined my style of teaching. Over the years, I moved from the novice I was in my first years, to the seasoned teacher I am today. Even today, I continue to learn something new with each class.

"Surprise"

This shenanigan still leaves me with a sense of disbelief and the question of "how could I have been so naive not to see the end result coming?" Naturally, if I remotely thought of the possibility of this happening, I would have reworded the instructions for the assignment. I was the one duped this time.

Literally, the students made me eat my words. At least one male in the class did, who was quite obviously the mastermind in the scheme. The two females in the group just seemed to go along with the prank. So here is…how, should I say this…well, let's see…I would have to say…my most embarrassing moment in teaching.

I taught obstetrics at the time in a religious-affiliated institution of higher learning. What a nice way to say College. Anyway, family planning is always included in obstetric-related nursing textbooks, and basically, a component of most curriculums in which obstetrics is taught. Healthcare providers such as nurses need to know how to educate women and their partners on various aspects of family planning. Such teachings included different methods of contraception ranging from natural planning approaches to the latest medical intrauterine implants.

To inform and teach others, nurses must first be versed in the information themselves. They need to be able to talk about different contraceptive options, demonstrate application of devices using models, explain techniques using pictures, and answer patient-initiated questions with current and correct information. Simply, nurses need to be informed and be able to discuss with patients what choices they have. Even if nurses find the topic embarrassing, or would never use the devices themselves, they must be informed.

Contraceptive awareness is one of those topics in nursing which comes with being a healthcare provider and a patient advocate. Nurses learn never to make choices for clients, but rather, to provide patients with correct and current information. With the proper information patients should then have the tools to make their own informed choices.

Knowing most nurses are visual learners, and they need to be comfortable explaining and demonstrating use of different products and agents on models, props, and mannequins, I am a proponent of "a picture is worth a thousand words." So with this teaching framework in mind, I always encourage students to see if they can find prototypes, models, pictures, diagrams… for illustration and clarification. To meet this visual expectation when teaching family planning to their peers in my prior classes, students typically obtained free sample products, models, and training videos from health-related agencies such as drug stores, product manufactures, and pharmaceutical companies.

Take note, the resources I mention above come from professional resources. The concept of "professional" was what went remiss in this assignment. I assumed students would use professional products for their demonstrations. I never conceived they might use less than respectable resources, and at the same time, put me to the test.

This particular group was charged with explaining to their peers the different methods of natural family planning. In similar past assignments, when groups had presented this segment of the family planning content they had drawn pictures of ovulation trending, brought actual basal thermometers, showed pictures of how cervical mucus differs, and explained withdrawal technique. Naturally, from this group I expected something similar. This group was moving smoothly through their presentation using various medical type pictures and even showed the class an actual basal body thermometer. As they were concluding their presentation they announced they had one last visual. That last visual I never anticipated. When they first started their concluding segment, my mind took a few seconds to register exactly what they had popped in the video player.

There it was on the television screen, a pornography film of the "withdrawal" method. Recovering from a second of stunned silence, I immediately asked them to turn the tape off. As I made my request, I realized all eyes were on me. Apparently the class had been prepped on what was about to transpire, that is, everyone but me.

They were testing me. They wanted to get a rise out of me, to see how I would react, and maybe have me eat my words. I am sure they got a major blushing from me, as I embarrassedly realized I did ask for visuals, and they were complying, just not in the way I imagined. Even more alarming, I heard a little voice telling me some of the Catholic faculties and parents weren't going to like this.

In the end, I learned to appreciate the phrase "watch what you ask for." For subsequent assignments, I gave totally different "visual demonstration" instructions. Never did it happen again. Nor did I get called to the department chair's office or the dean's office to explain what transpired. As a matter of fact, much to my surprise, I never heard a word about the episode. No parent called, no student brought it up, no colleague teased me about my naiveté, and I didn't have to call on "academic freedom "or the role of the "professional nurse" to support teaching contraceptives in the classroom.

Eventually I stopped holding my breath for repercussions. I truly learned a lesson, and survived to retell the story. Sometimes, though, when I reflect back on their trick, a part of me thinks "creative little buggers, I can't believe they tried to get away with that one!"

Psych Nursing!

Our Psych rotation had finally arrived. We knew all the crazy stories. We had heard them from freshman year. Accounts included anecdotes that familiarized us with the patients, nicknames bestowed on patients and staff, the locked wards, hidden keys, group therapy antics, late night card games, the joys, the fears….

Psych was legendary. Everyone liked to hear of the adventures and challenges. Start talking about Psych and those still awaiting their own experiences would be all ears. Everyone was captivated by the tales and hoped someday to have their own exciting stories to share. Accounts were probably spiced up over time, but who really knew where facts ended and fiction started. We didn't. We had no experience in psych nursing and were green to what was really true. Stories merged together. Nobody knew if the stories were exaggerated. It was Psych; anything could happen.

Just knowing we were going to a facility where not only the insane, but the criminally insane, were housed was alarming. We were told we would not be taken into the maximum security sections where the criminally insane resided because clients with such mental health histories easily manipulated students. "Easily manipulated" sounded insulting, but in this case with our limited psychiatric experience, I wasn't insulted. I am sure the professionals were probably right!

The stories passed down added a mystical component to our rotation. Just as intriguing as the tales, was the fact Psych was an "away" experience. Our hospital-based nursing program did not have a psych department. So instead, our program directors subcontracted the experience. Consequently, we were rotated to an institution in D.C. which happened to be the location of the oldest psychiatric hospital in the country. Here we were, nurses from the suburbs of Philadelphia going to D.C. And better yet, we were to live in the hospital dorms for seven weeks, right there on the property of the institution!

For us, living at the psych hospital was both thrilling and unsettling. Now, for the next few weeks we would be residing amongst the mental health patients our "Big Sisters" had told us stories about. If you were afraid, you didn't voice your concerns.

You just chalked the practicum up to what you had to do to graduate from the nursing program. We all knew if you wanted to be a nurse, gaining mental health knowledge was a piece of what you had to do. Psych came with the nursing territory.

In our minds, we were off to the big city to make a difference. We imagined the place had never experienced a group of students like our class. Surely, we would be the best group to ever set foot on their campus. Yeah, we had just a little ego inflation. Certainly, we felt our class would leave a mark. We would go down in the institution's history. In some ways maybe we did, but more than likely we faded into the woodwork. In reality, we were probably one of many nondescript nursing programs that rotated through the institution during its tenure.

We were going to the big city. Despite the fact our home school was also in a large city most of us came from communities on the outskirts of the urban area. Consequently, we were far from what one would define as city girls. Instead, I would say most of us were more like "country bumpkins" going to the big city. Philadelphia was a big city, but D.C. was a step above.

This particular hospital in D.C. was not in the best of neighborhoods. The crime rate was high and the area was economically challenged. I remember the day my parents dropped me off. They feared something dreadful might happen, but knew I had to broaden my horizons and complete my Psych rotation if I was to become a nurse. It was one of those times they had to let go. So they hid their apprehensions and left me amongst my classmates and the psych patients. It was good they did not hear our Big Sisters say, "If you go into the city, you might not be able to get back to the hospital, particularly after dusk, since many of the cab drivers refuse to come to this section."

Senator
One of our first introductions to the psych patients was a true testimony to our inexperience. It was an example of "country bumpkins" going to the big city. We had been assigned to certain care wards and instructed to mingle with patients and select two clients we would like to work with over the next weeks. One would be our primary patient, and the other a secondary. Unbeknownst at the time, we were to have our first lesson in manipulation.

A group of patients were sitting around a circular table when several of us (safety in numbers) got up the nerve to join them. As we were trying to make conversation, and at the same time sizing them up as potential primary and secondary candidates, a middle-aged man dressed in a black three piece suit came up to our table and introduced himself as Senator Roop. He asked us what we were doing in the D.C. area. After politely hearing our brief stories the dapper gentleman explained he was running for political office and would appreciate our vote.

Each of us shook his hand as we listened to his political spiel. We found it amazing we had only been in D.C. a short time and already had the fortune to meet a political figure. Didn't we say this was going to be a great rotation? All the signs were there. We were meeting "influential people" early on and now had an interesting story to share with folks back home.

Well, our bubble was short-lived when our psych proctor shared with us we had been fooled. That guy was no more a senator than the man in the moon. He was one of the residents on the ward. He could be one of our primary or secondary patients. Wouldn't that be a hoot? Hook, line and sinker, he got us. He pulled us in. What an embarrassing start! This story would definitely not be shared with those at home—at least not for a while. I wondered how many other student nurses this guy fooled.

We quickly learned some of the patients were good at conning people. Or, how did the staff put it...oh yes, "manipulate" the students. We had to stay on our toes. Hopefully, we would not be so easily fooled in the future. Lesson number one: we could be manipulated.

Psych Memories

Our days in psychiatric nursing were filled with adventure. We learned all about caring for individuals with mental illnesses. We participated in group therapy sessions, collaborated with the staff and did our best to make a difference in patients' lives; probably a minor impact, but a major impact in ours. There was one event which stands out as the hallmark of my psych experience. At this point, though, I will put aside telling that account because there are other psych memories to share first.

I have memories of many of my peers sitting around in the community TV room playing hands of pinochle into the late evening hours. It was a good way to chill out after our busy, challenging clinical days. All stages of players played: amateurs, card sharks and those somewhere in between. So many times, I was going to sit down and learn to play, to go through the painstaking process of learning, but for one reason or another, I just never did. In the end, learning to play was one of those things I wish I had done. A card game is a welcoming way of bringing people together and is a great icebreaker.

Psych North and South

When we were about halfway through our psych rotation we were greeted with a surprise. A group of nursing students arrived from another school to share the dorms with us while they also completed their psych affiliation. Our group attempted to befriend the new group. For some reason though, our hospitality was not well-received. We were shocked when our attempts to be social with our new dorm partners were shunned and we were given the cold shoulder.

One evening as a friendly gesture we invited the group to go out on the town with us. Only one student accepted the invitation. In our conversation with our guest we did discover why the others in her group preferred not to associate with us. We learned the problem related to our geographic roots. In their eyes, we were from the North, making us Yankees and their group was from the South, meaning they were Confederates. We were clearly different. You see, our new colleagues were a group of "southern belles" from the south, who perceived us as not quite of their caliber. Hard to believe in the twentieth century, but it happened!

Sadly, we never did get to know each other. I am sure given the chance we would have enjoyed one another's company, but that opportunity never came about. Thinking of myself as a Yankee was a whole new concept for me. I had thought the notion of the North and South died with the Civil War, but in this case the war still hovered over us like a haunting ghost.

Psych Dances!

When nurses older than me reminisce about their psych days they often recount the times they had to attend social dances sponsored by psych facilities. They would tell stories of how they were expected to dance with the mental health patients. The dances were seen as a therapeutic way of drawing the patients out and re-socializing them into society.

Notoriously, you can't have a gathering of student nurses and mental health patients without a few humorous stories unfolding. But for my generation, things changed. No more dances. We were never asked to attend a dance with clients, nor be put in situations where we were expected to ask clients to dance. Times had changed! We were nurses of a new generation. This was one of those times change was definitely for the positive.

Got a Light?

Psych dances may not have been a thing of my nursing generation, but smoking in psych wards was. Thinking about smoking on the units brings back flashes of patients coming up into our faces asking, "got a light…got a light" over and over again. No sooner would one frustrated patient walk away, since we could not light their cigarettes, when another patient would approach with the same request. You see, patients could have cigarettes on their person, but not lighters. So they would have to have one of the staff members light their cigarettes. And of course, there were rules and restrictions related to lighting cigarettes. One of the rules was students could not light cigarettes for patients. Though the occupants knew this rule, they would continue to request a light over and over again from us. So for me, the words, "Got a light, got a light" echoes through my mind when I reminisce of my D.C. days.

There were also those patients who decided the holes in their ears made good ash trays for the small butts they found lying about. Cigarettes were squirreled away and considered treasured items. Along with the lingering aroma of cigarette smoke, tobacco residue stained everything: the walls, the ceiling, patient fingertips, and of course, the teeth of patients. All the residents on the unit seemed to smoke. The smoking obsession was the way of the group, part of the behavioral reward system. Tobacco smoking was clearly a sign of the times.

An Array of Characters

There were people who held conversations with themselves, those who had habitual habits that impeded their ability to function, and then there were those individuals who saw things others did not see. I remember one lady who would spend her whole day catching the bugs flying in front of her, naturally which no one else saw. Then of course, there was always an array of famous characters on the unit: Cleopatra, Shakespeare, and George Washington… people were whoever they wanted to be. Princesses, queens, kings, rapists, and murderers also waltzed around talking to themselves and/or fighting with invisible opponents. Some spent the day swatting at bugs, asking for "smokes," rocking back and forth, and pacing the halls. Each day there was an assortment of colorful characters.

POW!

So what is the one memory from my psych clinical experience, amongst all these memories, which stands out above all the others? It was a unique experience for me. It would be the first time I was punched in the face. I was not only whammed in the face, but momentarily stunned. I felt like one of those characters depicted in comic strips where the illustrator draws stars around the person's head to signify their dazed state. Clearly, the star-struck individual was me.

I did not see it coming. I did not see the arm pull back or the clenched fist. I was listening for a response. We were all in a group participating in an art therapy session planned as a therapeutic intervention for the patients. I was engrossed in the artistic piece I was designing and simultaneously participating in a conversation between the staff and patients related to birthdays.

The older gentleman sitting next to me was part of the circle, but not really part of the circle. He formed a segment of the rim, but was not artistically or verbally sharing. Basically, he sat quietly staring off into space. Though I had not spent much time around him, I knew he was a patient and not a staff member. This I deduced by his behavior and the fact he did not have a visible set of ward keys dangling from his person, at least from what I could see. No patient carried keys.

Keys were the hallmark sign of being a staff member. Visible keys were the one clue nursing students learned to look for when unsure who resided on the unit as a patient, and who was a member of the staff. Sometimes, the difference between staff and patients were not as obvious as one would expect—a fine line. Scary! So since this man had no obvious keys, I deduced he was a resident. The unit was now his home.

At this point in time, things were fairly quiet as group members participated in the art therapy session. Various activities were underway in other nooks of the large room, but in this corner things were under control and progressing nicely. That is, until I turned to the gentleman next to me and asked, "Mr. Miller, what day is your birthday?" Seemed like a perfectly innocent question. However, the quick change of events suggested the question held a different relevance for Mr. Miller. There was an instantaneous transformation from the quiet gentleman sitting next to me, to an aggressive attacker. Was it the thought of a birthday, a flashback of some event related to his birthday, the tone of my voice, the instant eye contact, the fact attention was drawn to him… or was he just having a bad day? These questions would never be answered to help explain the quick turn of events.

What I did come to know was the impact of his fist. In the second it took the message to be transmitted from speaker to interpreter, came the shocking impact of his clenched fist against my right cheek bone. POW!!! I did not know what hit me! I was so physically stunned by the impact against my face, I blacked out for a few seconds. White stars literally floated in front of my eyes. I am sure the fact I was sitting was why I did not plummet to the floor. Thank goodness for the chair, otherwise, I think I would have awakened looking up into some very concerned faces. But even sitting, the anxious faces were there looking back at me. They were shocked by what had so quickly transpired. They knew I was hurt. They saw my bewildered look and dazed stare.

When I mentally returned to the moment, I recall feeling pretty shaky. The right side of my face literally burned, and felt on fire. Both Mr. Miller and I were immediately escorted from the room. My assailant was taken away by the staff to address his actions and I was taken to the medical clinic to have my injuries assessed. The medical practitioners feared the force of the punch may have broken or fractured facial bones and just as worrisome, caused neurological manifestations.

After a thorough assessment and reassurance to the healthcare providers the nasal bone changes on the facial X-rays was indeed an old childhood fracture, I was released from the infirmary with certain stipulations. I had to agree to the following: return to the dorm, lie down, apply an ice pack to my face, have my peers take my blood pressure and other vital signs hourly for the next twelve hours, and contact the infirmary's personnel if my caregivers noted any change in my neurological status. Even with these strict guidelines, I was more than willing to agree to their terms. I wanted to have the attention taken off of me. Plus, I wanted to return to my room and go to bed. My face was red and swollen, it still burned, and I had a horrific headache. Plus, I needed to hold ice to my face, lie down and close my eyes.

Friday evening and Saturday came and went without problems. It looked like other than the right side of my face being puffy, and a black eye on the same side, I was going to be fine. I did not lose any of my cognitive abilities and consistently scored in normal ranges on the neurologic assessment checks my peers diligently conducted. But things changed Sunday afternoon. Somewhere around mid-day, I started to get a toothache on the same side of my face where Mr. Miller's fist had left its imprint.

Each hour, as the afternoon wore on the pain in my mouth intensified. I tried whatever I could find: a heating pad, ice, and over-the-counter analgesics. Nothing helped. I hoped to control my discomfort until Monday, at which time I could see a dentist.

There were several reasons why I tried to hold off seeking emergency dental care on the weekend. I had medical healthcare insurance under my parents, but no basic dental plan. My parents always paid for dental services out-of-pocket. Second, only one person in our group had an automobile, and on this particular weekend the person who owned the car went home. Thirdly, I was short on cash. I simply did not have the money for a taxi cab. Fourth, "my" dentist was back in Pennsylvania, not in Washington D.C.... So, needless to say I tried to bear the pain until it became unbearable.

With all of these issues, and a throbbing, pounding, toothache which precipitated an earache, I could not keep from crying and feeling sorry for myself. Usually I am stoic and grin and bear what is tossed at me. This time though, the pain was too much. I was exhausted and needed to snooze, but I could not doze because of the excruciating, throbbing pain. As a result of the pain and my exhaustion, I ended up breaking a promise I had made to myself.

You see, quite frequently when I was in nursing school, I would hear some of my classmates on the hall telephone sobbing to their parents about some problem they were having. Mainly, they wept about how they could no longer endure nursing school because things were simply too hard. Because of distance, most times listening and reassuring their frantic child was all parents could do. Communication technology was pretty basic. There were no personal computers, no voicemail, no email…just mostly communicating by traditional black desktop phones or mounted wall units.

Anyway, from hearing these girls, and realizing all they were probably doing was upsetting their parents, I swore to myself I would never call my parents and whine about school. My parents lived too far away for them to come and reassure me. Believe me, there were many times I thought I couldn't take the stress anymore…that perhaps I should pack my bags and do something else. However, even in these weak moments, I refrained from calling and sobbing to my parents. I just pushed on and told myself I could do this. I could see there were seniors and they had survived, just as I knew I would. Despite what it felt like at times, I knew the intent of our teachers was to make us proficient nurses and not to fail us out of school. Nor was it their aim to crush our dreams of being nurses. Instead, they were there to help us fulfill those aspirations.

I kept the "no parent whining promise" right up to this point to the final weeks of my senior year. I was hurting, and so tired from not being able to sleep. But during this moment of weakness, I gave in to my rule and called my parents for advice. Even when I initially got punched in the face, I had not called my parents. I knew when they dropped me off they were worried about my safety, so I did not want to confirm those fears.

With my parents in Pennsylvania and me in D.C., I did not expect they would be able to do much in terms of helping me. I think I mainly just wanted to talk with them. However, despite the distance, my parents came through. Parents can do some miraculous things when concerns relate to their children. I am sure from the sound of my distressed voice, the late hour I called, my tears, and the fact I had never before called crying about anything related to school heightened their concern. My parents listened, assured me they would see what they could do, and promised they would get back to me with a solution.

There was one ace in our pocket. I was in D.C. and still my father's dependent, which meant I had military healthcare benefits. So from Pennsylvania my father was able to make the necessary telephone connections to get me an appointment early Monday morning at a dental clinic on a D.C. military base. My main task was to make it through the night. Somehow I did, and early Monday morning the classmate with the car was back and able to drive me to the scheduled appointment.

I am sure with my tear-stained, swollen face, tired look and black eye I looked pretty distraught when the military-affiliated dentist saw me. By that point, I did not care what he had to do to my tooth, just as long as he made the pain go away. After checking my mouth, and diagnosing the problem, he commented on how surprised he was I had managed to bear the pain for as long as I had.

It turned out, when Mr. Miller punched me in the face, my back upper wisdom tooth, which was still above the gum line before I was punched, also took a shot. From the impact, the wisdom tooth dropped down and a large abscess formed. It was the pressure from the abscess which caused the excruciating mouth and ear pain. The relief was almost immediate once the dentist drained the tissue. I could have hugged him and smacked him with a big kiss for relieving the pain. Instead, in place of such an outward display of gratitude, I merely thanked him and went on my way.

Regrettably, obtaining relief from the horrific pressure was not the end of the story. This military base dentist took care of the immediate problem, but then relayed I needed to follow up with another dentist.

Guess which clinic I was referred to? The dental clinic at the psych hospital! Talk about feeling panicky. All I knew was the dental clinic at the facility was mainly there to address the oral needs of the psych patients. Knowing this bit of information wasn't very reassuring to me. I am not really sure why the underlying mission of the clinic bothered me. Surely, care standards would be no different just because the clients had mental health issues. A tooth problem is a tooth problem, not a mental health problem. Anyway, despite my initial misgivings, everything worked out.

It turned out the clinic was staffed by a supervising dentist, but most of the actual dental work was performed by dental school residents. One of the residents was assigned to treat me. I was elated because he seemed to know what he was doing and was in the capstone of his residency program. Right from the start there was a student-to-student understanding. Plus, he voiced being glad to have a change in pace and to be able to care for someone "normal" again. Of course, the "normal" patient would be me. Just in case you had your doubts!

I also found out I could have gone to their dental clinic over the weekend, instead of having suffered with the pain. Someone was always on weekend call to cover emergencies. Too bad the information was after-the-fact. With the amount of pain I was in on Sunday, I would have welcomed their care!

Two Buddies

Knowing I could not miss much time from classes, I planned the surgical procedure for early Wednesday morning. I figured one day would be enough recovery time so I could once again attend classes on Thursday. This way I would miss very little time that could easily be made up. The procedure was not considered major surgery but one in which general anesthesia was needed. From past experience, I knew general anesthesia and me did not mix well. I typically became hypotensive and extremely nauseated afterwards.

The surgery went as planned, though on Thursday I still felt light-headed, weak and nauseated. Despite these feelings, I knew I needed to make it to classes. To help settle my symptoms, my friend and I surmised perhaps eating a breakfast would be curative.

We typically did not eat breakfast in the hospital's cafeteria for several reasons. First, we often did not have the money. And second, we usually grabbed something quick and uncomplicated in the dorm to eat. Having something available in our rooms for a breakfast snack meant we did not have to get up earlier than we already did. To us, getting up at 6:00 a.m. seemed hazardous to our health, so setting the alarm earlier to have time to go to the cafeteria in the adjacent building was unthinkable.

Anyway, that Thursday morning though breakfast was the last thing I felt like, we both agreed I should try to eat something of substance to make me feel better. Despite my hopes of food reviving me, I felt and knew I looked terrible. I was weak and my complexion was pale. On top of my pasty appearance, my legs were wobbling, I had abdominal cramps and still felt like I was going to vomit or faint. But, being a martyr and not wanting to miss classes, I pushed myself to walk the short distance to the employee's cafeteria. Each step was an effort!

I moved in a daze as I slid my breakfast tray along the metal frame running along the serving line, all the time feeling as if I was going to be sick. As I pushed my tray along my inner voice declared..."I can't do this...this was a mistake...I need to lie down before I faint...I need to get back to the dorm."

As I was mentally trying to suppress my negative thoughts, deciding whether or not to try to continue down the breakfast line, and contemplating whether to leave everything and exit before I fainted or vomited in front of everyone, I felt an arm on my shoulder. With the touch I heard a concerned male voice ask, "Are you all right, you don't look well." Ah...it was a familiar voice and belonged to my buddy's friend. Being a caring individual, and a surgeon, he could spot a person in distress. I also assumed because of their close friendship, my friend had more than likely shared with him I recently had surgery.

We left the food line. His arm and my friend's arm supported me as we went to sit at a close table. We sat there for a little bit as both of my onlookers waited for my color to return and the nausea to pass. They waited until I felt like I could walk. I insisted all I wanted to do was go back to my dorm and lie down. After some convincing, my friends reluctantly agreed to escort me back if I promised to contact them with any problems. I agreed just to be able to return to the haven of my bed.

I made it to my room, miraculously without passing out or vomiting along the way. I never did attend classes that day, or the next, but instead reported off sick and stayed in bed. As I succumbed to sleep, I willed myself to get better and prayed I would not flunk out of nursing school for missing time.

As students we had this misconception that any time missed from classes or clinical rotations would jeopardize our chances of successfully completing the nursing program. Somewhere as students, we missed the human side of our faculties and program director. We rarely considered their caring, nurturing side. Of course I did not flunk out of nursing school because I was sick. Instead, in a few days I recovered, gained my strength and went about my nursing school duties.

A Little Difference

You know, sometimes you can be the catalyst for a small change. Yet, when you think about the larger picture your one act just doesn't make a subtle change, but a substantial one. That is what happened in this account which transpired during the time I was a nurse educator. From my experience of feeling lousy and sick came something favorable. Certainly, I would not have believed good would have come out of the way I felt. However, in the end it did!

I had contracted some type of gastrointestinal virus, like a norovirus, which hit me hard and quick. It was one of those kinds of viruses which leave you wondering if succumbing to the organism would abate further attack. Perhaps, it would be better to just admit the bug is stronger and more powerful than you. To exclaim, "Yes, you win, now just leave me be!"

I did not think I could vomit one more time. My whole being felt as if I had vomited every last morsel, and all that was left was the acidic taste of bile rising with each convulsive retch. A few more episodes and surely the remnants of my stomach would come jerking out of my mouth. For hours after the initial upheaval of my stomach contents, my abdomen continued to knot and contract. Over and over, I hurled up what seemed like every drop of stomach excrement. With each episode of retching, I wondered how much more could possibly come up. How many times can you hug a toilet bowl or hold your head above a large basin as you expel your stomach contents? Oh, but vomiting is not enough! No, this virus needed to conquer. As the festering bugs descend down into the bowels of my body, the wonderful diarrhea kicked in. A little grumble, massive peristalsis and... off to the bathroom. Hopefully, in time of course!

So then, not only did I lose body fluid by vomiting, but I also lost massive amounts with each spasm of my intestinal tract. I was the illustrious picture of a person sitting on a commode, with one's head hung over a lap basin. I was hoping to catch any vomit erupting simultaneously with squirts of diarrhea. A vision of beauty!

Each bout of vomiting and diarrhea drained me further. I could feel myself getting weaker and weaker. No doubt my blood sugar and electrolytes were on empty. I had the shakes, felt lightheaded, was dizzy and had a pounding headache pulsating across my forehead. I knew my body could not take much more. I was definitely depleted. Probably would wilt like a prune, if I continued to puke. I had to cease vomiting and stop the nonsensical invasion.

Intravenous therapy was needed. I would have to climb into our car and make the trip to the hospital. Traveling seemed an impossible feat, almost unrealistic to achieve without vomiting or having diarrhea on the way. An up-chuck bag would need to come along. Better yet, bring a basin because then there would be less chance of missing the opening and staining the car cushions.

Making the trip was the only way to get some aid. So, there was no option but to drag myself out to the car, into the cold, and down the road! Thank goodness for little miracles. Someone else was available to drive.

I survived the ride without puking or having diarrhea, but the test was still on. The emergency room area was packed. It was 10:00 pm and we were told the wait time was approximately three hours. Worse yet, there were no available seats. Surely, I would die standing for that amount of time. As I stood there waiting, I tried to visualize what would happen if I continued to vomit in the waiting room. Would the staff then find me a place to lie down? Would they isolate me from the other patients so I did not start a puking frenzy? Perhaps, they would take me into an examining room away from everyone so I could lie down. Wishful thinking! Such thoughts, as irrational as they were, served their purpose. At least my fleeting mental badgering distracted me from the queasy feeling brewing in my stomach.

In between feeling sorry for myself, I chided myself for being so insensitive to the others around me. I knew they had to feel just as bad. As I wallowed in self-pity feeling utterly terrible, I thought about how I did not abuse healthcare. I contemplated how I only sought assistance when I really felt sick; a trait not uncommon of healthcare providers.

Usually when a person who works in healthcare drags themselves into an office or emergency room, one can surmise they feel pretty lousy. I calculated my last ER visit as being at least three to four years before. Certainly, my conservative use entitled me to this visit. At least my preoccupation with such self-absorbed thoughts was making time pass faster. Enough time for someone to be wheeled to the exit in a wheelchair, get up out of the chair and depart the building leaving the wheelchair behind.

"An empty wheelchair…that might help," I thought. I was too

weak and dizzy to stand much longer. The wheelchair truly looked inviting. I visualized gaining possession of the chair and positioning it so my back would be close to the wall. I conjured if I could sit like that I could tilt my head back to rest on the wall. Then if I could shut my eyes, I could do some type of meditation to possibly control the waves of nausea. I was in luck. My husband secured the chair for me. I aligned myself against the wall, just as I had visualized. What a relief to just sit and close my eyes.

After a substantial wait, I was called into the main emergency area, treated for several hours and then released. The next day, when feeling better and reflecting on my early morning ordeal, the brainstorm came to me. I thought of just how therapeutic lying down would have been when I was in the ER waiting to be seen. Then, I thought of the recliner chairs typically available in pediatric rooms for parents to sleep in when they spent the night. Why don't emergency rooms have such chairs available for individuals who need to lie down while waiting to be seen? Recliners would be perfect.

My solution seemed feasible and practical. Certainly, if the chairs were made of a washable leather/vinyl material, bed linens would not be an issue. A disinfectant wipe between users would address germ issues. I thought my idea was a clever one, and certainly had the potential of improving patient satisfaction, particularly if my wait time was typical. I telephoned the ER's patient care director, whose name was listed on my discharge instruction sheets, and left a message briefly highlighting my practical solution.

The director called me back, thanked me for my idea and stated how coincidental my suggestion was. She explained, due to some new renovations in progress there were some spare recliners available for use. She added that herself, and some other administrators had been actively contemplating what to do with the extra recliners. My advice answered their question. She assured me the available chairs would find their new home in the ER. So you see, from a horrific ordeal for one person, came positive change for others!

Florence and Me

Leaning in close to hear his heart rhythm with the ear pieces of my stethoscope in place, I did not expect to feel a hand run across my chest and a husky low voice with whiskey breath state seductively by my ear, "I've been told Florence Nightingale was quite the whore, is that how all nurses are?" Instantly, I stood straight up and backed away from his touch. I calmly informed him his perception of Florence Nightingale was wrong, and reiterated why I was there, which I clarified was to evaluate his need for continued home care services.

From the minute I had been given the assignment to go out and assess this individual, I had an inkling things might become complicated. The intake summary stated he had been injured in a bar room brawl while drunk. As a result of the fight, he now had a broken arm and shoulder. Both injuries were in the process of mending beneath the plaster cast now molded across his chest and down his left arm. His right arm remained free and still available to get him in trouble, as we have seen. He had a badly sprained left ankle, but otherwise, his lower extremities were fine.

His place of residence was a rented one room cubicle area. He shared the second floor space with five other guys living in similar one room spaces. Their living quarters and homes were located above a local tavern. The establishment was known for being rowdy, needing the police frequently, and rumored to have been a refuge for people in trouble with the law. But despite being knowledgeable of this information, and mentally wondering what I was getting myself into, this man's geographic residence was in my territory. Being in my territory meant, I would be the one to go to his residence and open his admission case. Although I would have loved to have had an escort, the agency I worked for did not offer this service. Nor did the administrators feel escorts for nurses were necessary or financially practical. They also felt using escorts would send a negative message to the community. This is one of those times when one wants to stamp his/her feet and yell out, "But what about us…what about our safety?"

When I arrived, the scene greeting me was no less than what I had anticipated. I walked through the main pub area just as the directions specified, ascended the steps to the second floor, and on the top landing was greeted with a cheerful, "We've been waiting for you." Maybe I should have turned around then. Instead, I walked across the hall where my client was visible sitting in his cubicle-like flat with the door wide open, "waiting for me."

He did not jest when he stated, "we were waiting for you." They were all waiting for me. All the doors of the six rooms were open with six somewhat questionable male characters lurking about. My client was sitting there, "waiting for me" in his boxer shorts. There he sat with his manhood freely visible along the cuff of his shorts. Whether this was intentional, or "his friend" just slipped out by accident, I did not give him the opportunity to address the subject. I deliberately ignored the spectacle, and displayed no facial expression indicating I had noticed the tip of his penis peeking out.

"This is not good," I mentally calculated. No dilly-dallying, just in and out, I thought. I closed my client's door about three quarters of the way to block out the view of the others and to leave an immediate exit. With his arm extended outwards in the cast, and his sprained ankle, I did not anticipate too much trouble from him. I was more fearful of the others who loitered in the hall.

One quick, visual sweep of the conditions and the environment put me in a "hyper" professional mode. As insecure as I was feeling inside, I worked to control any display of my fearfulness. When he referred to Florence Nightingale, and put his hand where it did not belong, I backed away, informed him I did not appreciate his touching me, and quickly but efficiently completed my assessment, explained things to him and exited. Thankfully, the individuals who previously were hanging about in the hall had dispersed and I was able to depart the building apprehensively, but uneventfully. My visit turned into his only visit. Further visits were denied based on the agency's evaluation of his care needs. So with this man, only Florence Nightingale and I would be the ones to have our integrity offended.

I did reiterate to the agency the need for an escort service when nurses are assigned to cases in which they anticipate safety could be a concern. Unfortunately, my suggestion did not result in any policy changes.

Lesson

I remember a practical lesson I learned in my first job. It was a simple thing, not something detrimental to patients, but something I needed to alter. The issue related to calling physicians during evening hours for some particular issue/report.

Working the evening shift typically meant call pages were answered at the physician's home or at some social event they might have been attending. But wherever they happened to be, or whatever the circumstances, some made you feel you were disturbing them, despite their being on-call. You never knew what might have transpired just prior to someone answering their page. It could be you had the unfortunate timing of calling during a domestic argument or when the person's child just shared a less than favorable report card, or the person you called had just fallen asleep. It is always a 50/50 chance that your call would come at a good time versus an adverse time. Sometimes calls are received well, other times, not so well. But calls related to care needs have to be made, and often occur at less than optimal times.

As a "fresh" graduate I had this habit of calling "physicians" to ask a patient care question or report some related information without having the patient's chart in front of me, usually I left it on the chart rack and relied on my notes. So while I was on the telephone, if the physician asked a question and the answer was not scribbled on my information sheet (my brain), I would announce into the telephone, "Wait a minute, I'll get the chart." One time too many, with the same resident, and a resident with an attitude, led me to be called on my "Wait a minute, I'll get the chart" response.

From my "talking-to," I learned to have the client's chart, or in today's times, the patient's computer page accessible before making patient care-related telephone calls. No more "Hold on a minute, I need to get the chart" responses. I quickly learned with the chart in front of me, I could answer questions efficiently and calls went smoother. Now the rule of having the chart readily available seems common sense. As a new graduate, and one who made few physician calls as a student, the simple task was not so obvious. But I learned. This was another rudimentary lesson highlighting my transition from an inexperienced to an experienced nurse.

Beyond Nursing

The school bell rings and they are not present again. Their absenteeism is noted, but not really missed; they are in school so little. Friendships are dwindling. Classmates no longer make an effort to keep in touch. School fades into the background and the hospital takes precedence. Such is the school pattern of children with chronic conditions or those battling terminal illnesses. I feel for them. I wonder how I can make a difference in the lives of these kids. I see home tutors employed by school districts. I hear parents question how long their children will be out of school "this time." I hear children bargaining to return to school and pleading not to miss a class trip, an outing, a prom, a football game....

Play therapists employed by pediatric units work hard attempting to "draw children out" and find ways to help them just be children within a topsy-turvy medical world. Unfortunately, the efforts of teachers and therapists are not enough. I see a gap. Nurses and school teachers don't seem to communicate. Both are worlds apart. The child is stuck between the two worlds, probably feeling lost and overwhelmed in both entities. I wonder if there are any professionals who function in dual roles as registered nurses and licensed school teachers. There should be a uniting of roles by qualified individuals that simultaneously addresses both the physical and educational needs of sick children. Imagine how such individuals could incorporate principles from nursing and from academia to help children understand their illnesses, and at the same time, assist them with their school studies.

I see an opportunity, and think it can be done. I need to lay the foundation before I take the steps. I have the nursing, now the educational piece. I go back to school to take more courses. This time my focus is not on nursing, instead on education. The curriculum is different, yet the topic is familiar, children.

Patience

My interaction with this particular patient would not have stood out if not for the events that followed our encounter. On this evening, I was working the 3-11 pm shift and the night was hopping. We had a number of patients in labor who were also delivering throughout the shift. Of course, deliveries occurring in labor and delivery had a rippling effect on the acuity level of the nursery and postpartum units. We coordinated our evening and employed a team approach to patient care. Such an approach simply meant patients were not divided amongst nurses, but rather we cared for all patients as a group. This meant we all answered patient call bells and worked together on care needs, so by the end of the night each of us probably had an opportunity to interact with every patient in the unit.

In our postpartum area we also cared for gynecology patients. The incident I am about to relay relates to one of the gynecology patients admitted to our department earlier that day. Apparently, on our shift this client received a dinner tray with an entree she had not selected, and the items she received she did not like. So to accommodate her wishes for different food, someone called Dietary and asked if they would send another tray.

I was told shortly after she received her second tray she rang the nurses to say she did not like the taste of the food and wanted something else. Again, another nurse answered the call bell and made the second call to Dietary for a new tray.

During busy times, complaints about issues such as food choices sometimes are put on the back burner to be able to address more pressing concerns. As nurses, though, we are schooled some patient complaints related to food dislikes are not really the true issue. Instead, other stressors may be disguised as dietary dissatisfactions.

Later, by her description to our department head, I was the one who responded to her third subpoena. Apparently, for the third time there was something wrong with her food tray. I am not sure of our interaction, but whatever transpired she once again felt her needs were not sufficiently addressed.

The next day, when I came on the 3-11 p.m. shift, our department head called me in and shared the patient had made a formal complaint related to her food issues and our interaction the night before. She told me she had spoken to the patient about the incident and the patient said she anticipated an apology. Though I could not remember any negative interaction during our food discussion, I agreed to apologize to alleviate any ill feelings. I made that apology, not even sure what I apologized for. I supposed if she was not happy with our exchange, then maybe under the busy circumstances, my frustration at her repeated request came through in my choice of words.

Each day this woman stayed her displeasure with the staff mounted to the point where she repeatedly issued complaints about individuals on the various shifts. As a result, she had everyone on pins and needles thinking they would be the next to be reported. Finally, something triggered her husband to make a meeting with the unit's director in which he disclosed his wife had mental health issues that she had not divulged to her hospital physician or to the staff on admission! He politely apologized for his wife's withholding of this information, asked the director to convey his thanks to the staff for being sensitive to his wife's needs, and voiced understanding of what we were experiencing in addressing her needs.

I wondered about sharing this story because the incident is not one of my best, but in the end I felt it was an integral passage to signify that a nurse's world is never perfect. That as nurses we are also human, and therefore will have good days and bad days. We will all have days when we might accentuate something a little differently on one day than on another; hence saying something we might not pose the same under different conditions. There will be days we can take anything that comes down the pike, but then there will be days that maybe if we had the opportunity to do them over we would do better. This is an example of such a day.

Today was a Difficult Day

Today was a difficult day. I found myself frustrated with my own profession. I could not explain why people said some of the things they did. Or why so few of the staff took time to explain what was going on. I asked myself, "How did our profession get to the point where tasks are more important than empathy?" We work with our emotions tucked away and feelings in check. We are so afraid to share information for fear of crossing the confidentiality line.

I wanted to scream! To let them know I was not stupid and understood what was going on. I yearned to shake someone and yell. "Just please talk to us…tell us what is happening behind those closed doors."

This day I wasn't a nurse, but rather a sister. I was sitting in a waiting room designated for friends and families of patients in the trauma unit. We were limited to checking on my brother in thirty minute intervals. Much to our frustration visitation opportunities came every four hours from 10:00 a.m. until 9:30 p.m. with each visitation time restricted to thirty minutes. Being part of a large family, the thirty minute interval ended up allotting each of us approximately five minutes to say hello. Not much, when you think of a whole life time of minutes and the few minutes of his life which could be left. As I sat there waiting out time, I wondered if he would still be with us when the next four hour interval arrived.

I understood all the professional rationale of why visiting hours needed to be limited in intensive care units. That day, though, all I could focus on was my brother being the one behind those closed doors. I wanted to stand up, stamp my feet, and yell like a child. "You just don't understand...this is MY brother!"

He was unconscious, just lying there while the ventilating machine breathed for him. Yes, everyone seemed to be meeting his physical needs, but I didn't get the sense any staff member was talking to him or telling him what was transpiring. I knew if he had any awareness of what was happening he had to be frightened. All the new sounds, everyone around, his extremities tied down, a tube down his throat....everything so strange and bizarre. I felt he needed his family. He needed to hear a familiar voice to tell him he was all right and we were all rooting for him. But we couldn't, we weren't there, we were locked outside.

Like the other families sitting in the ICU waiting room, we felt restricted and intrusive if we asked a question or ventured into the care unit. The fear was there. If we made too much of a pest of ourselves, then maybe our brother's care would be jeopardized. How care could be compromised, I am not sure. You just think it could. So, the fear keeps you from running through the double doors, during the off visiting hours, and demanding they let you in just to be sure your loved one is fine.

Instead, you sit in the waiting room and contemplate whether the person caring for your brother knows what he/she is doing. You pray the care provider's skills are sharp and the person is astute enough to pick up subtle changes. You hope the provider is not such a novice that your loved one crashes before the person says "Duh, I didn't even see that coming!" You've seen too much. You've witnessed the good and the bad of the profession. You have encountered those you would trust with your life, and those professionals from whom you would flee. And today, you simply ask from deep in your heart that your brother's nurse is one of those you can trust.

Reflecting on why I felt like a pest, I realized the answer was because I was in the role of sister. At this hospital, I did not know any of the nurses or doctors on a professional level, let alone as colleagues. Nor was my brother a famous celebrity or a relative of the hospital's CEO. He was simply the critical care patient in bed two. The emotional distancing amongst some staff was evident. There was no connection between my brother and his caregivers. He was just there, he was their assignment; a patient to treat, and pass on when their shift was done.

I had been a nurse for over twenty-five years. I had learned a lot, and seen a lot. I moved from novice to expert, but now I questioned my own knowledge. I believed I was seeing what I was seeing. My brother was having repetitive seizures. Many times I have seen people having seizures, and he was having similar body movements. So, please do not tell me he is reacting to a medication you are using to sedate him. I know what I am seeing. But today, I have to walk the line and not question those who are in charge. I am merely the sister.

How far can I push? How many times can I ask the same question, "Is he having seizures?" At this moment, I am a layperson. Not a nurse and not their colleague. They do not know me from Adam. They see me as someone who asks too many questions. I am not expected to probe or to challenge their expertise.

So what do I do? I need to be my brother's advocate. His wife does not know, she is out of her realm, unfamiliar with medical jargon. This is my world! I see no other answer, so I contemplate pulling out the big guns. I have to let them know I am one of them. In my own way, I have to let them know I know what they are doing, what they are saying and what I am seeing. Please don't try to pacify me and tell me I don't know what I see. Tell me what you are doing, what you are thinking, what you know and don't know. Don't merely tell me you are "doing tests." What tests are you doing? What are the results? Remember we hang onto your every word.

I doubt myself enough, without doubting you too. Before I speak or state what I think, I have played it over and over in my mind, validating what I know and questioning what I don't know. I have referenced my textbooks. I know the complications and the worse case scenarios. In this case, I wish I didn't know. The prognosis is grave. But I need to be his protector. I need to speak for my family. They trust I know what is happening, and believe in some way my answers can make his prognosis better.

I wish I had the power, but I am only the sister now, not the nurse, I have no power. I too am ineffectual. All my schooling, all my knowledge and all I can do is sit with everyone else in the ICU waiting room, thinking, bargaining, and praying he makes it until the next visiting hour. The hours tick by and together we wait, and pray.

White Light

I had read about the phenomenon and heard patients recap what they had seen. They talked of a bright white light. Is it what marks the here and now from the next world? Is this the phenomenon that helps one cross over? Does it beckon one into its warm embrace? I believe there are truths to such accounts. Too many people tell the same story. What I didn't expect was to actually experience the phenomenon, and for the event to occur early in my life.

I was a patient in the OB-GYN department where I was actually employed. Which meant my friends and colleagues were my care providers. Having your friends caring for you is different, yet reassuring. Not quite an hour had passed from the time I had left the surgical recovery room to the time of the incident. I was what we refer to as a "fresh post-op."

I had undergone a routine operation, received general anesthesia, and was trying to lie very still. Any movement on my part meant pain. My colleagues had already settled me in the bed, taken my vital signs, conducted their assessments, and were assured by their findings. I was progressing like every other post-op patient who had undergone a similar procedure. Nothing was out of the ordinary. My husband was sitting by my bedside as I dozed in and out of consciousness, most likely still feeling drowsy from the residual effects of anesthesia.

I did not have many tubes attached to me, just the intravenous tubing connected to the IV solution hanging at my bedside. I was lying there not doing much of anything except trying to transition back to myself and trying to lie perfectly still. As I lay there I felt this peculiar sensation come over me. I remember feeling very strange, like I was in my body, but not in my body, and my body or my inner being, maybe my soul, was being pulled out of my physical being. There was this feeling my body was moving forward, yet I could see my body still on the bed. I felt like this spiritual piece of me was being sucked out of my body and my physical being was simultaneously sinking deeper and deeper into the mattress. I had the sensation of floating within a long dimly lit corridor, with a vacuum nudging me forward towards a glowing light.

I recall trying not to advance towards the beam. Not that I was afraid, but I was telling myself I did not want to go there yet, I wanted to hang back, to stay where I was and not move forward. I mumbled to my husband I felt strange and to get help.

I heard orders being given to do this and to do that. All their voices and their rushing about seemed in another dimension. My visibility in the room was foggy and their figures were hazy. I knew they were there, yet not clearly aware of their precise movements. My mind was focused elsewhere. I was trying to stop my descent and attempting to pull back from the distant light. I did hear someone's voice saying I had passed out. I took a moment to chuckle to myself. I thought it sounded so absurd for someone to faint while in bed. Then their faces started to come into focus as their voices grew closer and I could see myself lying in the bed, once again physically amongst them. I was no longer separated into two entities. Nor, was I still being pulled through the tunnel and the bright light that had been in the distance had vanished. Now I saw faces, and concerned ones at that! I came back to my friends and to where I was; a patient in a room. I did not know what happened, nor did they. Could I have "just" fainted?

I am sure some physiological event like an extreme drop in my blood pressure precipitated the event. I knew what I had experienced was the phenomenon people who have near-misses with death describe. I had seen the bright white light at the end of the tunnel. I suppose I didn't move forward because it wasn't quite my time to end my journey. If the pulling and indecisiveness I experienced was because I was being given a choice, then I am grateful to have had the choice. Perhaps next time I won't be granted an extension.

Purchasing Ingenuity

I needed to think outside the box to get our administrators' attention. I had to find a way to make them see our department would benefit from the piece of equipment I wanted to purchase. Budgets were tight, so any purchases outside the ordinary were frowned upon. But expenditures of these dollars could bring something new and unique to our department. A product no other hospitals in our local area offered.

Our obstetrical department needed some clever marketing strategies and some changes to update the current practice standards. When I accepted the position as department director, I took on the challenge to try and revitalize the unit. Prior to my accepting the role, the number of annual births had dipped to a record low. Several obstetricians had retired without someone having the foresight to hire their replacements. Now a strategic goal of the hospital was to entice new obstetricians and attract expectant couples to choose our facility as their birthing center.

Many changes were underway, including a complete redesign of the department. The revamping was a great time to install this new product since special electrical wiring had to be secured within the walls of the renovated unit.

Prior to my pursuit of this piece of equipment, I had attended a conference on infant abduction. The presentation left me thinking how devastating just one attempt at abduction, successful or not, could be for an obstetrical unit. I learned the statistics, the typical profiles of abductors, what variables to be cognizant of, and what to do to prevent an incident. As a manager, I did not want our obstetric or pediatric departments to ever be victims of either infant or child abductions. Instead, my goal was to have our nursery and pediatric unit viewed by parents as a place where their precious off-spring would be safe. I wanted to install an electronic anti-abduction security system which would lock down our unit if any child wearing a special electronic device was taken beyond a designated area. Today, almost every nursery has such a system, but at the time I was contemplating purchasing the unit, the device had just come on the market.

I had to be clever to capture the attention of our administrators to receive their approval to submit my purchasing request. I knew I had to emphasize the financial loss the hospital could incur if they did not purchase the system and a tragic incident happened as a result. An infant abduction had not occurred at this hospital, or at any other local hospital. Unfortunately for me, the threat I needed to convey to our decision makers would seem an exaggeration and be perceived as unlikely to happen.

More than likely, unless someone was pregnant, or had a close relative or friend who was pregnant, the interest for installing such a system would not be at the top of their investment list. Therefore, to simply argue our obstetrical department needed this costly addition would mean little to these hospital administrators. I needed to show our executive committee the relevance of the system, how the hospital would benefit, and the gains for the birthing center if the new device succeeded in attracting expectant couples.

Being a visual person, I have a tendency when I want to make a point to find a way to make people visualize what I am speaking of. I look for ways individuals can experience the phenomenon. From such pedagogies of conveying information, came the perfect plan to convince our administrators to sign the desired purchase order.

First, I negotiated the purchase price with the company who had patented the product and made a deal with the designers. Our deal was to allow other hospitals contemplating buying the same product to come and see our device in operation. Naturally, the agreement to show this product included a discount on our overall purchasing price. The reduced price was a bonus I planned to present when attempting to sell the product to our administrators.

Second, I had to get their attention. Our monthly management meetings seemed the perfect venue where upper tiered administrators to mid-level managers came together. Obtaining a spot on the monthly agenda was easy. The challenge was to figure out a way to capture everyone's interest.

My goal was to immediately secure each person's attention as he/she filtered into the meeting room. If I could gain their curiosity for a few minutes, before they lost interest, I would have a chance of selling my idea. I needed to make them see it only takes one incident. Whether or not the attempt is successful is immaterial, the hospital's reputation will still take a hit. No new parents want to be the victims of such an assault, and no hospital wants to be known as the place where an infant abduction occurred. I knew if I could get our management team to see how this new system could provide new parents with piece of mind and how the system could potentially attract growing families to our facility, the board members would sign for the new electronic system.

Thus, I made an abduction come to life. I introduced them to the threat. They got to meet the type of person who attempts to steal hospital babies, and who would cause a hospital's name to be broadcasted on the six o'clock news and emblazoned across the headlines of local newspapers. They needed to see how easily such a disaster could happen to feel its impact. Additionally, they needed to realize though the system might be expensive to install, the startup cost was nothing compared to what would be lost in terms of reputation, legal suits, and dollars if a true abduction did occur.

Before people started arriving for the meeting I went to the room and set up an abduction scenario. I wanted to catch everyone's attention and stimulate conversation while people waited for the meeting to convene. I used my knowledge of what a typical abductor might look like and created an abductor from one of our adult size CPR mannequins. I dressed the female mannequin in our hospital's OR scrubs and applied a white lab coat with one of the hospital name tags pinned above her left breast pocket. She wore white nursing shoes and a stethoscope lapped around her neck. At the meeting I used a stand to achieve the visual image of a standing, fleeing woman carrying an infant (doll) wrapped in a blanket. I also placed signs close by the mannequin which cited statistics and facts related to infant abductions.

I had told very few of my mock abduction plans. I hoped the element of surprise generated the curiosity I needed to gain the interest of the meeting attendees. My attempts were rewarded when sparks of interest were evident as people filtered into the meeting and discussed the display. The exhibit spoke for itself. No one needed to stand by the mannequin and explain the significance. The message was evident!

My plan worked. I left the meeting with consent to purchase the infant abduction system. Some even congratulated me on my presentation and voiced a new awareness of infant abduction issues. However, my true reward was yet to come!

We installed the electronic unit and developed new policies

and procedures on what to do if an alarm sounded and/or there was concern of a potential abduction. One day, out of the clear blue sky, not long after we had our new electronic system in place we were compensated for having the foresight we did.

On the morning's television news, and repeatedly throughout the day, plus in bold letters across the local newspaper was the name of a neighboring hospital whose obstetrical unit had experienced an attempted abduction. The perpetrator almost pulled off the feat if it wasn't for one nurse overhearing something she thought suspicious. Remember, we were the only hospital in our local area with the new electronic system. So naturally, the hospital in the news did not offer their newborns the protection we did.

At our hospital the resonating buzz that echoed, centered around how thankful we were to have such a secure system in place. Our CEO had copies of newspapers to show me the headlines and even confessed how thankful he was we had the foresight to install such a valuable system. He was even more appreciative, as was I, that we were not the ones in the headlines. This was one of those moments when I really got to feel good about something we achieved and to be proud of our obstetrical department's image. This time we were shining! What more could a department director and a CEO ask for?

I, too, was on the local television news, but this time as the knight in shining armor! I was asked to share with viewers how our electronic system made infants safe, and to recommend what other hospitals could do to assure the same sense of security. After some of the initial commotion died down, a nursing administrator friend of mine who worked at the hospital where the abduction was attempted telephoned to inquire about our system. She was thrilled her administrators had given the green light to install a similar unit in their OB department.

Certainly in light of this incident, our department deserved kudos for our foresight and ingenuity. In the long run I would say our new infant protection system, though initially perceived as costly, more than paid for itself.

She Escaped!

Several other stories evolved as a result of our installing the new electronic security system. One tale related to carrying out a factitious abduction, which in the end did not have the success I had hoped for. However, knowing the event was a practice drill with the intent of identifying our shortcomings and ultimately tightening our system, I was not overly stressed by the mock abductor's outcome. In the end, I got what I set out for: to test our new system for functionality of the electronic device, the response of the obstetrical staff to an attempted abduction, and an awareness of hospital personnel of the significance of a Code White alert. Thus, when I saw my mother dressed like an obstetrical nurse in green scrubs playing the role of an infant abductor and waving to me with a "baby" in hand outside the front doors of the hospital, I knew we still had some work to do.

Only I, my assistant patient care director, a few key administrators and the head of security knew we were planning to test our system. I had recruited my mother to play the perpetrator since she was not a familiar face to others at the hospital. Our goal was to make my mother appear to be an employee. We set the scenario so my mother would start by looking for a set of green scrubs, a white lab coat, and a pair of white nurse's shoes left accessible to the wrong person. To our staff's discredit, she readily found the items and was able to dress in the appropriate attire. We then gave her directions on securing her way into the OB department so she could retrieve and carry away a newborn, which was really a doll.

We set the nursery scenario so one would believe the newborn was out of the nursery and visiting with the mother in a postpartum room. An electronic security sensor was applied to the infant's body so the alarm system would sound when the infant was taken beyond the designated area. This "out of range" step would cause the exit doors of the unit to automatically lock down and an alarm to sound when the infant passed by the protected area.

Several weeks before testing our system, a hospital policy was put in place outlining the procedure to follow if a Code White (attempted infant abduction) was announced over the hospital's announcement system. Designated personnel within the hospital were expected to respond and carry out specific tasks to stop the potential abductor before he/she exited the building. Our drill questions were: does everyone throughout the hospital know what to do if a Code White is called? Do they know their roles? Will we stop the attempted abductor from exiting the building?

My mother revealed her success in escaping related to her locating an open, back stairway left unmonitored by staff. As a result, she was able to make her grand exit. She performed no Houdini maneuvers, but rather, her success was due to our failure. Simply, we needed additional practice until all the kinks were ironed out, employees were well-versed in their assigned roles, and we presented a secure front.

Clinical Jeopardy

Sometimes, as traditional college-age students we used good judgment, and other times not so good judgment. Not so good judgment related to the times we went to fraternity parties on nights before clinical practice. To be on time for clinical one had to start their day by at least six o'clock in the morning. For us young adults, six o'clock in the morning seemed like the middle of the night. In my book, six o'clock in the morning is early, but now when I hear some college students say they won't register for any eight o'clock classes because the hour is too early, I think of our 6:00 a.m. starts.

Well, if you want to be a nurse and work day shift, six o'clock (and perhaps even earlier) is your reality. Our dorm curfew was midnight so we really could not stay out extremely late. But on those pre-clinical nights when we did go out, and knew we would have to be up early, we should have used better judgment. We did not do this regularly but the nights we did go out, getting up the next morning and physically making it through the next day was challenging.

On a few such nights, I can remember walking over to the hospital wondering how I was ever going to keep my eyes open throughout the day. I was always a person who needed at least eight hours of sleep, and one who did not do well with early morning starts.

On such mornings, despite just wanting to crawl back into bed and go to sleep, there was the personal challenge of performing well because you were someone's nurse. The true test was not to be caught half-asleep by your clinical instructor. What probably would have been the ultimate blunder was if you tried to go to clinical in the morning without having researched the pathophysiology of your assigned client's medical diagnosis, failed to develop medication information cards, did not develop a nursing care plan for the individuals you would be caring for, and did not know the pharmodynamics of each of your client's medications inside out and upside down.

There surely would have been no tolerance for being tired and not being able to intelligently discuss your client's disease/disorder and his/her related plan of care because you had gone to a party the night before. Surely, if you could not rise up to your clinical instructor's verbal quizzing, or did not have your written plan of care and medication cards to submit, you would be sent off the clinical unit. Inevitability, before you left the unit you'd be given a dissertation on how your lack of knowledge put your assigned patient at risk; the ultimate guilt for a wannabe nurse.

Being sent off the clinical unit because of poor judgment was never a good thing, and most definitely an infraction which could cause you to be dismissed from the nursing program. So, going to fraternity parties on nights before clinical days really was not one of our wiser decisions, but we were young and wanted to have fun. Actually, going to bed on a pre-clinical night about ten o'clock and skipping the fraternity parties on Monday or Wednesday nights before the traditional Tuesday and Thursday clinical days, would have been much wiser. Though, as I first said, we were young and did not always use our best judgment.

Patriotism

We had paired students up for the day. It was one of their first clinical experiences so we had taken the group to a local nursing home. Here the students could implement the basic skills they had diligently learned and practiced in the learning lab. They were nervous since they were finally out in the actual world caring for "real people."

For some, it was a challenge to just greet a resident and introduce oneself, to make an effort to bridge the gap between the young and old. For others, saying hello and conversing with someone entirely on one's own, and withstanding the lows when conversation did not flow and silence prevailed could be discontenting. This first clinical experience might be the first time a student touched another human to help them bathe, washed someone from head to toe, lifted another's body or ever repositioned someone in bed.

It was a morning of exhaustion as they learned what it meant to bathe, lift, feed and change someone. Novice students would rise from bent positions and wonder if their own backs and shoulders would survive. But most of all, some would wonder, "Is this for me…did I make a mistake in wanting to become a nurse?" And, others would feel they did a miraculous thing; that this day was the start of a fulfilling career.

As clinical instructors and nurses we bustled amongst the residents' rooms. Directing here, and hoisting, positioning and lifting over there. As teachers we modeled appropriate care, taught by example, and moved students along. We instructed students on care measures to help them with the residents' daily routines. So as not to throw off the tempo of the day, we kept students moving with the care they administered. We were cognizant of the unit's routine and attempted to ward off any disruptions which would alter the normal delivery of the resident's morning care.

Most of the students had survived the early morning "up and about" schedules of the residents. Students were now in the midst of wheeling residents out of their rooms and into the bright community room as they cautiously maneuvered around mobile clients clicking along with their decorated walkers. Other students were in the process of walking slowly down the hall holding someone's arm assisting them to the community room. In the common room students would position residents around the large circular tables which filled the room. Once in this beehive individuals could converse with friends, watch television, or participate in activities led by a recreational therapist.

The room was the center of activity where everyone congregated. For some, the room offered a change of scenery from their personal quarters. It was the hub where one heard all the gossip; clearly the place to be to catch up on who's who and what's what. For others, being in the room offered a form of therapy, an attempt to orient them to the here and now. Therapists hoped planned activities would bring the confused back to where they currently were and provide a moment's respite from the world of dementia. Some residents occupied the room to dine and sip tea or coffee. Others came to simply enjoy the sounds of life, and to catch glimpses of nature through the large glass windows revealing a picturesque countryside.

As usual, the large flat screen television was on. Another attempt at keeping everyone oriented to the here and now. "Television orientation" even worked for the staff who sometimes after a busy morning, needed their own reality check. Just kidding!

Try to visualize the room. You have seen it…a "happening" room. One with lots of activities going on, and different people moving in and out as a television blares on. Some folks are watching and catching every motion, while others tune in and out. And yes of course, there are those, who appear completely oblivious to any sound, but yet, one never knows if this is so.

Utters of "Oh, my God" and gasps of shock echoed. The television program had been interrupted for national breaking news. Many were now frozen in place or advancing closer to the large screen to listen and hopefully catch a recap of the shocking news. Mouths hung open, eyes were glued to the program as many watched and wondered if they were seeing and witnessing what they thought they were seeing. "Was this some television hoax?" "Was the first part of the show missed, and what seemed reality was simple out of context?" "Was one really witnessing this"? "It couldn't be." "No sane human could do this."

There was a plane crashing through a tall building in one of our country's major cities. The scene seemed to play out in slow motion as one watched the approach. The plane seemed to slowly glide through the supporting walls, effortlessly sending debris flying as the structure simply crumbled and chaos erupted in the streets below. Were we at war? Who would be so bold to commit this heinous act? And, why would they? What horrific thing transpired to cause such retaliation? Why us?

The tears, the cries, and the outburst of those around registered within your mind to confirm, "Yes, indeed, this vision was real" this insult did happen, and "they" were projecting more to come. Additional targets were anticipated the news broadcaster relayed. Chaos exploded across the screen.

Those in the community room seemed frozen in their spots, glued to the television as they listened for the next bit of news. Others were in their own world of confusion. Questions were posed. "What should I do? Should I leave? Should I take shelter? What happens to the residents? What do we do for them? Do the confused understand? For some, is this another nightmare: another D-Day? Bewilderment, helplessness and fear hung in the air.

Some expressed a need to get out of the room so they could make telephone calls to check on loved ones they suspected might have been in the vicinity of the disaster. It seemed many knew of a friend or relative who lived in the city or worked in the exact building which was now in ruins. It was a time of urgency. In reality, though, if one stopped to think, "What could they possibly do?" They were one, and this was a battle against many. And, they were not there; they were here, miles away. They could not help. Instead, they had to shoulder the burden of helplessness.

Many of the students attending this particular college were from surrounding states and a few were from New York. As a result, several students on the unit were personally impacted by what had transpired. We sent those students off the clinical unit to do what they needed to do. We consulted with the nursing home staff and changed our original plans. We would help to settle the residents the best we could in an attempt to provide some sense of security. Once the residents were settled, the staff would then take over so we could meet with students to debrief and discuss the ensuing events. Since most were having difficulty focusing, we cancelled the reminder of the clinical day. We felt comfortable doing this knowing the regular staff at the center would address the needs of the residents. In actuality, most of our students were too upset and to numb with fear to function effectively.

As I exited the door of the nursing home building, I remember wondering, "Now, what? What was to come? Was this the end? What should I do?" As for me, I was fortunate because I had no relative working or living in New York City or at the Pentagon. Ironically for my father, 9/11 was his birthday, and he was a veteran. And I knew 9/11 would be one of the biggest insults to our country, particularly for those individuals who were actively serving or had served in our country's armed forces.

Telepathy

This incident was so unique I have to wonder if it was caused by one of those universal phenomena which we as humans don't fully understand. It was an exceptional occurrence relating to energy fields, spiritual connections, mental telepathy and psychic marvels or to some other unexplained, bizarre force. The experience bore resemblance to the phenomenon when someone calls on the telephone and the receiver says they were just about to pick up the telephone to call him/her. It's the spiritual connection, or esotericism flowing between two individuals; the sense of oneness that transcends the essence of both beings when at precisely the same moment two people are doing the same thing or thinking the same thoughts. Some unexplained, unconscious communication exists between the pair. Naturally, it seems the closer two people are spiritually, the more likely this connection exist. How often has one heard mothers and daughters chat about having a sixth sense? The phenomenon which explains why they call each other on the telephone at exactly the same moment, or sense when something is not quite kosher with the other?

This connection occurred between me and a friend I had known for many years. I had met her at my first nursing job following graduation from the original nursing program I attended. We resided together for a short period while we looked for an apartment and then became apartment roommates. Over time our apartment dissolved, both of us married men with some type of military affiliation, each of us relocated multiple times, started families and pursued our careers. We always seemed to be living at two ends of the country, one predominantly on the east coast and the other on the west coast, and sometimes, the distance spanned across continents. Despite our geographic distances and the lows and highs in each other's lives, we managed some degree of correspondence and every couple of years were able to visit one another.

Close to thirty years after the beginning of our friendship is when these strange phenomena ensued. I was living on the east coast while my friend was living on the west coast near the U.S. Air Force Academy. The time was the summer before our daughter was entering her senior year in high school and contemplating possible attending the academy. Prior to her thinking about attending the academy, we had planned a summer trip across the United States to check out some of the national parks populating the Midwest and Western regions. Initially, stopping at the academy was not one of our destinations, but later became an add-on as we ventured out. Since we had not planned on visiting the academy, which was now the hometown of my nursing friend, I did not contact her to say we were driving out west and would she and her family like our company.

As we approached the military facility, which was fairly close to their home, and after much back and forth mental badgering on whether or not to call and say we were in town, I opted not to. At the time it seemed like a wise decision because notification of our visit would not have provided much advance warning, we were only planning on being at the school for a few hours, and we had lodging reservations at a national park booked within two days' time. But something was stronger than my indecisiveness, which later made me realize there was a stronger force at work.

We had arrived at the academy later than we had anticipated. Consequently, we did a self-tour of the area and viewed the parts of the academy grounds which were still open. Evening came fast, and being tired we decided not to continue our tour, but rather, to call it an early evening and secure lodging on the base for the night.

In the morning before leaving we opted to pick up some supplies for our continued trip. One of our stops would be the commissary on the base for some food items. From the minute I got up in the morning, I had this sense I was going to see my friend. Maybe, I was just feeling bad because I was so close and had not contacted her. Nonetheless, I had this strong premonition we would meet. And even stranger, I sensed our meeting would occur at the commissary.

Think about how peculiar this is. I am from clear across the country, did not call my friend to say I was coming out her way, and had not talked or corresponded with her for several months. Yet, at an exact moment we would both be in the same store, in the same aisle, both looking at bread. She spotted me first, as I was looking down weighing in my mind which one of the two gourmet breads my family would prefer. She came over to me and said in a surprised, uncertain voice (which was framed like she could not believe what she thought she was seeing), "Brenda?" When I looked up and saw her, I wasn't surprised, because I knew I would see her. But, I was certainly happy to see her

Like the old friends we were, our conversation sparked and we had lots to tell and catch up on. We readjusted our travel plans and spent the day with her and her family. For both of us, our meeting was an opportunity to reconnect. But what caused this reconnection; was it just a coincidence? Or, did some type of energy exist between us, pulling us together against all odds? Was this a natural mystical force not to be reckoned with, but meant to be?

Chapter Seven

TRANSPORTATION

*A small leak can sink
a great ship.*
(BENJAMIN FRANKLIN)

A Squirrel

This was a second time I came upon an accident on the roadside. It was me, our daughter and her friend in my car. The girls were fairly young at the time, about nine years old. We were heading out to a movie for some fun. The street we were on was in a rural area, but not so densely traveled cars did not frequent the road. Actually, if one traveled further down the road he/she would find the center of town, which is where we were headed. We were just coming over a small incline in the road when I noticed something peculiar about the scene ahead. Reducing my speed to approach with caution, I saw a car that appeared out of its lane. As I drew closer, I realized there was an automobile lying on its rooftop in the center of the road.

What initially crossed my mind was there were no other cars or people about except ourselves. More than likely the accident had just happened. We had probably missed the car flipping over by a matter of seconds. Unfortunately, even if we were there an instant earlier, we could not have prevented the accident. Thinking about it, if we were there at precisely the moment the car veered off the road, things could have been worse. Possibly we would have been involved as well.

There was no activity, no appearance of someone trying to crawl out of the car or someone crying out for help. There was a sense of stillness. Nothing was moving, not even the wind, not even the sound of the car's engine.

I pulled my car off to the side of the road just a little distance away from the tumbled car. I instructed the two girls to stay in the car and then headed over to see if I could help. As I neared the overturned vehicle, I saw a gentleman approaching from the back end of the capsized car. Evidently, he was driving up the incline on the opposite side of the road, which explained why I had not initially seen him. He must have arrived just about the time I did, both of us missing the exact moment of the mishap. With there being no witnesses, whatever made this person lose control of the car and cross the road would remain a conundrum. Later, I heard it was suspected the person swerved the car in an attempt to avoid hitting a squirrel, but no one was ever 100 percent sure.

Approaching the automobile we could see a lady trapped in the front seat. She was no longer behind the driver's wheel but now was positioned more towards the passenger's side. She appeared to be the only person in the car. She was so still, exhibiting no sign of life. There was so little space between her, the seat and the roof. The top of the car had crushed almost completely inward, leaving very little space for her body. Looking at her and the condition of the automobile, I figured there was no way someone could survive the accident.

She was contorted inside the car and almost completely out of reach of our hands. Only the roof near the driver's side had not been totally crushed. Enough space existed from a ground position that one could see her in a twisted, pretzel-like position across the front seat.

Realizing the seriousness of the situation I used my cell phone and called 9-1-1. The dispatcher's initial inquiry related to whether any fluids such as gasoline were leaking from the car. Broaching the question about fluid leaking was so practical and critical in this situation, it instantly occurred to me I did not even think about looking for any such fluids as I had approached the automobile. I was so focused on whether or not people were injured in the accident I did not appreciate the danger for those who stopped to render help. Of course, I knew why the trained person was asking.

We were all in danger of a gasoline explosion. Talk about instant awareness of a critical mistake in my thought process. I realized I hadn't thought like a trauma or disaster nurse. Such individuals would automatically calculate the environmental dangers. We didn't have such worries working in inpatient settings, so I was a little slow on the uptake. Truly not realizing the potential explosive danger was an oversight on my part which could have cost not only mine, but my daughter's and her friend's lives as well.

Not to get away from the story, but ponder this. What would you do if you and only you came across an automobile accident on a desolate country road involving seriously injured people, obvious fluids leaking from the car, and you had no cell phone or other communication means? Would you immediately approach the vehicle to help the injured, or would you hold back because of a potential gasoline explosion? Or would you note the scene, drive on, and try to find help to send back? Think about it. Certainly, there is no absolute correct answer, merely one of those ethical challenges to reflect on.

Although there was visible fluid on the ground near the automobile, the gentleman who arrived on the scene about the same time as myself, conveyed to me, that "yes" there was fluid, but it was "oil, not gasoline." With this critical variable addressed, I went closer to the car to see if I could help the trapped woman. Lying on the ground with my face against the cold pavement of the road, I could stretch my arm into a space created by a slight opening in the driver's window. I was able to reach just far enough to touch the extended arm of the lady. Even with my touch, whether gentle or somewhat harder (just to check her response) she did not react. There was no wincing, pulling away, or uttering of a sound. I could not tell if she was breathing because of her curved, anomalously angled position. However, I was able to extend my arm so the tips of my fingers touched the area of her wrist where I could feel her radial pulse. Though extremely weak, I was assured to feel a very light wisp of a pulse flicker against my fingertips. So faint, but nonetheless, a pulse.

The feel of a pulse confirmed there was still life. But there was little we could do to help sustain her if the faint flicker extinguished. Sadly, with her locked in the crushed car, and no way to reach her, there was not much anyone could do to help her physically until the rescue team arrived. But there was something small, but significant, that could be done. So as I retained my position on the ground, alongside the car with my arm extended as far as I could, just barely touching the tips of her fingers, I talked to her. I told her what was transpiring, informed her she was not alone, and help was on its way.

I could hear my teachers in our fundamentals of nursing classes emphasizing to us: "Hearing is the last sense to go… talk to your patients…particularly the unconscious ones…they can hear you." So, that is what I did. I positioned myself on the cold ground and talked to her as the crowd grew and we waited for the emergency response team to arrive.

Someone caught sight of a wallet lying within reach inside the car. With the assistance of a stick, they retrieved the wallet. As hoped, some identification was found in her wallet. Her name resonated familiarity with me. I knew of this person, one of those "friend of a friend" acquaintances. She was a religious sister belonging to the same religious order who founded the college where I taught, and the hospital where I maintained a clinical practice. She dedicated herself to caring for others, and now she was in need of help from others; the irony.

Shortly after her identification was made, the paramedics and rescue team were on the scene. Everyone was asked to clear the spot. I reported to the paramedics and police what I knew. Then, with a brief silent prayer, I retreated from the scene. She was in the paramedics' hands, but in all actuality she was in her Holy Savior's hands. Unfortunately, I did not have the opportunity to see how she was actually removed from the crushed car. I would have liked to witness the intricate operation, merely for my own knowledge of how rescue teams manage to remove people from crushed vehicles. But respecting the request of the rescue team for people to vacate the area, I left with some of the other bystanders.

I retraced my steps back to my car, where I had left my daughter and her friend. Amazingly, they had listened and not gotten out of the car as I had requested of them. After turning the car around and detouring another way, I took time to answer their questions. I was thankful their queries did not suggest they were overwhelmed with the graveness of the situation.

Because the woman involved in the accident was "a friend of a friend," I did hear bits of what happened after she was retrieved from the wreck. I know she regained short periods of semi-consciousness. However, in a day or so after the accident she died of complications related to her injuries. Maybe for my own resolution, and to facilitate closure for the other sisters of her religious order, I was able to share with them what transpired at the scene of the accident while we waited for the rescue team. I could reassure the other sisters she was not crying out in pain and people were there offering her support. From what I was told she never regained full consciousness long enough to tell the whole account of what caused her to lose control of her vehicle. Instead, everyone was left to speculate.

A Matter of Time

It was one of those nights that was horrific. A night when living in the moment you thought the events transpiring could not possibly be more dreadful, but each step got worse and worse. It was one of those times which seemed like "the longest night of your life." An occasion where the minutes crawled by and you would love to be any place but where you were. Only being in the mist of the unfolding catastrophe you knew you needed to continue on, you were in too deep. You just hung on for the ride, and hoped for the best. Most of all, you prayed there was an angel sitting on your shoulder, because you knew you needed one. You were dying a thousand deaths and had a gut filled with acid because you knew the events transpiring were not going to end well. If only you could write the story, before the story wrote itself.

It was like being on a perpetual merry-go-round. The hours just seemed to go on and on. Even after the birth, which could not have gotten any worse, the nightmare didn't end. My shift did, but my part didn't. We were now into the early hours of the morning.

The birth we witnessed and labored through with the mother resulted in the delivery of a beautiful newborn. Only the infant that was born was hanging onto life with a single thread. With time, the baby would let go of the thin strand and float away, leaving her grief-stricken parents behind. But first, we all went along on an epic journey, a sad and devastating crossing.

Everything was status quo when I first came on shift. I was assigned to labor and delivery with the usual task of assisting a happy, effervescent couple who were on cloud nine, ready to welcome their first baby into the world. It was a birthing experience I had participated in many times; events I never grew tired of, as each welcoming was different. There was always some little element which made one delivery different from the others.

I by no means perceived one birth as the same as the next nor the same as the last. Each experience was different and special in its own way. When I first received the shift report I was told things were progressing. The couple was doing well. A little augmenting of the labor with oxytocin was underway, but things were moving along, slowly, but surely. She was in early labor, only at the tip of the choppy waters. Eventually, I'd see the expectant mom's smiles change to deep pensive looks, and then to focused frowns. The amplification of her labor pains would be the culprit which would cause her demeanor to change. And in between, she would release some high and low pitched moans. I had seen it before, many times before. It is what I expected. I could predict the course she presumably would take.

As labor and delivery nurses, we've seen the transition in couples over and over, the smiles, the frowns, and then the smiles again. But this night, the early smiles would end. They would not return. The end would not end like most endings. It would have its own finale. And, to everyone's misfortune nothing would go as nature had intended. One thing after another, it was the domino effect. But for this story, let's begin with the baby's delivery.

When the baby was born we were surprised it exhibited any life. The child fought every step of the way into this world. She was clearly exhausted, and rightfully so. A rag doll was what I thought when I saw how limp her body was. The baby was listless, but had a heart rate and was making heroic efforts to breathe. We did all we could as we intubated the infant and placed her on life support. While we worked to sustain her life, others simultaneously made the necessary preparations to life-flight the baby from our facility to a larger tertiary center. Hopefully, one better equipped to care for such gravely ill newborns and that had a highly specialized staff to save the child's life. Even the weather was obstinate that night. Soft white snow was coming down, and had been doing so for quite some time. Visibility was limited. The flight team had been grounded. Only a local ambulance crew believed they could slowly and safely make their way through the blizzard.

The baby was sent out in the snow with the transport team. Mom and dad remained behind. There was no room in the ambulance, even for dad. And the mom, despite her pleas to accompany her newborn, needed to remain with us to stabilize after enduring a difficult and complicated vaginal delivery.

With the child's departure, the overall mood within the obstetrical department was mournful. There were tears along with questions of how this could have happened. There was disbelief. An overall sadness prevailed. We did all we humanly could, and yet we still couldn't change the outcome. We felt as if we had failed.

Being true parents and fearing they were going to lose their child, the only thing this couple wanted was to join their baby at the tertiary center. Following much pleading on the part of the mother, her physiologic state changing from immediate post-delivery to a few hours postpartum, time for road crews to do their magic displacing the fallen snow, and word from the tertiary center the baby would probably not survive served as stimulants for our hospital to arrange transport for the mother via ambulance to the larger medical center. An addendum to this agreement stipulated the new mom would have to be accompanied by one of the obstetrical nurses since she was still at risk for any of the immediate postpartum complications (e.g., hemorrhage) confronting all woman who are "fresh" deliveries.

I had been the primary nurse caring for this couple throughout the evening, from the time one would say she was in active labor, through the delivery, and from beginning to end of the infant's transport. By the time much of this activity had transpired my shift was over, but I had stayed beyond my normal departure time to see things through. The next shift had come in and was busy with other pressing issues and with cleaning up from our evening's plight. As a result, they were short staffed from the extra work left unfinished.

So the unit's recovery efforts meant there were no nurses who could be spared to make the trip with the mother. Either someone would have to be called in, or someone from the prior shift who had stayed to help would need to go on the ambulance run. Who would go? Some thought the answer was obvious. I guess it was, since I had developed a rapport with the family and been with the family through the whole traumatic ordeal. So I agreed to go, and wanted to go.

By the time we left our hospital the snow had let up which allowed the ambulance driver to make decent travel time. We ended up arriving at the tertiary center in much less than an hour. The plan was upon our arrival the new mom would be admitted as a patient to their postpartum unit. That way, like her child, her care would be assumed by the receiving hospital. The transfer of care from our hospital to the new facility meant I would give report of the mother to the receiving staff, and they in turn would update me on the baby's status. Not surprisingly, the summary I received on the baby's condition was not good.

As I had foreseen on the trip down, the trip home was a sad, reflective and lonely one. Sitting in the back of the ambulance, with just me and the stretcher and my thoughts of what I had just seen, made for a long, sad ride. I knew when I saw the infant in the ICU the staff was right. It was only a matter of time before the child would die. As the staff shared, "It's a good thing the mom's here, because it won't be long." All the way home, I thought of their words and wondered if even then the time had come.

Entwined Hair to Entwined Hearts

You know how sometimes when you first meet someone you sense there is something special about the person? There is some type of connection between them and you. You feel the draw, almost like a pulling force somewhere deep inside of you. In a flash, a charge finds its way to the surface, right through your skin pores, causing a strange tingling sensation to sweep over you. You can feel the force, almost like a magnet is drawing you forward. You attempt to repel the unexpected force, sensing if you succumb to the pull you will fly smack up against the equally magnetized person. Wham, you would be body to body! Such a strange sensation! You almost feel confused by how to respond. What should you do? What should you say? Stunned might be a good verb to describe how you feel, not in a bad way, but a good way.

"Stunned," I like the word, it's a good word. The word could be used to describe how I felt when I first met the guy who would become my soul mate. Naturally, I did not expect to meet him when I did. I was doing my own thing, occupied with my own thoughts (so very typical) and somewhat oblivious to what was going on around me. I was headed home for the weekend. Going home was always a welcomed treat. I wasn't able to go often because I either had too much school work or not enough money to pay the bus fare, plus I didn't have a car.

I was happy to have arrived in my hometown, glad the two and a half hour ride was behind me and I could begin enjoying the weekend by visiting family and friends. I was familiar with the bus terminal in my hometown, which was smaller, quieter and less congested than the bus depot in the city where I went to school. Typically when I got off the bus I headed right for the exit to meet my brother who would be waiting in his car to pick me up. I knew he would not be able to stop his car and park while he waited. Any vacant spot would be occupied by cab drivers waiting for potential customers. If he attempted to park, someone from the terminal would wave him on. As a result, he would have to keep circling the block and keep coming back around until I came out of the terminal.

Having to keep circling the block was a royal pain, so I tried to exit promptly. As I was making my beeline exit, clutching my nursing textbooks in one arm and holding the handle of my weekend suitcase in the other hand, and mentally thinking about a thousand different things, I pushed open the exit door with my body. Just as I stepped through the door, a gust of wind blew and wafted my waist length hair off my back, and into the air. Somehow as the door went to close, and my hair was returning to its rightful place a protruding knob on the door caught hold of my hair and inadvertently caused several strands to twine around the knob. My hair tangled so tightly that as I stepped forward I instantly recoiled back with a yank.

A jolt and I halted, right in my tracks. Between the stunned look I must have had on my face, and not having a free hand to deal with my twisted, tangled hair, I must have looked quite "the damsel in distress." Seeing a damsel in distress or just possessing well-bred manners, whichever it was, prompted a masculine voice coming from behind me to say, "Here let me help you."

At first, I really did not get a good look at him because I was too busy trying to help him help me. I was flustered, and desperate to just get my hair released so as to put an end to the embarrassing ordeal. Of course at my youthful age, I thought everyone was looking at me and that I was the center of attention. In all actuality, very few people probably even took note, except a certain someone. I suppose in this incident, it was good someone noticed my predicament because I definitely needed help!

To realize how embarrassing this was, you have to picture my hair so tangled in the bracket my head was pulled up close to the door. I could not move without my scalp hurting. So I truly did need help. My hair was wound so tight, I did not even have the capability to bend, ever so slightly at the knees. Being able to bend would have allowed me to gingerly lower the suitcase I grasped in my hand to the floor. Releasing the suitcase would have provided me a free hand to untangle my hair. I guess I was fated to be stuck in that position, at just that time with a handsome stranger behind me. Who would have thought with my hair caught in a door is how I would meet my special someone? Never in a million years. Anyway, he was lucky. He had his hands free and very little hair to worry about. No tangles for him, he had a military cut styling his head. No sir, no worries, free as can be.

It did not take him long to free my hair so I, he, and the other people stacked up behind us, thanks to "moi," could proceed through the threshold. Once released, I got a good look at the guy who stood before me. My eyes started from his toes up and ascended to the top of his 6'4" frame. I recall my initial response was, "Wow…what a physique this guy has." The shoulders, well, they were something most guys would die for. Complemented with his height, he was one handsome male specimen. Great for a gross anatomy course! No doubt he had to have been a body builder.

Something about me must have gotten his attention as well,

because just on the other side of the doors, he began to make conversation with me. Nonsense stuff I suppose because I really can't recall what we said. I do recall hoping my brother was going to be late and he would have to drive around the block a few times. Sisters can wish those ill-fated nuisances on brothers, it's an inborn right! I wanted more time to talk, and maybe make an impression in hopes we would exchange some form of contact information. As we talked, my rescuer revealed he too was waiting outside for a relative to "swing around" and pick him up.

I did find he recently returned home from a military expedition and was temporarily without an automobile, so his brother was coming for him as well. Lucky me! He would also be departing right away so there would not be much time to become acquainted.

Though good fortune was on our side in one way, it was not in another. My brother pulled up to the curb within a few minutes so we really did not have the opportunity for much conversation. Not even an exchange of telephone numbers. And as for email addresses, well at that time electronic messaging would have been a foreign concept to us. Probably the most information we learned about each other was he was in the military and I was in nursing school. Exactly where I was in school, or where he was currently stationed, we did not get to those essential bits of information.

When I got in the car, my brother commented on the "built on that guy" and how tall he was. I thought, "Yeah, and I'll probably never see him again…just my luck!" As you can imagine, since I stated earlier this guy did become my husband, we would meet again. Fate was even a stronger variable in our second encounter. Truly we were destined. You see, several months went by, probably even a change in seasons when another weekend came, and I had an opportunity to go home. This time the meeting happened on the going end, not the arrival end. So this encounter would be at a different bus terminal, a much larger and more crowded terminal, and one in a city versus a rural setting.

Because this departing terminal was bigger and more chaotic, my routine upon arrival was to immediately take my place in one of the many lines to purchase a ticket. Once I had my ticket, I would then locate the first free seat to sit and wait for my boarding time. Typically for something to do while waiting, I brought a book to read.

I was not looking for any familiar faces, and had my nose in a book so I did not notice "him" sitting amongst the crowd. Later, he revealed he had spotted me as soon as I showed up inside the terminal area. Apparently, he had arrived at the terminal some time before me. He had caught sight of me, watched me purchase a ticket, and take my seat. Those words "some time before me," would define why I have come to believe our relationship was meant to be. You see, in our era of time when customers purchased tickets the bus terminal personnel would stamp a seat number on the stub. As you might have guessed, though we both arrived at different times with some time lapsing between both our arrivals, when we boarded the bus we were assigned two seats next to each other! Window and aisle, perfect!

I had gotten on the bus first, and was settling myself into my seat when low and behold, as the line of people filtered down the tight aisle there he was. Just as I noticed him, he swung his masculine body plop down in the seat next to me. To say I was stunned would be an understatement. Not only did I never expect to see him again, but not on this bus. At the time, I did not know he was stationed in New Jersey while I was simultaneously in nursing school in Philadelphia. He could have been anywhere in the world, as far as I knew. I had only known he was in the military but not exactly where. So there he was, all six foot four of him. We had the seats next to each other, with no one in between, for a heavenly two and a half hours.

Well, one can cover a lot of territory in two and a half hours. We learned a lot about each other. We even found we had common high school acquaintances and lived in neighboring towns. Despite these commonalities our paths had never crossed. Or, at least we thought they hadn't, because we were sure we would have remembered each other with the chemistry we felt between us. Instead, it took a bus, some distance from home, and a little spark of destiny to bring us together.

He confessed he had a premonition I would be on the bus, and when he saw me walk into the station he wasn't surprised, he knew I would be there! After a talkative ride home, we again walked together through those same exit doors which had caught my hair so many months before. This time with him holding the door, and no noticeable puff of air to blow my loose flowing hair, we breezed through the exit chatting away.

Because of the issue of not being able to park and wait for someone outside the terminal, my brother and I had made new arrangements for my pick up. Instead of him trying to time my exact appearance, I agreed to call him when the bus arrived. Once he received my call he would depart to pick me up. My family only lived about fifteen minutes from the terminal so my wait would not be long. But this day, I never did call my brother. Instead, my new friend offered me a ride home. He escorted me to my parent's doorstep, right to the top step! He even got to meet my dog and greet my mother when she answered the door.

Knowing my brother had not left to pick me up my mother was surprised to see I was home, and even more surprised I was not alone. Unlike our first encounter, this time before I arrived at my house we exchanged telephone numbers and other contact information. We were not going to miss our second chance of connecting. So at the steps I said goodbye, but not really goodbye!

I could end here, but I would be remiss if I did not tell you one last piece of this story. At least I always saw this addendum as part of "our" story. You see, we would date for about a year and a half before "this guy" decided maybe it was time to go one step further and ask me to marry him. On the night of this next story, I did not know I would become engaged.

We had not discussed becoming engaged, so of course, as a couple we had not picked out an engagement ring. I had no clue he played detective and investigated my favorite stones, ring setting preference and obtained my ring size. Nor did I know, he was so thrilled with himself and anxious about asking me to marry him, he had shared his intentions and my ring with our housemother and several of my friends, just hours before he popped the question. Unbeknownst to me, they were all ooh-ing and ahh-ing over my ring in our school's infamous community living room, while I was one floor above gathering my bags for a weekend trip home. As I approached the community room, and they caught sight of me, my friends quickly switched the subject to some trivial topic as he slyly tucked the ring away.

Since he was stationed once again in the states, he had purchased his own car which we frequently used to travel the turnpike to visit our families on weekends. During this particular trip home he never mentioned the ring or becoming engaged. Rather, we discussed our social plans for Friday and Saturday. So on Saturday evening when we went to the movies I did not anticipate anything special happening. Rather, I presumed we would see a movie and have dinner afterwards, which was pretty much our weekend routine.

We went to a movie theater where the original Rocky was playing. A little clue to our age! Just before the movie's grand finale he asked me to leave the theater. I couldn't believe he wanted to get up and go before the movie's ending, let alone disturb those immediately around us as we climbed over them to exit the row. To my response of, "I want to see the ending," he whispered, "We can watch the ending at the back of the theater." "Why?" In a somewhat hushed voice I projected back. And, his response which was just as quiet was, "So we can avoid the crowds." "Crowds" I thought…"What's up with that?"

Despite being somewhat annoyed at his request, I went and stood at the back of the theater. At Sylvester's last words, he took my hand and moving quickly, steered me out of the building, across the parking lot and into his car.

Once we were in the car, he asked me to do what I thought at the time was absurd. He asked me to put this white scarf around my eyes in blindfold fashion. Between rushing me out of the theater, and asking me to put a blindfold on, I began to wonder about this guy's sanity. For a fleeting moment, I contemplated if he was perhaps off his rocker, and I was just picking up on his disturbed mental state.

After he mentioned putting the blindfold on, he proceeded to tell me he would drive his car, stop, get out for a short period, get back in the car, drive some more, then stop and come around and get me out of the car. As he outlined the steps in his plan, I caught some of the instructions, but not all of them. I was still trying to process the blindfold bit. So in response to his detailed explanation of what he was going to do, I merely bellowed out, "What...you've got to be kidding, I can't put this blindfold on, what will people think?" I couldn't imagine what people would think if they saw some guy driving around with a blindfolded passenger. Well, being the clever individual he is, he had the perfect solution for my debate..."Just put your head down," he instructed me!

Of course, I pondered whether or not to oblige his request. Finally the light bulb went on and I realized he was attempting to do something special. So when he added, "For once in your life, will you listen to me, and do what I ask?" I listened. But, you know, the comment about not listening, well, that was a surprise to me. I thought I always listened! Me, the perfect "little" girlfriend! Shows, you what I know...just kidding! Well, anyway, something about the way he uttered the words or maybe the sound of his frustration, caused me to put a cork in my mouth. I had no clue what he was up to. I only sensed what he had planned was something unique. Consequently, I agreed to go along with his escapade.

There I sat, in the passenger seat of his car with my blindfold on. Head tucked between my legs so nobody could see me. Thank God, nobody could see me, I thought. As we cruised along I did realize being driven around with a blindfold on and not having a sense of where you are is an odd feeling. Peculiar as the sensation felt, I was still able to distinguish when we were driving through highly populated business areas, as compared to neighborhoods, by the amount of light that passed through my blindfold. Commercial areas were definitely brighter.

He did stop the car at one point and told me he would be right back... and not to peek. Though I was tempted to steal a glimpse, I didn't. Instead, I stayed in the tucked down position and waited for him to return. Talk about trust. This is when you know you love someone. You trust them enough to let them do something like this. Much to my credit, the entire time he was out of the car, I didn't steal a glance. I did not want to ruin what he was working so hard to capture.

True to his word, after a few minutes I heard him open the car door and get in. As he once again settled himself he inquired if I had snuck a look. Why would little old me ever peek? Again, as he had outlined, we continued on our way as I kept my head tucked down and blindfold on. He drove for a little bit and then stopped the car. At this point he assured me he was going to get out of the car, come around, open my door, get me out, hold my hand and walk me a few feet. He went on to explain that once he had me positioned exactly where he wanted me, he would take my blindfold off. When he stopped the car I heard traffic and could sense bright lights, but had no idea where I was. I could not fathom where he had taken me. I simply had no clue. He planned everything, right up to the point where I was standing with my blindfold on waiting for him to take it off.

Did you figure it out? I didn't! Do you know where I was? I was smack downtown in front of the bus terminal where we met. We were standing at the exact bus station doors where my hair had become tangled. We were positioned right in front of those doors when he took my blindfold off. As I was staring up at him, stunned at my surroundings, he got down on his knees and on the busy downtown sidewalk proposed! Now, that is love! And… a little spice of creativity!

Oh…and maybe you have an unanswered question. I did. That's right, why did he stop the car the first time, get out, leave for a few minutes then get back in, and drive away again? Well, after all the initial excitement, and saying "yes," that question came to me. As I started to ask the reason, I knew the answer. At that moment, I noticed something was different about him. He was no longer attired in the blue jean pants and plaid cotton shirt he had on when we ventured out for the evening. Now, he stood before me, debonair as can be in a three piece black suit.

He had gone into a donut shop and changed from his jeans into the suit. He had on full formal attire to commemorate the next half of the evening. Thank goodness I had on a nice dress that evening. We had dinner reservations at an exquisite restaurant to celebrate our new life together. There we would toast too many years of happiness. A union we still share today!

Transports

Flight nursing, was something I always wanted to do, and was my original reason for looking into the nurse corps. However as things worked out, I would not care for people in the air, but would have the opportunity to be part of a land transport team.

I worked in a neonatal unit which "retrieved" sick and/or premature babies from smaller hospitals that did not have the technology, staffing, or specialization to manage the children at their facilities. We, being a larger tertiary center could offer the children such care essentials.

In some healthcare organizations, staff in some specialty units develop a sense of self-importance. Something like what happens between nurses working in intensive care units and nurses working on general medical-surgical floors. Somewhere along the way, some intensive care nurses assume a disposition which suggests they have evolved to a higher level than medical-surgical nurses. An aura seems to infiltrate their being to a degree that they project self-confidence which edges on arrogance. Such an egotistical nature, if not curtailed, can offend others, especially in transport situations.

It's such an arrogant nurse who goes on transport to retrieve a baby, or patient, and makes the relinquishing team feel whatever they did to stabilize the ill individual was in some way lacking. There's an underlying message suggesting the transport team receiving the baby could have done a better job at stabilizing the infant, when in reality the skill of caring for the child may not have been an issue of expertise, but rather of resources.

Having been on both sides, the relinquishing team while working at a small community hospital, and the retrieving side as part of a transport team, may explain why I was always cognizant of not projecting a condescending attitude to the relinquishing staff. Rather, I found these pick-ups a great time to share knowledge, and develop a rapport with other nurses. I also knew that by showing respect for the relinquishing team's gallant efforts they would not think twice about calling us back the next time they needed the assistance of a transport team.

I also remember the adrenaline rushes when ambulance drivers put sirens on and speed down streets. The warning sound and sense of urgency to arrive at our destination made one feel part of something important. Sometimes though, I have to admit, I worried about our own safety. On some occasions, it seemed we would have a driver who in his/her zealous way, rounded corners a little too fast and left all precautions behind. But overall, I loved being part of a team that went on transports to retrieve distressed newborns.

Swish-Swash we Need to Wash

This is another transport story for which we are lucky we

survived and did not have a major accident. Or, potentially cause a mishap for others. On this trip, a group of nursing faculties and I were taking nursing students via a charter bus to spend a day on our state's capitol hill. The students were to meet legislators, learn how healthcare reform proposals progressed from bills to laws, and explore the state's capital. First, however, to get there we had to travel on a bus for about two hours.

We managed to raise money and obtain funding from other departments within the college to rent a charter bus for the day's excursion. Arrangements were made and like any trip, we prayed for clear weather. Unfortunately, despite our hopeful thoughts the weather turned crummy.

What happened was when the bus was about halfway to our destination the weather changed. When we initially got underway, the temperature was cold but there was no precipitation. An unexpected wet snow mixed with sleet began to fall. The mix was the kind of snow which made for great ice balls in snow fights, but not a nice ingredient on a school trip. This combination created a wet sloppy snow which froze easily and adhered to the windshield of the bus. When the driver turned on the wipers to wash the slush away, only one wiper functioned properly. On top of the wiper malfunction, the defroster could not keep up with the condensation forming on the inside of the large bus window. Visibility through the front window on the passenger door side was nonexistent, and the driver's side, though a little better, was also compromised.

The driver was upset and quite apprehensive because he was having difficulty seeing. He radioed his dispatcher to explain the problem but they did not have him stop or initiate an exchange of buses. So, holding our breaths, we trudged ahead at a slow rate. One colleague, who was a little taller than the rest of us, stood at the bottom of the front window and used paper towels to wipe the condensation from the window. She was our internal windshield wiper. She stretched as high as she could and wiped from side to side. She kept her routine up for miles until we finally reached our destination. Thank goodness we had a substantial supply of absorbent paper towels to complement our human wiper!

When we got to the capital, this time I called the bus company and reported the incident. They thanked me for reporting the problem and assured me they would look into the issue. Our poor bus driver, not unlike ourselves, was pretty shaken when we finally arrived. More than likely, if it wasn't for the human wiper blade and one very cautious bus driver, we may never have arrived safely.

Going home was no problem. We had the same conscientious bus driver, the weather had cleared, the fallen snow had melted, and our wipers and defroster were no longer needed. As we headed home darkness began to engulf us, but thank goodness when the driver flicked on the headlights they came on!

Signs

I got lost a fair amount of times. To say it goes with the territory would be true. Every visiting nurse, whether seeing patients within a particular city radius or in a rural area, can expect to become lost at some point. My assigned territories consisted of both urban and rural geographic areas. One could easily get lost finding a house or apartment in the city, just as simple as in the country.

It doesn't take a visiting nurse long to realize there are many streets and alleyways missing well-marked street signs. Those visible landmarks which silently announce, "Here I am, turn here." Some signs just never were put up; some got put up but are no longer there; some are weathered so badly they are unreadable; some the lettering has been altered by someone's hand, or some of the lettering has been painted over; some are hidden behind bushes, trees or buildings; and some have been nicely repositioned so they now face either upside down or are hanging in an awkward unreadable angle.

Well, trying to find one's way can be challenging. You can get to your destination in a timely fashion and have time to care for the person, or you can drive about in circles. Sometimes when lost, by the time you finally arrive at the residence you have little time to spend with the person you were sent to see, and even less time, to spend with subsequent patients. It's easy to suggest, "Why not just call the person when you're lost?" Well...as amazing as it may sound, not everyone has the luxury of a telephone (including a cell phone). There are still Americans in our country living in remote areas that do not have telephone access for one reason or the other. Also, many elderly have difficulty using telephones for various reasons (e.g., can't see the numbers, fingers are to crippled with arthritis to peck the keys, can't remember the number to dial....).

Also, unless directions are obtained prior to the initial visit, and even then, the directions are only as good as the describer, the first nurse to go out to the home records directions for successive nurses. So that means, if you happen to be the nurse doing an initial intake there may be no directions available. Sometimes you could obtain directions from the patient before making the trip, but in some cases their directions included confusing statements like "you know where Joe's old place use to be, at the corner of the old barn, well, you turn there...."

Most times finding a home was no problem, and street signs and directions were not a problem, but sometimes, one could become very frustrated. Today, though, thanks to GPSs direction issues have essentially disappeared. But, on the other hand, the street sign issues still persist. Take note as you drive around how many street signs have related obstacles, which can easily interfere with someone trying to find his/her way!

Surprises

I made many new discoveries during my visiting nurse days. Whether the residence of a person was a house, apartment, one bedroom rental unit, assisted living center, senior high-rise community housing, a housing development, independent living facility, group home.... I quickly realized to never judge the establishment by its appearance. From the nicest home, to the most dilapidated home, I learned to expect the unexpected. I have walked into situations I would never have predicted from the overt appearance of the residence. Two old sayings come to mind: "Don't judge a book by its cover" and "What goes on inside ____ stays inside ____." Lots of secrets wrapped up inside people's homes.

Years have passed since my visiting nurse days. Now, whenever I pass through my old territory I find myself thinking, "I saw someone in that house, in that house, and that house.... I wonder how he/she is doing?...I wonder whatever happened to him/her...Could he/she still be living...Does he/she still live there?" Some sound will interrupt my thoughts, or someone's comment will jolt me back to the present. My thoughts interrupted, I will sigh and then reflect on how as nurses we so often wonder what happened to some of the patients we cared for. It would be nice to know how their life turned out. Did the problem get resolved, or did it get worse? Instead, time passes on and we're left wondering and remembering.

Before I end this chapter, I do have to throw this out there so as to add a little more to the mystique of visiting nurses. This piece illuminated the sense of adventure and what sometimes transpires out in the field to cause a nurse to wonder, "Now why am I doing this?"

At times, it was not the patients we were called to see who were of concern, but instead we worried about other household occupants: pets. These darlings came in all sizes and shapes. Some crawled, some walked, some flew and some hopped. Some were best friends, some were well trained and then some were just plain wild.

There were times we would have to call people to have them put their animals or reptiles away. You know like, "Could you please put your pet snake away, I'll be there in fifteen minutes." Or, you start to ascend the front steps of a house and snarling dogs come from different sides of the house like speeding bullets. You're so shocked by their unexpected presence you stop dead in your tracks. Mice, well lots of people have them around. They can be a pet, or simply a nuisance. However, most times they are just creatures of the territory. We dealt with cows on roads, homes that were overrun with cats, different species of reptiles, pet birds having free flight, house pigs and large pet spiders. You name a pet and some visiting nurse has probably dealt with it. Plus, more than likely, he/she has a related story to tell. But, you know what? Such challenges are what make the tales…our nursing stories.

Taxi Ride

This is one of those stories you keep from your parents until time passes and the events are part of the past. And when you do finally let them in on the story all they can do is listen and be flabbergasted they never knew the incident had happened. They're amazed you never shared the tale before. At the time, you did not evade telling the story to be hurtful, but rather to keep them from literally "flipping out" or "stroking out." How else would parents react knowing their child felt threatened or feared for his/her life? Certainly not calmly!

As this story was unfolding, I could hear my parents' sermons on taking chances. My parents' words of ..."It only takes one time" echoed in my mind. Their words were there, co-joined with the fear which was mounting. I was frightened enough to chide myself for putting myself in the situation. Still, I promised myself if I survived I would change my present approach and take a new route. Next time, if there was a next time, I would find a different way back to my dorm.

Years after the incident, at a Thanksgiving dinner when our family sat around exchanging stories and memories, I told my story. It was only a memory then. But for my parents, the account evoked a disbelief they had not heard the story before, but yet, at the same time they were glad they had not heard about the event as things were unraveling because of the alarm it would have aroused in them.

Only now, being a parent, can I appreciate the not knowing piece. As contradictory as this statement may seem, sometimes as a parent you are better off not knowing when your child is at risk, particularly when the child is an adult and making his/her own way. Parents would experience a thousand deaths if they knew each time their child was involved in some threatening encounter.

Such risks were pivotal to the account I shared that Thanksgiving—a personal danger. My plight transpired because another human being thought invading my space was okay. He crossed personal boundaries.

Some weekends when I went home from nursing school I traveled on a commercial bus. On Friday afternoons when I headed home finding transportation to the bus terminal was no problem. There were plenty of city buses, subways, and taxis available. Most importantly, there were plenty of people about. I just moved with the crowds, getting on and off the city buses. Everyone seemed to be in a hurry to be somewhere for the start of the weekend.

For me, those weekends when I could afford bus fare to go home were special. Going home wasn't something I could afford to do regularly, maybe every three to four weeks. My parents had five children, so extra funds for weekly transportation was not something they had readily available. Therefore, to help my parents with some of my education expenses, and to have money to purchase a bus ticket, I would work some weekends as a nurse's aide.

Going home was something I always held dear. Maybe it was because of the familiarity of my surroundings or because I could forget the demands of nursing school for a weekend. There seemed to be a sense of balance. Things pretty much stayed the same. When I returned, I found people basically doing what they usually did. Our residence didn't change, and my brothers and sisters were still my brothers and sisters, through thick and thin.

Despite circumstances at home not changing drastically, going home felt different. Even my old bedroom took on new meaning. Though my room was not physically changed, I sensed an underlying difference. My old haven was now becoming a place of memories; a tribute to days gone by.

I traveled by city buses on Fridays to make my way to the bus depot. Getting to the terminal translated into standing in crowded bus aisles, swaying back and forth as I grasped on to the bus's overhead security bar, staying alert so I did not miss my stop, and enduring drivers weaving their way through busy city traffic. All this bustling wasn't bad, just part of the weekend exuberance. Plus, my level of tolerance was high. I was going home.

When returning to school on Sundays, I experienced different emotions. I typically put off departing until the last possible minute. However, I could only delay returning for so long because my return was dictated by the terminal's bus schedule. During winter months, the last bus I could take departed at 2:30 p.m. Two and a half hours later gave me enough time to be back in the city before nightfall. The distance from the terminal to my school residence was too far to walk, and since the city buses did not run on Sundays, I took a taxicab back.

There was never a problem locating a taxicab. As a matter of fact, I believe the cab drivers had the bus schedules memorized. At certain times, cabs lined up along the curb just outside the terminal doors. On nights when the temperature was warm, drivers would huddle outside their cabs conversing as they awaited the arrival of weary passengers and potential customers. As passengers exited the terminal doors the cab drivers reminded me of vultures swooping down on their prey. There was competition between cabbies in approaching those exiting so as to be first to "scoop-up" the next customer.

Typically, when I went home for the weekend, I had delusional thoughts I would study on the two and half hour bus ride. If I studied both ways, I could rack up five hours of study time! Inevitably, on my Friday trips home the last thing I wanted to do after a long week of classes was study some more. And, as you might suspect, despite my admirable intentions, I rarely studied on my trips home.

Instead, I would converse with the person sitting next to me or enjoy a nap. I'd promise myself I would study on Sunday when I got back to the dorm.

Sometimes I kept those study promises, and other times, I gave in to distracters. Don't get me wrong, I did keep a regular study schedule. Nursing school is far from easy, and to stay there you have to stay on top of your game. So study you do—and lots of it. But sometimes, when one is a nursing student, a weekend mental break is vital.

Well anyway, I just went through this whole dissertation about studying to make a point. My intent was to explain because of my commitment to pseudo-studying is why I would lug textbooks home with me. Carrying books and my suitcase through the terminal meant I did not have a free hand. Thanks to one arm wrapped around textbooks, and my other hand clutching my weighty suitcase, I would exit through the terminal doors by pushing through them with my backside. Once through the doors, needing a minute's break from carrying my heavy load and to survey the lineup of cabs, I would set my suitcase down on the sidewalk.

One particular night, when I placed my suitcase down on the sidewalk for a mere second, the bag was immediately snatched up. The scooping up of my bag was reminiscent of a hawk after a mouse. As I watched my bag in flight, my brain tried to process what had happened. In that split second as my mind reacted, I acted. In hindsight, what I did next was not wise. Rather, my response was impulsive and not very sensible.

I went after my possession and ended up putting myself in danger, for a suitcase of all things! A replaceable item merely filled with clothes purchased on a student's budget, nothing extravagant. We are talking a student's salary here: no minks and no expensive jewelry. But, you would have thought there was a million dollars in my suitcase because I immediately went after it. Why, because he was taking my belongings. He took something of mine. Within seconds, by the time I mentally processed what just transpired, he was already a distance from me. So I did the "sensible" thing any rational thinking human being would do: I went after him. Right to the cab parked away from the other cabs. Of course, his taxi was not one of the cabs lining the curb. No, his was parked off by itself further down the road and isolated from the others. Nevertheless, I went after my suitcase, my personal property. He opened the backseat door and tossed my suitcase across the seat. Still obsessed on retrieving my bag, I slid into the cab. This guy was fast. By the time I hopped in, he was already around the front sliding into the driver's seat.

Instantaneously, once inside, the fact registered the cab really wasn't a commercial cab, but rather someone's car. Thankfully, I knew some taxicab drivers use their own automobiles and convert them into cabs by simply adding special odometers. Knowing this tidbit of information kept my brain from overreacting. Instead of panicking, I rationalized the man was probably just making a living by starting his own cab service. My misgivings calmed even further when I spotted a large odometer affixed to the dashboard. "Okay," it flashed through my mind, "He's a taxicab driver and not someone trying to steal my luggage." "And maybe, he's just being an aggressive entrepreneur who is trying to solicit business." At least, I was united with my suitcase and had secured a ride back to the dorm.

I appeased my gut instinct that was telling me the whole scenario wasn't right, that something was wrong with the picture. Not listening to my inner voice was a mistake. But you know what, for some reason, I kept patronizing my intuition and waiting for the scene to get back on track. Also, although things seemed to be moving in slow motion, in reality they were transpiring quite quickly.

I heard my inner voice telling me to leave the suitcase, get out of the cab, and go back to the terminal. But my thoughts did not match my actions. We pulled away from the curb and I was still contemplating what I should do. Even then, it crossed my mind to jump out of the cab. We were moving slowly, maneuvering our way into the now dark street. But no, I stayed in the cab and watched as we pulled away, my body pressed against the door and my fingers wrapped around my suitcase handle. I assured myself if I had to I'd jump out the door with my bag in hand.

My mind was active and my thoughts erratic. I could not even recall if he pushed the odometer lever when we pulled away. Was he clocking the miles? I did not know. I only knew he pulled away from where I should have stayed.

The conversation starts. He inquires. "Why are you going to the hospital?" A string of probing questions followed. I tried to answer without giving away any personal information. Echoing in my ears was the warning we all knew, "Don't talk to strangers." I was a little old for the warning, but in this situation I knew it was applicable. I tried to be polite knowing I was in a compromised situation. He was my ticket back to my dorm, my beloved dorm. Plus, the sun had set and we were driving through a less than desirable neighborhood. Not a good place to be dropped off or to jump out of a cab.

In this particular neighborhood I figured if I had to get out of the cab, and walk by myself, I might not be safe. I had two options. I could stay in the taxi and politely evade his questions, or jump out when the vehicle slowed. One option seemed no better than the other. So I sat there numb.

I did not know if his questions were a way of distracting me from noticing our route. I realized the route he was taking was not the same prior drivers had chosen to take. As my apprehension rose (hard to believe it could get any higher), I wondered if he was trying to rack up mileage as an attempt to earn extra cab fare. Thinking such thoughts, made me worry I would not have the extra money to pay the additional charges. I only allotted so much money for traveling. If I didn't have enough to pay, I wasn't sure what I would do.

Along with the fear of not having enough money, a new fear surfaced as his questions continued. His probing became more personal and bold. He asked if I had a boyfriend. I lied and told him I had a fiancé. He wanted to know where my fiancé was and how long we had been dating. I probably stammered over my words, because he then questioned why I was not wearing an engagement ring. I was surprised he had noted from the front seat of the cab that I did not have a ring on my finger. He was clever! I made up some excuse, which seemed a shallow explanation, but one I hoped he would accept and move on. He did move on, but to a new challenge. Would you believe, he then asked me to go out on a date with him? "Now I'm done for," I thought. I reasoned if I said "no," I would probably tick him off and never get back to my dorm, and if I said "yes," then I would be nuts.

This is not the kind of guy one goes out with, especially a guy who might be abducting you. So in the midst of being lost in a strange neighborhood, I refused him. I fell back on the fiancé story. How my fiancé would not appreciate if I cheated on him. Nice try, but my excuse did not work. He tried another approach. "Are you prejudiced?" "Is that why you won't go out with me?" "Do you think you are too good for someone like me?" Oh, my God, this was getting worse and worse, and I was getting in deeper and deeper. "No, no, no…" I assured him, as I pressed closer against the door with one hand on the door knob. I was not prejudiced, that had nothing to do with why I would not go out with him. I reinforced I had a boyfriend and was happy with him.

What a mess! I felt like I was drowning and just about holding my head above water. But one reassuring thing happened. I began to recognize some familiar sights. He was taking me home! We were going in the right direction and he wasn't planning on abducting me. Maybe, I just had an overactive imagination. We just had a little further to go. At least now, I knew a new way home. You can get through this, I assured myself. Just stay calm, don't upset him, and stick with the boyfriend scenario.

What a long and unnerving ride. In the end, he did pull up outside our dorm building. Yes, my cab fee was more than usual, but not much more, I could cover the cost. I gladly paid the extra money, anything to get out of his cab. As I paid the charge, I wondered what he would do with the information of now knowing where I lived. Would he leave me alone? I hoped so, as I vowed in the future to find other means of transportation back to school.

D.C. Runs
Just those little things…..

Half of our class was in Washington, D.C. to do our mental health rotation. For some of the girls with boyfriends back in Pennsylvania, heading home to Philadelphia at least every other weekend was top on their agendas. For others, having an opportunity to go home to see family was also inviting, so many spent free weekends traveling the turnpike. With little money to spend on transportation we pooled our cash for gasoline and highway fees. One of our classmates, the only student with a car in D.C., had a boyfriend back in Philly so she made frequent trips back and forth. On the trips she appreciated having company, which worked out in everyone's favor. When we were making our "D.C. to PA runs," she drove a Chevy Vega which was a popular vehicle at the time.

The only problem was this compact car only fit four comfortably. If everyone was fairly thin, one additional person could squeeze in the back seat, but space would be tight. Fitting five meant nothing to us. We were on a mission when we wanted to go home. How we fit as many as we did, I am not sure. We crammed probably seven into her car. Sitting on laps and sitting on top of one another we managed to achieve the needed traveling space.

Seat belts, yeah, they were there, but we didn't use them. We took the risk. A safety risk I would say today was pretty dim-witted of us. We paid little attention to the seat belt detail so we could all fit in the car. Heck, we were young adults with that invincible mentality. Truthfully, it was more like we had angels on our shoulders. Luckily, we were not in an automobile accident or pulled over by the highway patrol. We had some amusing moments on those trips. They were fun-filled times which built friendships and made for entertaining stories.

I particularly recall one time in which we never expected to make it home without first being pulled over by a police officer and given a ticket. Since money was always an issue for everyone in nursing school, our friend with the Vega rarely had extra cash to fix little things which broke on her car. To us, the fact these items were not fixed was no big deal. All we were concerned about was if the car's motor could make it up the highway.

This time, as we were traveling along the beltway, we started to hear this odd clanking sound. Pulling over we jumped out to see what was causing the noise. What we found was one of the car's front headlight fixtures, which had been jimmied into place, had fallen out of the socket and was dangling by wires. The clamoring noise was caused by the light banging against the car fender.

We had no string, no wire and no logical way to temporarily reset the light. And naturally, darkness was approaching so we would soon need to utilize the car lights. What other time would such a dilemma occur? Certainly not during broad daylight, when car lights weren't needed!

What creative device could a bunch of females come up with to solve the problem? Something we had access to, were familiar with, and had on us. For us, the practical answer was pantyhose! Amongst us, we had plenty of pantyhose tucked away in our overnight bags. So we tied several pairs together like a rope. And, "voila" we had something temporary to secure the light in place! Of course, we imagined everyone on the freeway could see our panty hose solution, and we would indubitably be pulled over and fined. We did not think we would be in as much trouble for the headlight stunt, as we would be for violating the law with so many bodies in the car, and bodies without seatbelts!

We had our little jokes about the situation, which kept us laughing and chuckling on the way home. Despite all the comic anecdotes we knew we would be charged with major violations if we were pulled over. We were breaching a number of safety rules, but we were young and just wanted to get home. Imagine the report the cop could have made if he/she pulled us over and had to bring in seven student nurses, each minus a pair of panty hose!

First Wheels

More memories...recollections of events which may not have seemed memorable or nostalgic at the time, but now with the passing of time are remembered differently. The frustration and fear are no longer evident, but have faded with time. Instead, we are left with humor and now can laugh at the "good old times."

Our stories bind us. They are common threads, which years later link us together. They are what we laugh about. They are the pillars of our "remember when" stories. The events seem like yesterday. Yesterday, when the four of us lived in an apartment and we each purchased or acquired an automobile for transportation to our jobs.

Me, I had a royal blue Mustang, a Mustang Gia, to be exact. Unfortunately, one could not win a race in my mustang. Just turn a corner and there was a 50 percent chance the car would stall. Certainly not a trait my car exhibited the first months of purchase, but revealed in time. Was my Mustang brand new, fresh out of the showroom? Of course not, I was living on a new graduate's salary, a beginning salary. There was no nest egg when I graduated. Nor did my parents have the extra money to buy me a new car or help me with payments. My parents still had my younger brother and sister at home in the midst of their high school years and anticipating college in the near future. I had my knowledge and my diploma as my "money in the bank."

I could not afford one of those nice shiny, reliable, brand spanking new models. No, my first car would be a model bought from a used car lot. An automobile the "honest" dealer would guarantee was the perfect car for a young lady. One he would assure me was totally reliable, "won't need a thing" and "you'll have nothing to worry about."

My Mustang was shadowed by another roommate's Volkswagen

Bug. That car was unbelievable. I believe it was handed down from one of her brothers. Despite having no heat, a poorly functioning defroster, and the car sometimes needing a push down an incline to start, the car never died.

So what do I remember most about our cars? I recall the times we worried whether our cars would get us to work. Times of seeing our breath and hearing our teeth chatter as we endured the cold without a heater. I recall worrying whether I would be plowed in the rear as my Mustang stalled in the middle of a turn. But now, all these old memories cause us to laugh as we tell our "can you remember when" stories....

Keys

Driving home after one's shift was a good time to unwind, especially after a hectic night. This particular night was one of those fast-paced, chaotic times when we did not stop running all night. I can't remember if I had an opportunity to eat supper that evening, or ate on the run as we often did on busy nights.

We were inundated with post-operative patients and admissions. The only uplifting part of the evening was when the next shift started filtering in. A welcoming sight, a reminder the evening was coming to an end and we would soon be heading home. On busy nights such as this one, you commonly left at the end of the shift praying nothing had been missed or a mistake made. I remember one hectic night when something vital did get missed.

The shift had finally ended, but I was still in overdrive. After hectic nights it usually takes me some time to wind down. My trip home from this job was approximately an hour's drive so I had time to level out and regroup before arriving home. The first part of my drive was spent recounting the evening's events and conducting a mental self-check to validate if I completed what was expected. This night, as I was going over the evening's events, I realized we had forgotten to do the change of shift narcotic count. Counting narcotics was a ritual RNs did at the end and beginning of two shifts. Basically, the task consisted of counting narcotic medications in the medication cart or cabinet to be sure all narcotics, used or unused, were accounted for.

This night, as I was driving home cognitively recapping the evening events, I could not recall completing the narcotic count. Things had been pretty turbulent, so much so, that getting through the shift report had been a task. Did we forget? Could we have been so distracted we forgot to do the narcotic count? Did someone else do the count, and I just didn't notice? Did I hand off the narcotic keys to someone?

"Could I still have the keys…Oh my, gosh, they're in my pocket!' "I can't believe I have them! How did we forget to do the count… it's a routine we do all the time? How will the patients get their pain meds?" This means I have to turn around and go back. I'm so tired, but I have to return the keys. They won't be able to open the narcotic box if I don't. They're probably frantic right now, trying to find the keys. But hey, at least I didn't get all the way home before noticing the missing keys.

I was about thirty miles past the hospital and it was already close to 1:00 a.m. We had not left the unit until after midnight. Unfortunately, unlike today when this episode transpired, cell phones weren't commonly owned by the general public. I couldn't just use my cell phone to alert the new shift I had the narcotic keys and was on my way back. No… it wasn't so easy. I would have to find a phone booth somewhere at 1:00 a.m. to notify my colleagues I was returning. Finding a place to make the call was not easy, since the road I was traveling was not densely populated. Consequently, I figured my best course of action was to head straight back, and if I happened to see a phone booth, stop and make the call (which I never did).

When I walked on the unit, the night shift nurses were in the process of looking for the keys. Clearly they were grateful to see me with keys in hand. My return saved them from continuing their search when activity on the unit was already in full swing. If I had not gone back, I would have worried all night. I would have felt I was letting the patients down and causing my peers undue stress.

Making the mistake of taking the narcotic keys almost home never happened again. I learned to empty my uniform pockets before leaving the department. And serendipitously I found at the end of the night, one often finds a collection of gadgets lining their pockets.

Today finding narcotic keys tucked away in uniform pockets is unlikely. Many facilities are using keyless computerized medication systems. Being keyless means narcotic keys are no longer necessary, and have become tokens of the past.

Monkey in the Middle

This is a short account, but is it relevant enough for me to share? I believe so, because at the time the incident was significant to me. The event touched me so deeply, I can still visualize the scenario, and recall the unease it provoked. Ask me the exact date, and I will not be able to recall that detail. But ask me the event, and that's simple. The occasion was the morning I was traveling to take my nursing state boards after graduating from the diploma nursing program I attended. I was driving by myself, focused on keeping my anxiety under check because it was "the big day" and I wanted to do well on the examination. Obtaining a passing score would mean I was authorized to use the title Registered Nurse.

In my blue Mustang I was heading for a testing site about an hour and a half south of my home. I had never driven the route so I left my home early enough to allow extra travel time. However, despite my precautions I still was apprehensive something would go wrong and make me late. I feared making a wrong turn, getting lost, and arriving at the testing site to find the doors locked because the exam was in progress. Just a little something I gave myself to agonize over! This of course, was before the time geographic navigational systems became common household commodities. Instead, I had an old fashioned road map to guide me.

So map, mug of hot tea, a little apprehension, directions from a friend and some soothing radio music, and I was on my way. The roads I was sent on wined around mountainous terrain. It was a route truckers used to bypass turnpike traffic, particularly if there was road construction.

The twisting and bending of the road around the hilly mounts was dangerous. Any responsible driver would gladly heed to the posted speed limit signs. Some of the truckers I believe possessed more self-assurance in their driving skills than the authorities who specified the speed limits. Some of the haulers seemed to round the curves at a greater velocity than the posted speed regulations. I found being part of this fast flowing mix a bit unnerving.

Two truckers in fairly large rigs decided, most likely via their CB radios, to break up their monotonous drive with a little fun, of which I was the target. They were the tag team and I was to be the "monkey" in the middle. On a section of straight highway, both truckers made their way over to the lane I was traveling in, and locked my faithful Mustang between their rigs. One traveled in front of me, and one behind me. They kept up a good speed causing me to feel like I was being pushed up the highway.

Being locked between two vehicles I had nowhere to go. I could not slow down because the truck at my rear would have rammed me straight into the back end of the truck in front of me. Any wrong move and me and my Mustang would be crushed like an accordion. I'm sure watching their stunt play out they were having a hoot communicating back and forth on their CBs. They locked me in their clutches for about five miles before they decided to end the game. I guess they grew tired of the diversion, or maybe heard on their CBs there was a "bear" lurking about.

For them the game might have been laughs and giggles, but for me my heart was pounding. I was definitely sweating, and about to jump out of my skin before they finally decided to break up their clutch.

Their little act only added to my pre-state board examination jitters. My saving grace was I still had a fair number of miles to travel before I reached my destination. Time I could use to calm and refocus. The worst part of the experience was nobody I knew was there to witness what happened or share the experience with me. And of course, telling the story later would never hold the same impact as living it. So…it just happened. And, I am thankful I survived. Simply, a memorable account which is a recollection of my state board testing day!

Caution, Dads at Work

"Drive slow, my daddy works here" are words posted on construction site signs to caution drivers who have a tendency to speed through work zones. When I drive past these signs, the words resurrect an image of three small children in my mind. All three youngsters were probably under the age of six.

They made a beeline, right into the living room when they heard the opening of the rusty hinged screen door. They came in force. To see what I had come to do, to see who had come to disturb their dad. "Was he okay"…and, "What was this stranger about?" Their words were never actually voiced, but they resonated in the air. They were standing guard. Their father was in agony and a stranger had come into their house. Mom was somewhere about the house so they were the first to dash, as children do, into the room.

I could see him lying in his hospital bed in the living room, now bedroom, as I approached the screen door. He was lying there with most of his thin body suspended in traction. A step through the threshold revealed a man who appeared much older than his stated thirty-five years. His ordeal had aged him, so much so, he could now pass for the grandfather of these children rather than the father. He was tired: tired of being in bed, tired of being out of work, tired of not being able to play with his kids, tired of seeing how exhausted his wife had become, tired of having others care for him and tired of needing his pain medications to get through the day. Why, because someone did not heed the drive slow signs posted in the work area. Instantaneously, he had become the victim of a hit and run accident.

Knowing he was a hit and run victim only made him feel worse. Someone had hit him and taken off. So now it was questionable whether he would walk again. He already knew he would never be able to return to his utility job; he now was too disabled to resume this line of work. So there was despair. Despair in his eyes, in the eyes of his wife, and those of his children.

In an instant, and in the hands of another, their lives had been altered. How drastically their lives would eternally change, I would never know. But when I saw him, I would have bet the transformation was going to be life-altering.

Thunder

Sometimes illness brings people together, and sometimes it makes them pull away. Sometimes people send cards with kind words, and others come together and pray. Sometimes people turn to religion, and some turn away. Sometimes people see miracles in minute change, and others mistakenly interpret reflexive behavior as positive change. Sometimes people express their support through monetary contributions, and others through sacred medals. And others, like bikers, well they give through their cycles. They ride with pride, for the person they sponsor. Nothing compares, except maybe also being a rider, to watching a fleet of motorcycles roar by in thunder. All on a ride to raise money for someone's loved one; a contribution from the heart.

Sailing the High Seas

Reflecting on transportation stories makes me think of another inner aspiration I have. I suppose the desire to travel and to experience new adventures lives within me. Along with dreams of being a flight nurse, I have always thought of trying cruise line nursing. You know the image of standing on deck of a large luxurious cruise ship, with the ocean breeze blowing through one's hair, as the ship courses the blue waters to some exotic island.

Standing there one feels that refreshing and exuberant feeling which sweeps to the core of one's being. The sensation is manifested as one stands at the ship's railing and takes in a refreshing breath of ocean scented air. If one closes their eyes, an almost natural response when looking out over glittering water, and draws a breath, they can visualize the salty air being pulled into their being. The flow of air up into the nostrils drifts lightly down the back of the throat and proceeds to the chest. In the upper chest, the wisp of air hovers for a millisecond then settles ever so gently in the gut of the abdomen. The air lingers, and drifts about, forming a circular puff-ball before converging and moving down. Almost in a funnel shape, the floating breath of air begins to filter down....down into the lower pelvis where it collects then splits in two. A tributary descends to the left and to the right. The strips of air now course down each thigh, coming to rest in the knees—like small clouds drifting about. There is a tingling, as puffs of air once again thin out and float down the legs. The soft air streams continue downward where the original breath of air settles, ever so gently in the very tips of the toes. Now at its final resting place, it lingers than slowly dissipates once again into the salty air only to be followed by yet another invigorating breath of air. With this inner cleansing, one feels exuberant. Life seems to have taken on a new tranquility, a new inner peace.

Of course, one can experience such pleasures as a cruise line nurse, yet still attend to their nursing responsibilities with the highest priority. At least in my mind one could. Truly, work should be both fun and rewarding. Ah, so easy to let the mind wander to the finer things of life.

In truth, this is probably an exaggerated and romantic image. I imagine healthcare providers working on cruise ships can be extremely busy with the volume of people traveling. More than likely, providers have little time to leisurely stand on deck breathing in fresh, tranquil air. But it's a dream, and a nice one at that. Don't you agree?

My dream of becoming this romantic cruise line figurine has

faded over the years. However, even in the passing of time, I still hold on to that spark. Though now there is a different picture to my vision, a somewhat tamer one, a mature one! Today, when I think of being on a cruise ship, I see myself as a nurse, but not one standing at the bow of the ship catching the breeze in my windswept hair. Rather, I visualize myself sitting in a chair, below deck, listening tentatively to some motivational speaker enlighten me on the finer qualities of our profession. I am earning continuing education credits from a specialty expert.

Only now, I have a fear. My new trepidation...the ship might wreck and I could find myself in shark-infested waters. Imagine that! Maybe cruise line nursing is a fantasy I have to put to rest. Well, for some less fearful nurses, the profession still holds those buccaneer options!

Gas

This story has a little twist to where it is placed in this book. Many of the stories I have told have a serious side, some a learned lesson and then some have elements of humor. This is one of those stories, though it has a serious undertone, there is humor. By placing this short account in my transportation chapter, I am jesting. Really this episode does not relate to the type of gas one uses for automobiles, or any other form of transportation, but is rather associated with the gas or flatus humans, being creatures of normal physiologic functions, commonly pass.

The individuals in this event happened to be myself as a clinical faculty member, a student nurse whom I was observing perform a procedure, and an elderly male with an underlying diagnosis of confusion. We were at the man's bedside, in the process of treating his leg ulcer, which was a complication of his diabetes, when this memorable moment transpired.

The student had learned all about treating diabetic leg ulcers in the classroom, simulated dressing changes in the nursing learning lab, been passed on the procedure and was now performing the skill at the patient's bedside for the first time. So naturally, she was nervous for never having completed the skill on a human, and secondly because she was doing the procedure for the first time with a faculty member hovering. As faculties, we all know most students would love to omit doing their first bedside attempt, of any procedure, with their clinical faculty member standing alongside them. Can't blame them, I was always nervous when being watched.

As I typically do in such learning experiences, so as to ease some of the student's anxiety, I instructed the student to gather all the necessary supplies to do the dressing change, had her talk with the patient about what she was going to do (despite her patient being confused), and then had her lay out all the supplies, using sterile technique needed for completing the procedure. I would send students off by themselves to complete these tasks, hoping by the time I came into the room some of their anxiety would be defused. With their apprehension in check, I anticipated they would be able to proceed with greater confidence and focus less on my presence. Only this time, I guess my well-intended approach wasn't quite successful.

All was correctly in place when I joined the student in the patient's room, so we commenced with the procedure. I would say we were only into the process for about a minute when the student, as she proceeded, began to pass a string of flatus. The student made no comment, the patient excused himself for the sound of the gas he thought he passed, and I not expecting to hear this puttering sound, said nothing and acted like I heard nothing. But then, there it was again and again...throughout the entire dressing change.

Of course, after enough episodes there was no doubt where the sound originated from. But what really made it laughable (of course to myself) was every time the student would pass the trumpet sounding wind, the confused patient would excuse himself for passing the gas. Really it was comical! Other then, the patient apologizing, the student worked through the procedure as if nothing out of the ordinary was happening. Me, I continued to observe silently, but snickering inside. The whole ordeal was quite laughable.

Only after the student finished, put her supplies away and we were leaving the room did she acknowledge the passing of gas. What she said was, "I am sorry about passing gas during the procedure, but when I get nervous I get gassy. It always happens to me."

Chapter Eight

TREASURES

Don't judge each day by the harvest you reap but by the seeds you plant.
(ROBERT LEWIS STEVENSON)

Words

"Hey, Brenda...congratulations," greeted the hospital's security officer as I passed him on my way into the building for work.

"Congratulations, for what?"

"You were in the newspaper."

"What?"

"In the editorial section...a lady wrote in thanking you for the care you gave her. She shared you were exceptionally nice to her."

"Really... thanks." I was perplexed. I could not recall a recent event that would strike someone so deeply that they would take the time to write to a newspaper about, and I was equally surprised the guard knew my name since we mainly only exchanges greetings of "hellos" and "goodbyes."

I walked away figuring he was mistaken and the newspaper article must have been referring to someone else. As I made my way to my unit, I heard similar comments by other coworkers, so I decided to check out the editorial. Sure enough, the woman had to be writing about me. She knew my first name, had the right unit, right hospital, and correct shift. Plus, there was not another person with my same first name who worked on our unit.

Though it was complimentary to read this woman's praise for the care and personal one-on-one attention I gave her, I was disappointed she did not singularly stand out in my mind. I recollected a similar situation she described, but I could not say for sure whether I had the right incident in mind. Regrettably, if enough time lapses between patients, picking out one person's story can be difficult unless something exceptional transpired. Somewhat like the stories I am telling, wherein something special happened enabling me to vividly recall details years later. If such a connection does not happen, many faces fade with the passing of time.

It did feel good to know I made even a small difference in someone's life. Sometimes as a nurse, when day after day you do what you do, you begin to wonder if you are making an impact. You wonder if you have become toughened to your everyday nursing life. Does your job end up becoming just a job and you lose that special touch? Fortunately, some incident usually comes along and erases those mounting self-doubts. Once again, you know you are doing the right thing. You have pursued a fitting profession.

I believe the woman who took the time to write the thank you letter, and actually submitted it to the newspaper should be complimented as well. Many people have admirable intentions of doing such deeds but never quite get around to the task. Once time and distance take them away from the situation such plans easily become displaced with life's everyday demands. So, I say to her, and to all the others who have done the same: Thanks for taking the time to say "thank you!"

Jewels

As a team we went down the hall asking patients to look in their beds. We turned those who could not move to search their beds and back-tracked my steps. "Who did I care for last?" "Who did I recently reposition...Where could it be?" We knew despite our looking it could easily be missed. Perhaps, if it just sparkled ever so slightly we might find my valuable possession hidden amongst someone's sheets.

We had just finished giving back rubs to everyone who wanted, or needed one. Sleeping pills had been administered to those who requested hypnotics. Now with my discovery, we might have to disturb everyone, unless the item surfaced in the first room. Otherwise, as lights were turned on, we would be bound to awaken many of those individuals just beginning to doze. Or worse, startle some awake with our sounds, flashlights and touches.

Clearly my other option, instead of arousing everyone was to accept my loss and move on. Only part of the original was missing, so all was not lost. There was also the possibility someone would find my prized gem the next morning and turn it in. However, accepting the object might never be found without even an attempt to search seemed unacceptable to me.

I had only owned the item for about a month. Aside from its monetary value, it had sentimental significance. I realized the one missing piece could be replaced fairly easily, but not without a substantial monetary cost. Then again, in my mind, replacing the one original piece would cause the entire item to seem tarnished in some way, even if by a technicality. The setting would never be the same, an original piece would be gone.

I was not sure exactly where it had fallen. Nor, did I know how much time had lapsed. What I did know was it happened within a six hour span of time. I knew it had been intact when I started my shift, which meant it had to be somewhere on our unit. I had not left the department, even for dinner.

As we were congregating to write our final nursing notes and the evening's pace was at last winding down, I happened to look at my hands. With a shock, I noticed one of the diamonds which sat on one side of the central sapphire stone of my engagement ring was missing. I got a sick feeling in my stomach. I could feel my heart skip a beat as I thought of my fiancé's pride when describing the value of the ring. Now, I wondered how I would tell him one of the diamonds from the ring dislodged and was lost. I knew he would understand and take it in stride, but I would feel badly.

I had to find the stone. We had to retrace my steps. At least we had to make an attempt. Within no time, almost everyone within our unit, including some patients, started looking in their own beds and in their rooms.

Patients were giving back to me. I had helped them earlier in the night, now they were helping me. For the immobile patients, well they got some extra turns. A little added precaution against bed sores.

The supplemental turning paid off because while we were boosting a patient up in bed, we found the diamond tucked within the sheets winking back at us. The stone must have fallen out when I gave the gentleman a back rub and straightened his sheets for the night.

We were truly amazed we recovered the stone. In actuality, we never thought it would surface. Looking for such a small item, in such a large unit was like looking for a needle in a haystack. Once found, I had the diamond replaced in the original setting where the diamond has remained steadfast. Never again has the jewel fallen from its ornate throne.

There was another time I lost a ring, but this keepsake was never retrieved. I believe my possession went for a ride down the laundry chute. The ring symbolized what I had achieved. Hard work, tears, laughter and joy were embodied within that ring. It was my nursing school ring. The ring was silver with a mother of pearl stone in the center. The sides were etched with the school's crest and coat of arms. Affixed on top, in the center of the mother of pearl stone was a small silver medical insignia. It was a stunning ring!

Each groove and every symbol was a representation of the tradition of our program; a replica of the accomplishments of many. Now, these same rings which some graduates may still possess are even more unique since the nursing program, and reason for the ring, no longer exists. Over 100 years of educating nurses has come to an end. We were a tribute to the many stellar nurses who graduated over the years. All of us exemplified the school's high standards and esteemed values. Today, some might perceive the ideals we were taught a little extreme or confining. Perhaps some would define the values we held as stifling our free choice or that critical thinking was subdued. At the time, though, the teachings reflected the nursing code of standards. We were taught qualities that defined nurses, what nursing was.

Anyway… back to losing the ring. I am not sure exactly which night I lost the ring, although I do think I know how it was misplaced. At the time, I worked in a newborn nursery so as a nursery nurse we went to the operating room for all Cesarean deliveries to "receive" babies at birth. Going to the operating room meant changing out of my personal scrubs and into another clean set of scrubs supplied by the hospital. Once dressed for the OR, a thorough scrubbing from fingertips to elbows was protocol. Whenever I scrubbed, I would take off my class ring and put it in the breast pocket of my OR attire for safe keeping. Some female nurses would secure their rings to the outside of their scrubs by clasping a safety pin to a bra strap beneath their scrub tops. Me, I would pop the ring into my breast pocket and leave it there until after the delivery. And then afterwards, I'd put it back on. Today, being wiser, if I wore my ring at all, I would utilize the pin approach, just to be safe!

Well, I did forget. At least I think I did! More than likely what happened was I forgot the ring in my pocket on a night when an unhealthy baby was born and we were consumed with stabilizing the child. My mind was probably thinking about a thousand other concerns and not about the ring in my breast pocket. I am sure when

I finally changed out of my OR scrubs I failed to empty the breast pocket. Instead, being exhausted I merely rolled up my scrubs, put them in the laundry bin, and left. Later, when someone sent the laundry bag sailing down the laundry chute there went my ring concealed in the scrub's top pocket.

Exactly when, and in what laundry bag my class ring sailed down the shot is a mystery. When I finally realized my ring was missing from its place in my jewelry box I checked with the laundry department at the hospital. Naturally, with no specific details, and an unknown amount of lapsed time, my ring was never found.

Fondly Named

At one time in my career friends affectionately nicknamed me "Taber's". Some may recognize the name "Taber's" and understand the association, but for those unfamiliar with the reference book, let me explain. You see, Taber's is the name of a commonly used medical dictionary often found on reference shelves in hospitals and in other healthcare entities.

A few of my colleagues gave me this nickname because whenever someone on our nursing team had a question, to which none of us knew the obvious answer, instead of just blowing the question off I would say "let's look it up." I did not solely use the Taber's dictionary to find answers, but rather used whichever textbooks or journals we had on the unit. Keep in mind at this point in my career we did not have computers at our work stations (nursing stations) to "Google" answers. We predominantly used textbooks housed on the nursing unit to search answers. Unfortunately, many times because of unit budgets, the references were often dated or limited in number.

I earned the nickname because I took the time to look questions up. Referencing questions was my way of learning. By taking time to look items up, I could then answer questions posed by my friends. In turn, this practice prompted colleagues to seek me out with other questions. Naturally, doing this over time built my knowledge base and caused some of my peers to see me as smart in terms of medical/nursing knowledge. Since the nickname was somewhat complimentary, I never minded being greeted with "Hey, Taber's."

M&Ms

No matter how much someone prepares a person for seeing the surgical changes in their abdomen following this particular surgery, especially with the initial swelling, there is a sense of shock. "How will I ever survive this" must be a common reflection.

The whole concept must be life altering. In this story I am thinking of a man who most of his life wore pro-boxing shorts because of his career. Now in his sixties and retired from the boxing arena, he talks of how he once had a flat, well contoured abdomen that was rippled with muscles. He recollected how people use to admire his solid physique. But now, his finely sculptured abdomen had been altered by the surgical blade. Today when he peers at his abdomen what he sees are scars, a stoma and a colostomy bag looking back at him. A "bag" he is told he would have for the rest of his life.

He knew somehow he would need to learn to manage his bag without the support and guidance of his wife. She had passed away several years before he became ill and his body began to change. Now he talked of how he would have to battle this match on his own. He assured me he was a "fighter" and was not about to be beaten by this new opponent. Instead, he was resigned to the challenge. He was ready to "dance."

I did not meet him during his initial stay when the abdominal surgery was first performed. Rather, I met him on re-admission several days after he was discharged following the surgery. In morning report I was told he was returning because he was having problems managing his new colostomy and performing stoma irrigations. He needed someone to spend time with him and instruct him on how to self-manage his stoma appliances.

In the hospital where this man was being cared for, and where I worked, there was not a certified ostomy nurse. The staff did not have the luxury of picking up the telephone and calling for a consult with a colostomy specialist. Instead, nurses and doctors offered advice. For the already anxious person, such teaching approaches can translate into confusion. Typically with multiple teachers, patients hear conflicting and inconsistent information which cause them to feel overwhelmed. This man was no exception. Before I knew just how discombobulated he felt, and how unprepared he was to care for his colostomy, I was introduced to him in what he later defined as a "very embarrassing predicament."

It was early morning and when he awoke he found his colostomy bag had fallen off during the night and the semi-liquid contents had spilled onto the bed sheets. Even worse for him was the offensive odor permeating the air.

I met him when I was making my morning rounds to check on those patients I was assigned. When I first saw him he could not apologize enough for what his body had done. He was mortified I would have to help him with "his mess."

While controlling my response to the pungent aroma in the air, I suggested we immediately start with his morning care. I proposed he shower and later I'd return to show him how to manage his colostomy.

I looked forward to sharing with him what I knew about colostomy care. I considered myself fairly knowledgeable and current on what care supplies and appliance options were available. At an earlier point in my career, I had the opportunity to spend time with an ostomy nurse. This specialist had shared many secrets of the trade with me and taught me about different ostomy devices. I had enjoyed learning from this specialist and from the clients she worked with. Most of the recipients were genuinely grateful someone took time to work with them. As a result of my positive experiences, I found I enjoyed this part of nursing and considered becoming an ostomy nurse specialist. In the end, though, I settled for being ostomy knowledgeable.

As I promised, I spent time sharing my expertise with this man so he would feel confident in his own care. As part of our general conversation we talked about favorite foods. I shared one of my favorite snacks was peanut M&M candies. Love those crunchy, hard shelled candies!

Feeling secure in his new self-care abilities my new friend was discharged. Hospital life went about its normal course: patients were discharged, new patients were admitted and one day rolled into the next.

Several weeks had gone by when one day I was called on the intercom system to come to the nursing station. When I rounded the corner, there he stood with a big smile of greeting and holding a glass canister full of M&Ms. A priceless gift he extended to me in gratitude for "all I had done." He truly surprised me by recalling my confession of loving peanut M&Ms and for taking the time to stop by with such a precious gift.

Tatting

She was not one of the clients I typically saw. Whenever her regular nurse, Ann, had some other assignment or was off for the day, this elderly woman's visit would be scheduled for later in the afternoon when I came on duty. She had a multitude of problems, all related to the systemic and inflammatory manifestations of rheumatoid arthritis.

During the early phases of the disease process, she developed her own self-help protocol for delaying the crippling effects the disease had on her hands and fingers. Maintaining some degree of digital function was foremost in her mind. To her, loss of the use of her hands and fingers meant succumbing to arthritis. So to maintain hand movement she developed a plan and adhered to the daily regime.

We knew what to expect when we made a visit to her home. There would be the occasional mouse scurrying across the floor, the offer of a slice of homebaked cake or cookies, and the odor of urine permeating the air. The mouse we would just ignore, he was now her pet. The food we would politely refuse, always with the excuse of having just eaten, no matter the time of day. And the odor, well, we would evaluate the degree of incontinence and determine whether she could continue to maintain her independence, or if additional services were warranted.

Since she had ongoing issues, the agency staff saw her pretty regularly. Ann being her primary nurse was the recipient of several of the woman's "special gifts." The elderly woman spent hours manipulating a tatting needle with her fingers to create beautiful trim work she adorned to the edges of floral handkerchiefs. Every visit, she would reiterate how vital it was she continue her tatting craft, her therapy.

Over time she developed a beautiful collection of handkerchiefs she proudly showed visitors. You knew she appreciated something you had done when she kindly presented one or two of her prized gifts to you. Not a costly item, but a nursing treasure. I have two of her tatted masterpieces, nested in my memory box.

Rose Scented

The rose scent greeted me as I opened my office door. Twelve ruby red buds in full bloom elegantly displayed in an ornamental floral vase were placed on the center of my desktop. I was surprised when I saw the arrangement. A gift I had not anticipated.

This day, though an eventful one, did not conjure up the joys and thrills which usually relates with receiving flowers. It was a day of firsts, but not the kind which leaves one jubilant. I was about to deliver my first nursing lecture to a classroom of excited nursing students. Anticipating the unexpected, I wasn't thinking flowery thoughts. My thoughts were more like: "Why did I think I could do this?" "I hope I have everything" and "What if they ask me a question I don't know?" Of course I knew the answer to, "What to do when you don't know the answer." You simple state you will look it up and get back to them. But on my first day I wanted to have all the answers.

A glimpse of the card tucked securely within the roses revealed one special person in my life saw I needed a little ray of sunshine to bring a smile to my face. The sender, my husband, sent the flowers as a message to take a deep breath, enjoy the moment, and to celebrate the beginning of a new chapter of my life. Indeed, this was a day for flowers! I was embarking on my first day as a nurse educator!

Friends and Colleagues

Three colleagues, three friends, and over a hundred years of nursing experience is what I see when I look around our table. A hundred years of nursing experience! What an exuberant amount! As much as I say the number with respect and honor, one hundred conjures up an image of three very old, weathered nurses. Poof— erase that image from your mind. The likeness is far from such a vision!

Instead, visualize three colleagues sitting under a canopy in a beautiful garden with the soothing sound of a spilling water fountain, sipping refreshing herbal ice tea, laughing and sharing their stories. Each disclosing their aspirations for the future, intermingled with memories from the past. It is a celebration of what is yet to come. Toasting, laughing, and well wishing; these are the images you should envision.

As we talk there is a pulse of power, of self-assurance coming from longevity in the profession, all punctuated with accomplishments. I am aware of the extent of our professional knowledge, a depth which took years of cultivating and refining to achieve. I can't help but associate our knowledge with the image of an overflowing treasure chest. There is a wealth of expertise amongst us. Wisdom not just shared amid us, but with others. We, the three laughing and sharing, are nurse educators, practitioners, consultants, researchers… the list could go on! Our credentials stack up behind our names, but aren't exhaustive. The future could bring more. For we know learning is a lifelong endeavor, and we are forever on the road to learning.

Another year has gone by and once again we come together. Naturally, there won't be enough hours in the day to rehash everything which has transpired, but we will do our best. Like forever friends we talk, converse, and talk some more. We catch up on family, on our health and on our recent antics. It feels great to hear we are each doing well as we progress along life's path and build our worlds. We eat, we drink, we laugh, and we have fun. We solve some problems...then move on.

We reflect on nursing and discuss its issues. We offer solutions and explanations, knowing despite our counsel nursing will be nursing. We see ourselves changing within our profession. We move from solidified answers, to reflective resolutions. We offer our wisdom and well wishes, as we take on new challenges. Each of us has new adventures to look forward to, new chapters in our nursing lives. A new job, promotion, data collection, semi-retirement and life-career changes, these are what we celebrate today. We salute change and longevity. Three friends, three colleagues, three new dreams, and three new adventures...our stories continue on for our next meeting; our next celebration.

Best wishes, my dear friends!

Kudos

A couple of us were talking in a small group. Elaborating on new projects we had in mind. I was voicing my thoughts about a nursing invention I had been toying with. When I rattled on and conveyed my passion one of my colleagues said, "Someday, I can see you on one of those famous talk shows." I looked at her somewhat bewildered because I was taken aback by her response. I suppose I expected her to comment on my idea and not make such a general statement. Probably seeing my look, she went on saying, "No, really. Someday you are going to come up with something really special...If anyone of us is going to make it, you will be the one."

Though taken by surprise, it certainly was nice kudos to receive. In response I said, "Thanks for the compliment and support, but I can't honestly see that happening...at least not in the near future, but it certainly would be worth aiming for." My invention was far from tangible so I didn't perceive I had anything "great" going on at the moment. Since any thoughts of greatness seemed so remote, I put the compliment to the back of my mind.

Sometimes, particularly when I struggle to understand why I push for an idea or for a personal goal, I remember her words and think she must have seen something in me. Perhaps she saw a spark, maybe not on the surface but as kindling inside of me. As for her prediction, well being a guest on a television talk show isn't a bad goal to keep in mind! A jewel of a thought to refuel my passions!

Memorabilia

Symbols of love, tokens of gratitude, all treasures received long ago and tucked away. There's the note card which was sent by my Big Sister in nursing school received the summer before classes commenced; words of welcome and hospitality....part of my memory box.

Two handkerchiefs beautifully tatted by arthritic fingers. She called her work "her therapy." She tells me, "I have to keep my fingers moving....so now I have so many. I work on them every day...please pick some." A piece of art, a dying craft, a therapy tucked away and never used, found amongst my treasures; these are my memories.

There are two pins, not safety pins, although such memorabilia could make me think of my "nursery days." While safety pins conjure up images of babies, my nursery days were signified by newborns wearing disposable diapers secured with adhesive tabs. During my nursery days we did not stock cloth diapers or safety pins. Such "nursery" items were before my time.

Anyway, the pins I talk of are two exquisite and very symbolic embellishments received while in nursing school. Each pin is unique in its splendor and tells the story of a nursing program. One is gold plated, completely circular with blue and gold etching depicting the coat of arms of our school. My favorite, not only because of its beauty, but because this was the first pin ceremonially presented to me after much hard and dedicated work. It denoted my passage into the nursing profession and was bestowed to me during our "pinning ceremony" at my first school of nursing.

Pinning has always been a well-celebrated nursing passage shared by family, friends and colleagues. Even today, "pinning" is still a ritual most graduating nurses ceremonially partake in.

My second pin is also a remembrance of the many years I worked to progress from my diploma to bachelor's degree in nursing. This star-shaped silver pin, etched with white and black colors was the medallion I received upon completing my RN to BSN studies. This symbolically different, but similar pin also represents years of struggling and hard work to achieve a goal.

As I lift a pin from my jewelry box and feel its metallic coolness against my palm, each brings forth in my mind unique stories of its time. As my nursing career evolved, and I moved from wearing the traditional white uniform to wearing scrub attire both pins spent most of their time tucked safely in my jewelry box, but they are never forgotten!

A yellow afghan knitted by the niece of a frail dying man. Each patterned row was a reflection of hours of tedious work. The result: a delightfully comfortable, snuggly blanket, truly a gem amongst store-bought comforters. A well-used treasure, a motif of friendship and caring, and a loving memory from a family once encountered.

A nursing cap placed in a hat box and stored away, eventually to become a remnant of the past. I wore my white, starched cap throughout my diploma school education as part of the "nursing" uniform. On my head sat the cap and on my body a blue pin-striped dress overlaid with a white apron. I appreciated being of the times when the uniforms of nurses had some style, rather than when uniforms had a matriarch-puritan look; a fashion which seemed to foreshadow all nurses as grim and haggard. In my day, graduation marked the day we put our pinstriped uniforms away and adorn traditional whites.

I continued to wear my cap following graduation, right through each work day of my first nursing job, a medical-surgical/orthopedic position in a large, tertiary hospital. A place where white caps bopped along on moving heads and nurses scanned passing heads in hopes of finding a friend, an alumnus. Your cap was your icon, the symbol of your school, a representation of values, training, and professionalism.

White caps reflected pride, accomplishment, and successful passage. Each shape was distinct with no two schools exactly alike. Some you looked at and wondered about the design. There seemed a fine line between the unique and hideous. Regardless of its outward appearance the cap was worn with distinction. The starched, crisp caps could "stand up" on their own thanks to the entire content of a bottle of liquid starch... such joyous memories!

In my day white pant suits or tunics with matching pants were fashionable. I favored the pant and shirt combination—easier for maneuvering and less likely to reveal all when a nurse was bending and lifting. The all whites made us look fresh, starched and pressed and a pair of highly polished white leather shoes topped off the sterile look.

For about a year I looked traditional in my whites. Then I moved into a specialty where scrubs were norm. Off came the white uniform, and on with the scrubs. Blue was the color I initially wore. Caps were not worn in this specialty unit. Head gear was considered a hazard amongst the heating coils of the radiant warmers used as beds for ill newborns. There was a fear our caps would catch on fire.

So my cap came off, was put in a hat box, and stored away. With time, the sentiment of its glamour diminished. On top of this change, came an awareness that at one time nursing caps served the purpose of keeping head lice confined to the head. It was a necessity of the times. Quite understandably a public health need, however, learning this little bit of trivia in my RN to BSN program transformed the emblematical meaning of the cap for me.

My treasures would not be complete without mentioning the many gifts I value that have been given to me by former students. I have statues of nurses in all forms, shapes and ages of life. Nurses as angels are common themes, particularly from the Willow Tree collection. There are placards with original words and those with inspiring quotes. Students have left me with their own treasured books. Some books were given because of their antiquity, others for their words, and then some because they tell some nursing story.

I have two of these placards, both identical except for the recipient year etched on the metal plates affixed to the wooden frames. These memorabilia sit upon a shelf in my home and are both cherished pieces. I was taken aback and surprised, yet honored, when I received each award. They were a gift from two different graduating classes at a university where I had taught. Each class of students acknowledged my dedication and love of teaching. Both were symbolic gifts from students to faculties, presented to the honored teacher on a very important day in the lives of students... graduation! From their international travels students have presented me with small tokens so I could share a piece of their ventures. And then there are the lovely cards that simple thank me for conveying words of nursing wisdom, for simple being part of their career path or for taking a moment of time to listen and to see them for who they are. Another one of my treasured gifts is a holiday cookbook signed by members of a graduating class, which is a reminder of the core value of hospitality.

Kind Words

She wrote me the summer before I left for my first nursing school "training." She described herself as my soon-to-be Big Sister. "That was so nice of her to write," I remarked. Her encouraging words provided me a sense of connection with the school. What I found comforting was she was successfully doing what I was about to set out to accomplish. Knowing she was a senior and soon finishing made me feel I too might be able to achieve similar successes.

Going away was a little frightening. More worrisome was how academically challenging the nursing curriculum might be. My grades were commendable in high school, but I lacked the self-confidence to believe in my achievements. Thankfully, it would be our Big Sisters who would allay some of these pre-school fears.

Initially, I did not know what having a Big Sister truly meant. In time, I would come to understand much like one's own blood sister, a nursing school Big Sister was often one's saving grace. They were the ones who looked out for naïve, klutzy "little sisters."

Her welcoming letter was the beacon of hope that there would be friendly faces when I arrived my first day, so unsure and insecure. A simple letter, and a kindly gesture, left me with a treasure from years gone by....

Baby Faces

I have a treasured book, but not an ordinary book, rather one I have made. It is a photo album. I use it to teach, to convey what we should think. It is simple, but powerful. It is not of people I really know, but rather images of children. They are not babies I physically touched, or children I actually saw. Instead, they signify the many newborns that are born each day with birth defects. Actually, the album is simply a collection of medical photos, mostly of babies with some type of neural tube defect (brain and/or spinal column) or other physical anomalies.

Once you move beyond the initial amazement of the physical defects you realize amongst those images something deeper is missing. You can feel the deficit with the turn of each page. Then it dawns on you, just as it was meant to. It jumps right off the page and one finds themselves wondering...what about their souls? There are no pictures of their souls! The camera has not captured the humans these children are.

As one continues to turn the pages you realize their souls are evident, their essence is there. It floats off the page and transcends your mind. It captivates you, and shakes your core. You ask the questions you were meant to ask. You can't help but ponder, does one being have a greater right to life than another? Beneficence, nonmaleficence and justice, the words are there floating before you and weaving their way into your mind. You close the book, but your disturbed thoughts continue. You walk away, but the questions remain. They invade your thoughts and interrupt your sleep. I hope they stay, and make you think, "Who am I to say?"

I have other treasured books, but they are not as profound as my photo book. Rather, these books I keep more to relive history, or to simple enjoy the stories for what they are. The one book I view as my obstetrical history book. The content takes me back in time and makes me marvel at how far medicine and nursing has come. This book, with the mustard-colored cover, is a medical book dating back to 1905. In it are instructions for "women in waiting." One passage reminds woman not to ride in an automobile traveling over cobblestone streets for fear of activating labor. Another section shows a picture of a breast shield used for breastfeeding. The shield is made from a hard blackish-colored metal. When I look at the picture, I ponder how the people of the times visualized a child could get milk from such a contraption. Or, maybe that was the problem: he/she didn't? Can't imagine, but on the other hand, someone introduced the products, and women bought them. I look at the picture of the inflexible, cold shield and compare it with the soft silicone breast shields of today. True, today's shields are much more flexible, and have better milk transfer, but still they are not 100 percent efficient. In comparison...to the metal ones...we've come a long way baby.

And I have my collection of nurses' stories. I collect books written about nurses, mostly by nurses. However, I do have a favorite series written about nurses, but not by a nurse. When I first began collecting books in the series, I was not aware the stories were authored by a woman in the 1950s who was a social worker. Her original intent for writing was to entice women into nursing. Sound familiar?

As you may know, I am referring to the Cherry Ames series. The nursing character the author developed was Cherry Ames; hence, the Cherry Ames series. The stories begin with Cherry Ames as a student nurse, takes one through Cherry's years as a senior nurse and then her experiences in different nursing roles: army nurse, country doctor's nurse, private duty nurse and several others. Of course, Cherry always finds herself in some dilemma. The stories are predictable and lighthearted, but enjoyable. I have managed to acquire several books from the series. Not having the complete set is okay, because treasure hunting for other original books in the series is part of the fun!

Now and Then
What we had ...

Medical diagnoses, kardexs, nursing care plans, narcotic keys, verbal narcotic counts at shift changes, pin striped nursing uniforms with aprons, white starched uniforms, pantsuits, nursing caps and nursing stripes, nursing hat boxes, white polished leather nursing shoes, call bells, stock medications, eight hour shifts, paper and pencil national state licensure examinations, a predominantly female profession, conformity, emerging autonomy, handwritten nursing notes, SOAP (Subjective, Objective, Assessment, Plan) notes, team nursing, glass intravenous bottles, refrigerated insulin, back rub rounds, patients became clients and clients became patients, tertiary centers, head nurses, Vietnam nurse veterans, National League of Nursing (NLN), Joint Commission on Accreditation of Healthcare Organization (JCAHO) standards, "training" of nurses, big sisters, nurse's aides, extended length of stays, bed sores, radiography, pre-surgical admissions for OR preparation, bedrest, emphasis of mother-child dyad, mercury thermometers, shaking down a thermometer, cardiac monitor technicians, manual blood pressure machines. And there was ... lots of cancer, stories of buccal pitocin, parlodel prescribed to postpartum moms, expansion then downsizing, grandfathered LPNs and RNs, hidden tattoos, low wage disputes, long hours, unions, end of shift reports, nursing care plans, patient satisfaction surveys, medicine and nursing turf disputes, acuity studies and timing of tasks, losses and births, young and old, womb to tomb care....and so much more!

And now we have ...

Nursing diagnoses, standardized nomenclature, North American Nursing Diagnoses Association (NANDA) list, Computerized Medication Administration Records (MARS), portable electronic medication units, scrubs, khakis and polo shirts, no caps, white nursing sneaker like shoes, portable telephones, single dose medications, twelve hour shifts, computerized testing centers, male nurses, creativity, autonomy, computerized charting, flow sheets, primary nursing, plastic intravenous bags, unrefrigerated insulin, optional back rubs, "clients," "patients" or "consumers"... whatever, magnet hospitals, patient care directors, Desert Storm-Afghanistan-Iraq veteran nurses, National League for Nursing and Commission on Collegiate Nursing Education (CCNE), "education" of nurses, nursing science, mentors, certified nurse's aides, shorter lengths of stay, bed sore prevention protocols, medical imaging, "in and out" or same day surgeries, rarely written "complete bedrest" orders, emphasis of mother-child-father triad, electronic ear thermometers, calibrating machinery, nurse extenders, electronic blood pressure machines, auto-immune disease and HIV, intravenous pitocin, elimination of parlodel use to "dry up breastmilk," downsizing and restructuring, advanced practice nurses, clinical nurse specialist, visible tattoos and multiple body piercings, overtime, unions, mandatory overtime disputes, bariat-

ric nursing, genetics, stem cell transplants, open-heart surgery and transplant teams, concept maps, informatics, quality assurance and quality improvement, simulations, technology, teleconferencing, interdisciplinary care, global healthcare, Doctorate of Nursing Practice (DNP), Electronic Medical Records (EMRs).... and we will evolve to even more!

And then, there continues to be ...

Different entry levels into practice, caring, diversity, the art of nursing, nursing process language, dedication, mentoring, ethics, clinical expertise, collaboration, healthcare reform, excitement, passion, life-long learning, the Nightingale pledge and our memories....

Chapter Nine

Soaring: Today

Believe you can and you're half way there.
(Theodore Roosevelt)

Nurses

Today is a reflective day. It is a beautiful day in my new home. I am on spring break. I always think of how much I sound like a student when I mention spring break. Actually my days of writing papers, grading papers, reading textbooks, and preparing presentations have not ceased, merely meshed together with my everyday life.

However, feeling like a student is not why I am writing today. Rather something else is weighing heavily on my mind. To try and put my thoughts to rest, I have decided to go outside and enjoy the blissful weather, to go for a walk. In my new surroundings, as I am assimilating to the Carolina coast, I have learned taking a walk is synonymous with "a walk on the beach." There's no place like the beach to make one's worries seem insignificant in the greater cosmic picture. Worries seem to vanish and are replaced by a personal affirmation of "I can do this."

I have always loved the outdoors so when I want to think and reflect I head outside. Despite loving the fresh air, I have one self-restricting variable; I do not like the cold. I don't mind looking from the inside out; particularly, if I would be sitting by a warm fireplace, in a cozy log home, peering out a panoramic window watching snow freshly falling. Or another of my favorite moments is being in the comfy inside, looking out a window watching a doe with her fawns grazing on winter shrubs.

Somehow by sitting there and looking out things take on a whole new perspective, almost like a sense of innocence and peacefulness prevails. It seems, if one gazes long enough, the stillness settles into one's inner self. You are overcome with a sense of awareness that you can do whatever had been gnawing at you. You will manage and undoubtedly do fine.

When you finally separate yourself from your tranquil world and bring yourself back to the here and now, you have greater inner strength and renewed optimism. This is my path to self-reflection. I go outside, walk, think and ponder.

On this particular day I am contemplating where I am today. I have advanced to another phase of my life. I am mulling over whether I did, or did not, make the best choice for myself and my family. I can see benefits of both positions. My unsettling quandary relates to an unanswered feeling in my mind that where I am right now, in this very moment is where I should be and where I am meant to be. So I go for a walk the Carolinian way. To surroundings that are so vast and beautiful: the coastal waters.

There are lots of people about today. The Carolina sun is shining. A perfect time for shorts and sun exposed skin. I see numerous sunbathers, though secretly I think they are a bit crazy. Why, because it is April and the sun has not had the opportunity to sufficiently warm the ocean waters. I begin to walk a paved pathway that runs parallel to piles of beach boulders placed along the coastline. I can see a few surfers sitting atop their boards. They are drifting in the distance. At least I see by their black minute figures they have the sense to wear wetsuits. As I continue my walk I pass two others returning from the water's edge and I hear the child exclaim how numb her feet are from the ocean's cold temperature.

As my paved path ends, I too opt to cut down to the beach and continue my walk. Shoes in hand, hair blowing in the breeze, sea gulls squawking overhead are all touches of heavenly bliss. I venture to the water's edge to look at seashells strewn along my path, but not so close to the lapping water that my feet become numb like the little girl's. As I enjoy the cool breeze, catch the beach sounds and see people simple having fun, I realize how much I love the ocean scene. Looking around, feeling an innate pull towards the ocean and being warmed by the bright sun redefines why I am here. My whole being needs this sense of the now. I discern I am exactly where I should be and need to take a cleansing breath and walk, not run, through this new phase of my life.

I will continue to learn, put myself out there, and reconfigure as I venture down this new path. I am from the east, and now live in the south. There are cultural differences, but not so diverse our worlds can't mesh. It takes time…and time is what I have. Time will mold me. In this time I will come to know and help graduate other classes of nurses. I will continue to teach new students with similar issues, values, and hopes. Their needs will parallel other students I have taught in the past. New sets of young eager faces will cross my path.

I saw something on my walk today, which I sensed added meaning to my being here. Though at the moment, I was not 100 percent sure of how. I don't think she would have caught my eye if the connection did not matter. In a second, I felt that fleeting sense of knowing, of nonverbal affirmation. There was a passing sense of awareness, a sharing and an understanding.

It happened as I was walking along the water's edge, further down the coastline where there were less people. Only a few individuals were meandering about. Some fishing, some just walking like me, some lying on their blankets soaking up the sun, some walking their dogs, and some hunting for just the right seashell that had washed up on a little island of sand about ankle deep in the ocean waters.

She was just a few feet away from the seashell pickers when my inner radar directed my gaze in her direction. Despite my eyes being concealed behind tinted sunglasses, this lady looked straight into my eyes. With her arm extended and smiling at me, she silently held out her hand. Nested in the palm of her hand was a dish-like seashell with the body of a sizable starfish consuming the center. The aquatic specimen's legs hung over the seashell's edges. An impressive sight!

I don't know if she smiled at me because she was pleased with her find or because she sensed I was struck by what I saw held in her hand. Though momentarily captivated by the magnificence of the starfish, I then realized she in all her splendor was clad in a sky blue-colored nurse's scrub jacket with matching blue cuffed-up scrub pants. I thought I should have known… a nurse…a nurse enjoying her time alone, hunting for sea treasures. Something unique, something simplistic….maybe that was it…a nurse… the beach…a simple life….maybe this is where I am suppose to be at this moment…at this very flash in time. Walking with this nurse…sharing our silent treasures!

School Again?

Maybe it is a midlife crisis, or maybe, I just need a chance to feel I am making a difference. Some tell me teaching is where I belong because I make a difference, but everything inside of me is telling me something is missing. Selfishly, I need a change. Intrinsically, I feel lost. The sense of who I am has become lost somewhere between students and me. I am missing the feeling of kudos when you achieve a high five because you made a difference in a patient's life. Not a big sparkling fire cracking difference, but one which achieves a simple smile or a heartfelt "thanks."

But now I am hidden under everyone else. I have given "it" away. It is time for me to build more patient stories and re-experience my own profession on a personal note. I sense it is time for something new. I see the change coming as a winding down and one that accompanies me into my retirement years. It is my future.

Repeatedly, I have used the word "it" above. A word any good teacher would tell you should be swiped from the English language. You can just hear the nagging voice of some not-so-favorite elementary level, blue-haired old spinster teacher saying, "Just what is 'it'?" "Define "it"…as her pointed finger jabs at the word on your paper. So to my fifth grade teacher, "It" relates to me; "it" is me. "It" here does not stand alone, rather it encompasses more. Tied up within this one word is a whole lot more. "It" is why I am doing what I am doing. "It" is foundational to my response when I am asked, why I would even considering going back to school again or "what other degree could you possibly need?"

I guess I have never gotten "it" right. Or maybe, I just accept learning is ever evolving as a lifelong endeavor. Understanding and accepting this fact will always lead one back into the classroom. Or maybe, "it" will be the means to once again define myself and redefine my thinking.

That is my answer after all this babbling. The answer to the question that was brewing…"why are you going back to school, again?" And, my answer…"I am going back to school to re-tool, as I begin a new dimension of my profession and once again begin to redefine the nurse I have become." How's that for an answer. "It" works!

To Be Me

Where am I going, I do not know.
Where have I come from, I am not sure.
What do I want, I do not know.
At what point in my life am I me?

I do not know.
I know I have questions and have lost sight of me.
But what direction to take I do not know.
I know I want to stop and look around, to stop the rush and live.
I do not know where I am going, or where I have been.
It is not the journey I wish to continue, or where I want to go.
Help me get off- help me to find the way, what is the way?
Bear with me, for I know not where or how or what I want.
Is it my age—or is it my life? Do I need more? But I want less.
But what is less? Can I make others understand I am not who I am, I want to be less.

I want to stop, to look around, to stop this whirlwind, to blow away for awhile, and feel carefree. To leave all behind, to walk away, walk away to another way, towards an open field with nothing in sight. Into the barren desert towards a path leading exactly nowhere; where nothing is there. No expectations, no pressures, just nothing. But where is there? I do not know. I don't want to know because I have to think, and thinking is what this is all about…I don't want to think. I just want to be!

How can people say they know me, when I don't know me? Something is missing—there is no connection. They see what they want, but only I know I am not who they see. I am lost in the depths of thee. I feel so small in the scheme of it all—like an ant crawling amongst the giant Tetons. Lost in what they can't possible see.

I need time to be me. Oh just let me be. For I cannot see… who I am to be! I really need… to feel free… to understand me.

Blending Role

When I decided to pursue certification as an advanced practice nurse, many asked me why I was going back to school, "again!"

"What more can you possibly learn," they challenged. Oh, but there is more to learn.

I knew when pursuing this degree, which challenges one to integrate principles of nursing practice with a medical model, the blending would be challenging. I realized I would need to learn to think differently, use a diverse set of skills and see the healthcare world through a new set of lenses. Though nursing and medicine work side by side in the healthcare arena, each has its own unique philosophical frameworks. While at times both might have similar focuses, each discipline has its own distinct functions.

Nursing revolves around assisting individuals to meet their own self-care needs, whereas medicine focuses on diagnosing, treating, and curing individuals of illnesses and debilitating conditions. Though both address basic human needs and are built on human dignity, there are fundamental philosophical differences which guide practice within each of the two domains. Our differences and commonalities allow us to care for individuals in holistic and complimentary ways. We learn to work as a team to address the care needs of patients. We must continue to work in harmony.

Emerging from Death

As I opened my eyes this day the first thing fluttering across my mind was today is my brother's birthday. As I thought about how sad his being gone was I wished him a happy birthday and hoped he was looking down from heaven. I wanted him to know I also remembered his birthday without a prompt. I think about the times we reminded each other of one another's approaching birthdays. We used to have this practice in which a day or two before one of our sibling's birthdays, one of us would put out a reminder phone call. The "reminder" call was initiated so no one forgot to wish their sibling a happy birthday. The celebrating "kid" was just pleased all his/her brothers and sisters remembered. Of course, the birthday person grasped onto the vision everyone remembered his/her birthday without the ceremonial call.

For me, my brother Nick's birthday was a sibling's birthday I never needed to be reminded of. We were close in age and our birthday months were merely one apart. He always seemed to remember my birthday as well. I like to think it was always without a prompt.

As my brother's birthday was nearing, I found myself wondering if there truly is a heaven, or whether one's body goes into a state of "nothingness" following physical death. I am not sure "nothingness" would be so bad, if one's counter-state was destined to be a condition of anguish. Maybe everything just ends…there is no thought…no observations…no color…no beauty… just "nothingness."

What about purgatory? Does it exist in some spiritual way? The purgatory concept is something I try to shut out of my thoughts. It is a phenomenon I can't conceive anyone I know being eternally sentenced to. I only hope I or anyone else does not end up there. Though with crimes some people commit against one another, it is hard to believe those who maliciously kill aren't condemned to some form of purgatory. Atonement seems only fair and just.

How can God, or some other higher being, possibly overlook such acts as murder? Yet, if I fall back on my religious upbringing in which God is perceived as all forgiving, I can't help but wonder how he/she cannot forgive. No matter the degree of sin. Is a sin a sin no matter the degree? What makes one offense forgivable over another, if both were committed with the intent to harm? A part of me stills holds onto these basic teachings.

This purgatory is not a place I would find my brother. Actually, I don't think there are many people in that forsaken place, except maybe only those who repeatedly committed malicious crimes. I can't think of anything my brother could have done condemning him to such a status. What troubling thoughts, they're going down some strange avenues. Yet, they're all related to this day, and what it means! And so I continue....

By no means do I believe he was an "angel." He was the brother I grew up with! Certainly he never intentionally hurt someone or did anything so bad the deed could not be fixed. No, knowing his personality he was either destined for the place called "heaven" or the existence I coined as "nothingness." Anyway, even if he had some big dark secret and did something one might conceive as "unforgiveable," I think suffering through the course of a malignant brain tumor more than balanced the scales. Maybe it was his restitution before heaven. Who knows? Such thoughts on his birthday!

Can my brother hear my thoughts? Does he know I think about him and hope he is doing well? Hope he is not suffering. Does he feel? I know what I should know and hold as gospel from my faith. Now, as death is real, I cannot help but challenge what I was taught to believe.

I have been around death oodles of times in nursing. I have held the hands of dying humans, retrieved loved ones from cold morgues so family members could say one last goodbye, I have dressed deceased babies in beautiful outfits to be held one last time by grieving mothers, and I have even become certified in palliative care. So death's experiences are not new passages for me. I had learned what to expect, what to say, and what to do. Over the years I had found a place within my cerebrum to park deep philosophical questions related to death. This tucking away makes it easier for me to function and to accept what cannot be changed.

I think as a nurse you have to find a neutral place within yourself to house such thoughts. Or death, and all its associated sadness, will overwhelm you. One has to find a place in your intellect where you can park some experiences and hold them in check.

Despite my many passages with death, my brother's death took me into a new dimension of understanding and questioning. Probably it released the flood gates for all those thoughts and questions I had so wisely repressed back in the deep recesses of my mind. Those thoughts I store for "another day." A place where I house the emotions attached to all those end-of-life encounters nurses witness, the heart wrenching grief of families, or the trauma experienced by someone who is just distant enough, in terms of our relationship, to allow me to cope.

Thus, as I took a few moments to just lie and let thoughts of my brother run through my mind, something came to me. I want to believe he lodged the idea in my mind. This would be a new venture, a new direction within my profession to pursue. I can see its purpose and how others will benefit. Even the name has come to me, Memory Writers. It fits and permeates the aesthetics of nursing. It signifies another dimension of caring.

So, what is it? And will I be able to develop this brainstorm? Will people be interested? I don't know, but I hope so. We'll just have to wait and see what evolves along my path of destiny.

Professional Growth

Ever hear the expression, "Nurses eat their young?" A statement which makes one step back in his/her mind and wonder how "caring" nurses could behave in such a manner. A cliché nursing has recently rallied together and worked hard to dispel.

To help eradicate this practice, nurses have brought the notion of bullying amongst nurses to the forefront. Nurses are writing articles on the topic, holding workshops that foster civility, building programs to mentor one another, and turning towards offering kudos instead of criticism. Today, the expression of eating our young is uttered less often. Unfortunately, not hearing the expression does not mean struggling new graduates are not victims of prey.

If one looks hard enough, he/she might catch a glimpse of a nurse in an area of solitude shedding a tear because of a peer lashing or because they were the recipient of some cunning remark. Perhaps, one might even be so fortunate as to witness a sly, curt comment released by a "collegial" perpetrator. Or overtly catch the impatient gesture of a behind the back eye roller. All subtle attacks bore from some underlying sense of competitiveness and rivalry which are now labeled "lateral violence."

We preach empathy, we talk about empathy, and yet, sometime we forget to bestow empathy to each other. We need to continue to strive, to work together and to destroy the venom of those "snakes at the nurse's station." Our new graduates need to be swimming amongst the dolphins and not the sharks! We need to respect one another and to soar with each other!

Their Day

I am the spectator today. I watch as students proceed across the stage amongst cheers and the occasional blasts of fog horns to retrieve their conferred degrees. They walk tall, with bounce in their steps, and broad smiles etched across their faces. This is their day. Yet, I sit here and have flashbacks of the last four years. I remember what they were like on their first clinical day, I can hear their groans when a test is announced, and see the spark in their eye when the light bulb goes on. Another class moves on. Another year has gone by. Today we celebrate their success and pay tribute to the parents and teachers who have seen them through. No scrubs today, but instead the distinguished black gowns; the ensemble of a graduating senior. Yes, it is their day, the culmination of four years of grueling work. The ceremony ends, the accolades are thunderous, and plain black caps amongst glittering, decorative caps of self-expression are tossed into the sky, soaring along with hopes, dreams and aspirations.

A Reminder Written to Me
Just a few words ....

Life is an exciting venture; the road of one's journey is full of twists, turns, bumps, and dips. The thing to remember is the road always becomes true again. It allows you to catch your breath for the next set of turns and dips. The excitement is living, and life cannot be penned on paper, nor disguised.

Existence cannot be analyzed; there is nothing to compare, no quantitative value. It has no price tag. Existing is pure and simple.

With each simple inspiration and expiration there is one cycle in which so much occurs physiologically to maintain existence. You cannot help but think it means something beyond the term "common." We, each in our own way, are so special, so very perfect! We need only exist to be a marvel.

The positive mind, the optimistic way of thinking is all required to maintain an even keel. We must navigate through the fog and surf knowing the calm is always waiting.

To compensate for weakness is simply thinking of another

means. Congratulate yourself, on finding another route, or discovering something new. No apologies. Think of the new. The excitement continues, follow the road. Go ahead, smile.

Your Friend ....

Ending Thoughts

Sometimes, when I sit in front of my computer typing out these memories and reliving, I wonder about the direction of these stories. I question if anyone will wish to read them. Perhaps all my efforts are in vain and my stories are only meaningful to me. I think about tucking them away and reserving them for only my family and my future grandchildren. Or, I wonder, has too much time gone by and the youth who I hoped would read and be inspired by my thoughts, end up viewing the stories as antiquated?

Will reform in the healthcare milieu and advances in technology make it impossible for similar experiences to transpire? Will our youth miss the underlying and timeless lessons of dignity, of passion, and of love? Instead, will their lenses only allow them to see dated anecdotes told by an out of touch, "nice to have known" nurse? Will this happen? Will all the times I mentally dictated my stories, and stopped what I was doing and ran to a computer to jot down my fleeting thoughts before they soared away, be in vain? Will my tales be understood and appreciated? I can only beg.

My instincts say yes, but what do you think? Now as you finish reading my ongoing journey, I have to ask.... Did you see yourself in any of my memories? Was it you not listening to a guidance counselor or you with an illness......were you right there with me... were you me?

ORDER FORM

"Every Step of the Way"

Individual and Group Orders

◊ Yes, I want _____ copies of *Nursing Shoes* at $14.95 each plus $7.00 shipping per book (PA residents please add $0.90 sales tax per book). Canadian orders must be accompanied by a postal money order in U.S. funds. Allow at least 15 days for delivery.

◊ My check or money order for $_____ is enclosed.

Name _____

Organization _____

Address _____

City/State/Zip _____

Phone _____ Email _____

Please make your check payable to:
Brenda Pavill
2759 Memorial Hwy.
P.O. Box 493
Dallas, PA 18612-9998